AMERICAN FIGHTS & FIGHTERS SERIES

Colonial Fights & Fighters

THE CARAVELS OF DE SOTO.

AMERICAN FIGHTS & FIGHTERS SERIES

Colonial Fights & Fighters

Pirates, Early American Conflicts and the
French & Indian War 1754-63

Cyrus Townsend Brady

LEONAUR

Colonial Fights & Fighters
Pirates, Early American Conflicts and the French & Indian War 1754-63
by Cyrus Townsend Brady

First published under the title
Colonial Fights & Fighters

Leonaur is an imprint of Oakpast Ltd

Copyright in this form © 2011 Oakpast Ltd

ISBN: 978-0-85706-765-4 (hardcover)
ISBN: 978-0-85706-766-1 (softcover)

http://www.leonaur.com

Contents

To
Edwin Wilson Morse

Prefatory Note

The generous reception and kindly criticism which was accorded *Revolutionary Fights and Fighters[1]*, the first book of this series, has inspired me to continue my efforts looking to the completion of a Battle History of America, in which the stories of all the conflicts, wars, and adventures, which have taken place on the continent, will eventually find a place. This time I have gone farther afield in choice of subjects and have wandered from the beaten path. The reader is here introduced to some of the racial struggles which went toward the making of the nation. As there were soldiers before Agamemnon, so there were battles in which we took conspicuous parts before the Revolution, notably in the French and Indian War, the principal campaigns and exploits in which are set forth in the latter part of the book.

It has been said sometimes that American history lacks the elements of romance. As I consider the great names which appear successively even in these few pages, I am constrained to contradict the statement. The proud, cruel, domineering, indomitable Spaniard; the gay, debonair, dashing, brilliant Frenchman; the merciless, rapacious, lustful, yet courageous buccaneer; the base, brutal, bloodthirsty pirate; the cool, stubborn, persistent, persevering, heroic Englishman; the hardy colonist, adding to his old-world stock the virtues generated by the new life in a new land, and the plumed and painted savage with his fearful war cry, his stoic endurance, his subtle strategy, pass before me in brilliant panoramic procession.

Believe me, dear reader, if these things be not interesting to you, if you do not find them full of tragedy, mystery, romance, the fault is in the teller, and not in the tale.

I have made a selection of events to be discussed, in accordance with my fancy, but I have tried to select those which would show

---

1. *Revolutionary Fights and Fighters* also published by Leonaur.

some of the diverse elements and conditions which are met with in pre-revolutionary history. As I have said, I have freely made use of every source of information which would throw light upon the subject.

No one who writes of this long period can fail to feel a sense of indebtedness to Francis Parkman. His books should be in every library, and should be read by every lover of his country. He stands alone among American historians in the greatness of his conception and in the way he carried it out. For many hours of pleasure and for much valuable information I stand indebted to him, and I gratefully make the acknowledgment here.

C. T. B,

Overbook, Phila., Penna., 1901.

1

De Soto and the Mississippi

1. THE BEST OF THE CONQUISTADORS

In the year 1536, a magnificent cavalier of noble presence and princely bearing, arrived at the court of Valladolid. The richness of his vesture, the profusion of his equipage, the magnificence of his household, for he was attended by a number of young officers scarcely less splendid than himself, dazzled the eyes of all—and it was no light thing to excite the astonishment of the court of the great emperor, Charles V.

The cavalier was Hernando de Soto. He was the scion of a noble though impoverished family, in whose veins flowed some of the bluest blood of Spain. He was born in the year 1501, at Villeneuva de Barcarrota at Xeres near Badajos. Like Cortez and Pizarro, he was an Estramaduran. There must have been something in the air of that province which produced heroic men.

When but thirteen years old, with no fortune but his target and his sword, he set sail for the new world which was opening with such dazzling *vistas* of romantic possibilities before the chivalry of the age. He was a page in the train of Pedrarias, the infamous governor of Darien. All the conquistadors wrote their names in blood upon the records of the countries, which it were a mistake in terms to say they governed, but Pedrarias earned a name even among his bloodthirsty contemporaries which indicated his character. Like Attila of old, he was called the "Scourge of God" (*Furor Domini*). In such a school was de Soto trained.

He met with the favour of Pedrarias, and in ten years' time was a captain in an expedition into the wilds of Nicaragua. His chroniclers relate of him that he joyed in the hunting of savages. In April, 1532, he landed with a troop of horse on the Gulf of Guayaquil, a needed reinforcement for the detestable Pizarro. The courage and ability of de Soto were soon recognized by the keen conqueror of Peru. Responsibilities—gladly welcomed—were thrust upon him. It was he who discovered and made way over the passes of the mountains. With Hernando Pizarro, he headed the embassy which boldly entered the camp where the Inca Atahualpa sat enthroned amid a multitude of wild warriors. He is reputed to have been the best horseman among the Spanish, and he took occasion, incensed by the coolness with which the Peruvian emperor met their advances, to give him a sample of his skill at the *manége.*

He caused his horse to curvet and prance madly about the square, finally rushing him at full speed toward the Inca as if to over-ride him, checking him within a few feet of his sacred person by so powerful a wrench that he threw the animal on his haunches at the foot of the throne. The Peruvians were dreadfully afraid of a horse, but the manoeuvre of the cavalier had no effect whatever upon the impassive Inca, who never raised his eyes, though it was gravely related that he caused some of his warriors who shrank back from the avalanche of horseflesh and steel, to be beheaded after the departure of the embassy for having shown fear before strangers.

He was one of the company which participated in the capture of the Inca on the 16th of November, 1532, and the dreadful slaughter in the square of Caxamarca. At the storming of Cuzco he was the first over the walls, and in all the battles and marches he bore a prominent part. It is to his credit, that being absent at the time the Inca, who had paid the unheard-of ransom of fifteen million dollars in gold for his release, was basely executed, he protested against this incredible treachery when he returned to Caxamarca.

When the country was entirely subdued, he returned to Spain, having received as his share of the ransom of the Inca, about two hundred and seventy thousand dollars in ingots of gold and silver. He met with a warm welcome from the needy emperor, who proceeded to bestow his royal favour upon him and borrow some sixty thousand *ducats* forthwith. It is to the credit of Charles, that he subsequently paid back this money—a most unusual act of royal condescension!

With a halo of romance and a more substantial gilding of treasure adorning his handsome and stately person, he had but to choose for a wife the fairest of the fair dames of Castile, purchase an estate, establish himself as a *grandee* secure in the favour of the emperor and pass the rest of his days in the enjoyment of his treasures. His choice fell upon the beautiful Isabella de Bobadilla, a daughter of old Pedrarias, and a connection of that grand dame the Marchioness de Moya (Beatrice de Bobadilla), who had been the friend of Columbus. His present and his future appeared certain, when there came to the court, early in the year 1537, a little man named Cabeza de Vaca, who had been a doer of doughty deeds, as we shall see, and was now a teller of strange tales.

Of six hundred who had set forth to explore Florida in 1528, with visions of conquest before their eyes, he and three others alone survived. They had passed eight years in wandering across the continent from one savage tribe to another, from Florida to the Gulf of California. He had marvellous accounts to relate of a country in the interior of Florida, then the generic name for North America, beside which the riches of Mexico and Peru lands where the precious metals were so base that the horses were shod with silver!—were inconsidered trifles. He refused to divulge the exact location of this fabulous Ophir, but he said enough to inflame the passions—which a year of idleness and enjoyment had not quenched—of de Soto. Unsatisfied by his tremendous booty and his future prospects, he determined upon the enterprise in which he hoped to acquire more glory and more gold than had been found by Cortez and Pizarro.

The emperor was pleased to accord his gracious permission— which cost him nothing—and reserving for himself a fifth of the gold which was discovered—which brought him nothing either—he created de Soto a marquis, made him governor of Cuba and lord of Florida, and pretty much all the rest of the western hemisphere which was not yet discovered, with the title of *Adelantando*. As I read the chronicles of the past it seems that everybody who bore that magnificent appellation was destined to misfortune.

When the news was passed among the young courtiers of Spain that one of the conquerors of Peru was about to take the sea once more, he was overwhelmed with applications to join the expedition. It was an age of chivalry, romance and credulity. The experiences of the cavaliers in the new world had lost nothing by the telling in the old. Gold and silver were supposed to be so plentiful that they could be had for the taking. With this embarrassment of volunteers, de Soto was able to select those best suited for his purpose. Among those who flocked to his standard were a large number of noble Portuguese under the command of Vasconcelos. Wise de Vaca did not go along.

On Sunday, the 6th of April, 1538, being St. Lazarus' Day, the expedition, comprising some nine hundred men, set sail in a noble squadron of ships from the port of San Lucar at the mouth of the Guadalquivir. Such had been the profuseness of their preparation, that great quantities of luggage, for which there was no room on the ships, were left behind on the wharf to the pillage of the people, but what did any man care for the reckless expenditure of a few thousand *ducats* in Spain in the face of uncounted ingots in Florida?

De Soto was followed by many of his old comrades in arms in Peru, the chief of whom were Luis de Moscoso and Nuño de Tobar, who were next him in command. The beautiful Isabella de Bobadilla accompanied her gallant husband. *En route* they stopped at the Canary Islands and were hospitably entertained by the governor. At the entreaty of the wife of de Soto, the governor allowed his daughter, a left-handed descendant by the way but withal a dainty and charming lady also named Isabella de Bobadilla, to accompany the expedition.

Nuño de Tobar fell in love with her. She was unable to resist his importunities, and though de Tobar promptly married her when the consequences of their indiscretion were apparent, his presumption withdrew from him the favour of the governor, he was dismissed and reduced to the ranks. After spending some time at Santiago and Havana, and putting all things in order in Cuba, on Sunday, the 18th of May, 1539, with five great ships, two *caravels* and two *brigantines*, they set sail from Havana. Donna de Soto and Donna de Tobar, the latter with a little baby in her arms, stood on the Morro Castle and watched the white sails wafting their lords to fame and fortune, as they supposed, sink out of sight beneath the horizon.

2. Vitachuco's Bold Stroke for Liberty

On the 20th of May, being Whitsunday, they landed in the Bay of Tampa, called by them the Bay of the Holy Spirit. They numbered over six hundred perfectly appointed men, perhaps two hundred of them being horsemen. Among the number were twelve priests, eight inferior clergy and four monks, who could minister to the soldiery and convert such of the natives as the sword of the secular arm spared. One recruit named Juan Ortiz unexpectedly joined the army in Florida. He had been captured by the Indians from the party of de Narvaez ten years before. He had mastered the Indian tongue and was able to make himself understood by the savages. He was a re-enforcement of great value.

Nothing that the forethought of de Soto could suggest had been omitted in the preparations. He expended the greater part of his private fortune in fitting out the expedition. There were shackles for the slaves, savage bloodhounds, spare armour, tools, portable forges, and a small falconet, or cannon. They had with them thirteen breeding sows in farrow, from which they expected to procure large numbers of porkers.

On the 15th of July, the army, trumpeters and drummers in the lead, plunged into the depths of the forest and disappeared in the Everglades. Twenty-five years before, on the 27th of March, 1513, being Easter Sunday, old Ponce de Leon had first caught sight of the green and smiling shore. Confident that within its confines flowed the wonderful fountain of youth for whose rejuvenating waters his soul pined, he had named it, in honour of the day, and the luxuriant vegetation which sprang from the very edge of the sea, Pascua Florida. Surely never was there a land so miscalled! Not finding the fountain of youth. Ponce de Leon returned in 1531 and was killed. In 1520 Vasquez de Ayllon had coasted along its shores and in 1525, with the witchery of its beauty still over his soul, like de Leon he had returned and had been slain with many of his followers.

In 1528, Pamphilio de Narvaez, who is remembered only for his vanity and his misfortunes, landed with six hundred men upon its shores. It was that de Narvaez who had been sent to supersede Cortez in Mexico. Cortez had defeated and captured de Narvaez and his men in a night battle in which their commander lost his eye, then with an address as great as his valour, Cortez persuaded his prisoners to desert de Narvaez and enlist in his service!

"Count yourself fortunate," said de Narvaez to Cortez, "in having captured me!"

"It is the least of things I have done in Mexico," calmly responded the conquistador.

He rated his captive so low that he released him and sent him back. In spite of this failure, we find him in 1528 at Tampa, with his devoted six hundred. Their adventures were one long tale of misfortune. None of them save de Vaca and his three companions whose incredible adventures have been noticed, ever saw civilization again. In the gloomy forests, the malarial swamps and the depths of the ocean their bones lie bleaching.

The land of flowers? Rather the land of blood! Yet in spite of these things the army of de Soto set forth with a stout heart.

The ships having been unloaded, all but the caravels which were kept for service were sent back to Havana. The soldierly de Soto insti-

15

tuted a strict regime. The army was drawn up in regular order, as the military science of the day indicated, and the companies marched and preserved their different stations in due course. It is neither profitable nor indeed possible, to follow the daily wanderings of these gay cavaliers in the hitherto untrodden wastes of the new land. In spite of constant attacks, with their superior arms and equipment they overbore opposition and daily penetrated farther and farther into the continent. Their method was extremely effective.

De Soto got possession of the chief of any tribe he chanced to come across and compelled him to furnish a sufficient number of his subjects to carry the baggage of the little army into the territory of the next adjoining ruler, where a new levy of forced slaves would be made and a certain proportion of those already impressed, released and sent back to their own land. The plan had the merit of simplicity and expedition, but it left behind a smouldering train of revenge, and it raised before, by means of rumour and message, a flaming barrier of war and rebellion. The Spaniards were brutal and licentious, but they did not descend to the horrible excesses which had disgraced almost every other expedition. De Soto was an angel of light beside men like Pizarro, Pedrarias and Alvarado, the fierce lord of Guatemala.

Sometimes the difficulties they encountered were trifling, sometimes of such alarming proportions that their very existence was threatened; sometimes they travelled through great forests, sometimes through cultivated plains teeming with broad-bladed Indian corn; sometimes they struggled desperately to extricate themselves from the vast swamps in which they became enmired; sometimes their way was barred by rushing rivers, or, as they reached what are now Georgia and South Carolina, by long broken hills.

One of the most serious encounters which they had with the Indians occurred in the domain of a chief named Vitachuco, in what is now Florida. In other circumstances and with other chroniclers, he would have been called a patriot. He was a politic savage, and on the approach of de Soto's army, though he had threatened them with annihilation, he dissembled and received them with complaisance, offering them hospitality. The old chroniclers love to dwell upon the splendid appearance he presented, his royal dignity, the stately and gallant band of braves who attended him, whose feathered head-dresses lent a touch of grace and softness to the fierce-eyed faces beneath them. The courtesy of the savage was no less Castilian than that of the Spaniards, and the meeting of the savage-hearted but courtly de Soto and the courtly hearted but savage Vitachuco, in this new corner of the old world, is a scene upon which the mind, like the eye, would fain dwell. But there was black treachery in the hearts of both men in spite of the veneer of politeness.

It was Vitachuco's plan to appoint a meeting at which de Soto would be invited to inspect his army. Twelve trusted followers were told off to seize the unsuspecting Spaniard and a general massacre was to ensue. But the Spanish commander had not come there a boy. Suspicion, scrutiny, and treachery discovered the plot. At the meeting de Soto had every Spaniard under arms. When the deluded Indian gave the signal, instead of being able to seize his enemy, he found himself, in spite of his gigantic strength, a prisoner. His naked warriors threw themselves upon the mail-clad Europeans with a courage that deserved a better fate. They made their attack in vain. Their arrows, though shot with amazing skill, fell back blunted from the steel *cuirasses*, the spears hurled by never so powerful arms had not the range of the deadly *arquebuse*, and the rude war club was no match for the Toledo blade.

After being slaughtered by hundreds, seeing their chief an impotent captive, they broke and fled. There were two lakes near the battle ground. The terrifying Spanish cavalry headed them off from the larger, forcing them to make for the smaller. With their relentless pursuers close on their heels, the Indians plunged into the sparkling waters. They were great swimmers apparently, for the old historians relate that they swam about for thirty-six hours!

The night fell and the Spaniards encircled the lake and prevented a single savage from breaking through the cordon of steel. As an evidence of their implacability, the Spaniards state that half a dozen men would swim together to form a platform in the water, upon which another would kneel and discharge his bolts so long as he had an arrow left in his quiver.

As the next day wore on, the Spaniards stopped shooting at them, their capture or death being inevitable; it was not good policy to waste ammunition, so the two parties waited in grim silence. I suspect there must have been shallow places in the water of which the Spaniards were ignorant, in which the Indians rested from time to time. The persistence of the conquerors finally wore out the resistance of the conquered, and one by one they came out on the bank—all but twelve who refused to surrender and remained in the water until they were so exhausted that de Soto sent in some of his men who were good swimmers and secured them. Their lives were spared.

The plan of Vitachuco had entirely failed. His warriors were enslaved, and his women the sport of the Spaniards, but the spirit of the savage was not broken. A fierce heart still beat in his breast. Hero-like, he determined to make one last effort for freedom. His men still outnumbered the Spaniards. Upon a given signal he arranged that they should rise and with whatsoever weapon they could compass, be it nothing but their fettered hands, they should overwhelm their captors. He was well treated by de Soto, and one night as they sat at supper together, he gave the signal by a mighty war whoop, then leaping to his feet, he caught the Spaniard by the throat and dealt him a furious blow in the face with his fist.

De Soto sank senseless to the floor. His nose was broken, his face smashed in, his teeth knocked out. With a cry of exultation the savage sprang upon his prostrate foe, and it was not until the sword of an attendant was plunged through his body that he relaxed his iron grasp. In obedience to the signal the savages attempted to follow the example of their chief, but the attempt never presented even a possibility of success. Many were massacred and the rest punished, loaded with the baggage and forced to move on. That was the end of Vitachuco's bold stroke for liberty.

3. The Defence of Mauvila

The adventurers spent the first winter in the fertile country of Appalache. D'Añasco, at the head of a detachment, discovered that bay upon the Gulf of Mexico from which the unhappy expedition of de Narvaez had set forth upon that last voyage, from which they had never returned. Thirty horsemen were sent back to the camp at Tampa to bring up the remainder of the army which had been left behind. The cavaliers fought their way down and the rear guard fought its way up. The caravels sailed up the coast and under the orders of de Soto made their way westward some distance along the shore and finally discovered the harbour of Pensacola. Thence the governor sent the vessels back to Havana with letters to Donna Isabella, and glowing accounts of what they had discovered and the brilliant prospects before them. The ships under the command of Maldonado were ordered to procure a re-enforcement of men, horses and ammunition and return to Florida the next October.

When the spring came, the men and horses refreshed by their pleasant sojourn in the land of peace and plenty, took up their march to the northeast again. The year was a repetition of the preceding one. When they advanced as far as the Savannah River in South Carolina, they entered the land of Cofachiqui, which was ruled by a woman, a princess upon whose beauties of mind and person the Spanish chronicles have dilated. She probably had no more claim to beauty than Dulcinea del Toboso!

At any rate, draped in grass cloth and cotton, crested with feathers and gleaming with pearls, she came floating down the Savannah River like Cleopatra coming to Antony. There was more Castilian courtesy, and black treachery, the latter being on the part of the Spaniards only. There is another fine story of a string of pearls as large as hazelnuts which the princess removed from her dusky neck and threw over the shoulders of de Soto, after some bashful hesitation and an exhibition of maidenly modesty, which show that there was not a great difference between the women of the old world and those of the new. There was a ring, too, which de Soto plucked from his own finger and placed upon that of the princess; which he meant to get back later on (I am happy to say that he never got it).

The usual demand for slaves and so forth—things too grim to be told on pages polite covered by that *et cetera*—was made. The little princess was made a close prisoner and her people were treated with the usual rigor. Observing the desire of the explorers for pearls she led them to barbaric temples and decaying sepulchres and exposed to their greedy gaze piles of the translucent gems. With their usual extravagance, the writers tell us of heaps so large that they could only be estimated in bushels. Save a necklace or two for each individual, a handful which even the commonest soldier could carry, a few hundreds for the royal treasury and a choice boxful for his own use, which the princess was allowed to carry, de Soto compelled his followers to leave the bulk of them until they should return. It is pleasant to relate that the princess escaped with the box of choicest pearls and de Soto's ring and was not recaptured.

In one place after showing the people the terrible power of the weapon by firing at a large tree until it was knocked over, they left their only piece of artillery, too cumbersome for transportation. The explorers pushed their way upward and westward into South Carolina across the foothills of the Appalachians, and gazed in admiration upon the mighty mountain range which barred their path. They then turned to the south and moved down through Alabama and entered the domains of a renowned chief named Tuscaloosa, a giant in stature.

His welcome was none of the warmest, but with careless indifference to anything the Indians might do, they persisted in their advance. The wily savage with specious promises of royal entertainment led the army toward his capital city of palisades and thatch, which he called Mauvila; a name perpetuated by the modern city of Mobile, a few miles farther down the same river. It was a well-fortified place according to Indian standards, located on a beautiful meadow, upon a neck of land surrounded on three sides by the rapidly rushing Alabama River. It was enclosed by a palisade fastened together by vines; the spaces between the logs were filled with thick masses of mud and straw and many of the tree trunks had taken root, so that the town was surrounded by a wall of living green.

The main body of the army halted one night five miles away from the village. The next morning, October 18th, 1540, de Soto, with one hundred cavaliers and footmen, followed by the usual melancholy train of slaves bearing the baggage, set forth for the town. He left orders for Moscoso to break camp and follow him with the main army at once.

Led by the chief, de Soto and the advance guard entered the walls. The slaves and the baggage were left hard by the gate outside. The place was crowded with warriors, and while there were many women, scarcely less fierce looking than their lords, the absence of children was noted. The Spaniards, however, fearlessly occupied the houses assigned to them, and by de Soto's orders prepared breakfast. Tuscaloosa had withdrawn upon some pretext, and when breakfast was ready he was summoned. Juan Ortiz, who carried the message, was treated with contumely and compelled to repeat it several times. In the thatched houses of the Indians a fierce debate was going on. The discussion was as to whether they should attack immediately, or wait until the whole army had been gathered within the town and finish the affair with one blow. The latter plan was favoured by the elders, but the impetuosity of the young men could not be restrained. One of them followed Ortiz out of the house and lifted his bow, shouting defiance.

De Gallegos saw the movement and whipping out his sword cut him from the shoulder to the waist. The son of the dead chief drew his bow and launched six arrows in quick succession. They all rebounded harmlessly from the armour of de Gallegos, and, seeing their futility, the Indian sprang upon him and dealt him such a blow with the oaken bow that he only succeeded in saving his life by passing his sword through his assailant's body.

From every house and hiding place the Indians came running with yells of hatred. They struck the astonished Spaniards with the force of a tempest. Resistance under the circumstances was suicide. The Spaniards turned and fled at their highest speed to get out of the town. They broke through the gate which the precipitate attack had prevented from being closed and then ran toward their horses, which were tethered outside under the trees. Some of them were shot down on the way. A few mounted and most of the others cut the bridles so that the priceless animals escaped. The horsemen threw themselves upon the advancing Indians and checked their onrush until the rest of the band formed up and advanced, and the Indians were driven back into the walls. The Spaniards attempted to storm the place but they were met with such a volley of arrows that they retreated once more, again pursued by the Indians. This advancing and retreating was kept up for four long hours of hard fighting.

Meanwhile the slaves had carried their loads within the walls. They were freed from their fetters and given weapons. The hatreds engendered in their captivity made them not less desperate than the savage Alabamans. Finally de Soto determined to break into the town. The Spaniards were smarting with wounds and mad with rage. Dismounting from their horses, under the cover of their shields they advanced to the gate. In spite of the arrows which were rained upon them they beat it down with axes and broke into the enclosure. The Indians met them in solid ranks. They were cut down in numbers but came on with most determined fury.

By the command of the chief the women, seeing weapons from the strewn ground, threw themselves upon the foe. The Spanish position was desperate. Bidding the men hold on, de Soto and de Tobar ran back outside, sprang upon their horses and charged up the narrow streets through the seething mass of Indians. Back and forth they rode, hewing and slaughtering, the iron hoofs of the horses crushing the life out of the prostrate savages. Missiles were rained upon them, but they bore charmed lives. Sounds of their war cries infused new spirit into the men. Finally as de Soto rose in the stirrups to deliver a blow, an arrow pierced him in the unarmoured thigh. There was no time to take it out then, and he rode through the rest of the battle standing in the stirrups, a great feat of horsemanship and courage of which his followers were justly proud.

The Spaniards finally succeeded in setting fire to the thatched houses, and flame added its terror to the scene. The battle had raged for eight hours, when about four o'clock the main body of the army under Moscoso, which had been loitering along under the trees, came in sight of the village. The crackling flames and rolling columns of smoke, the wild yells of the Indians, and the war cries of the Spaniards apprised them of the situation. Throwing aside everything but their weapons, the cavaliers galloped forward with the foot soldiers close behind them and entered the town. Throwing themselves in front of their broken, exhausted companions, they swept the Indians resistlessly before them.

Men and women were indiscriminately slaughtered. The brave savages fought until they were cut down to a man. It is related that the last Indian left alive ran to the wall and sprang upon it. When he saw that escape was cut off by bodies of Spaniards he shook his fist in defiance, caught his bowstring about his neck and hanged himself from the palisades! Spain in its palmiest days never produced a more devoted soldier.

There was not a living Indian, not even a wounded one, to be seen. The village was a roaring furnace. Eighty-two Spaniards had been killed outright,, eighteen of them having been shot in the face. There were two hundred and fifty badly wounded and fifty horses had been slain—an irreparable loss. The inefficient surgeons had hundreds of serious wounds to dress! Most of their baggage had been burned in the town, including all of the medical stores. In default of anything better they dressed their wounds with the fat extracted from the bodies of the dead Indians.

The vessels for the celebration of the mass and the wheat flour for the bread had been lost as well. Henceforth there was no mass on that journey. The priests, robed in vestments of skins of wild animals, would stand before the rude altars and repeat the service from memory; nothing more. Dry mass, the soldiers called it.

They were not troubled by the Indians of that tribe any further, for the reason that there were none left—all were killed. As Tuscaloosa was never heard of afterward, it is supposed that he perished in the destruction of his people. His brave efforts were as useless as Vitachuco's. The Spanish accounts of the slain range from eleven thousand to twenty-five hundred, the latter figure probably being more nearly correct.

From messengers and Indians they here learned that they were but six days' march from Pensacola, which was the place where they were to meet the ships. They had found no gold, nothing but marching and fighting had been their lot, and a natural longing for home filled their minds. Seeing no way of bending their inflexible leader, a conspiracy was hatched among the most discontented, to seize his person and abandon the expedition. If they had succeeded de Soto would have been carried back to Spain broken in fortune and ruined in fame. He was resolute to press on. In spite of all he still dreamed of conquests, still hoped to retrieve his fortune, He knew too well what the royal gratitude was. It was only consequent upon success.

For instance: in the year 1544, an old man forced his way through the crowd of courtiers to the carriage of Charles V.

"Who are you?" asked that monarch, looking wrathfully at the presuming intruder.

"A man who has added to your empire more kingdoms than the number of cities you inherited," replied the broken and disgraced Cortez.

"Drive on," said the king brutally to his coachman, turning his back on the man whom he had abandoned. Such would have been the greeting to de Soto if he had failed.

The conspiracy was detected, the conspirators severely punished, and under the orders of the chief the little army faced to the northwest and abandoned its last chance of getting home by way of the sea.

On the 17th of December, 1540, at the village of Chicasa, which they had occupied for the winter, they were surprised at midnight by an overwhelming force of Indians who set fire to the negligently guarded camp. The Spaniards, at first panic-stricken, were rallied by de Soto, de Tobar and Vasconcelos. De Soto, who slept in doublet and hose, was the only man to mount his horse in this action. In the middle of the fight his saddle turned and he pitched headlong among his enemies. There was a furious *mêlée* over the body of the captain but he finally escaped. It was found afterward that he had fought for an hour on horseback in an ungirthed saddle. It was not for nothing that he had the reputation of a finished horseman.

Fourteen men and fifty-seven horses were killed here, and over four hundred hogs, which were penned up in the middle of the city and carefully guarded, were burned. Only the young porkers who were small enough to run between the logs escaped. The Indians regarded a hog as a valuable prize, and every savage came to the attack with three ropes—one for a Spaniard, one for a horse, and one for a hog. The explorers spent that winter in the country of the Chickesaws, in a deplorable state of destitution. In the successive fights and

DE SOTO DISCOVERING THE MISSISSIPPI

MENENDEZ DE AVILEZ

fires everything they possessed, even to saddles, had been lost. With an energy which cannot be too much admired, they made a bellows out of hides and two old *arquebuse* barrels, and set to work to re-temper their weapons and make new saddles, lances, and such other rude equipments as were possible. They had no clothing except a few skins and they almost perished from the winter cold, until a soldier who had been a weaver, Juan Vega, made some grass cloth with which they covered their nakedness. They made forays throughout the surrounding country and treated the Indians with most brutal and implacable severity. In another village of the Chickesaws which they had gained by hard fighting, they put everybody to death.

4. THE FATHER OF WATERS

On April 25th, 1541, they set forward once more upon the march. They were a rude array of savage men, clad in the skins of wild beasts, a few of them riding horses, and driving a small drove of swine, their rude weapons scarcely differentiating them from the surrounding savages. Heading ever westward and northward, early in the month of May (the exact date is not known), the advance guard broke through the dense woodland and from a high bluff (Latitude 35° N., near Memphis, Tennessee) beheld the tawny, turbid flood of the Mississippi rolling swiftly at their feet—Espiritu Santo, de Soto named it. Up and down as far as the eye could see, spread the great river. A half league away the other bank confronted them.

The discovery of the Mississippi, together with his misfortunes, are the incidents which have served to perpetuate the name of de Soto, otherwise he would be remembered as lightly as de Narvaez or the others whom the primeval forests of the new world had swallowed up. The importance of a moment, the value of an incident, is rarely known until viewed through the perspective of centuries of time. The broken de Soto, who saw in the hurrying flood only an obstacle in his path, little dreamed that this river valley was to be the central artery of a great empire, not yet conceived in the womb of nations, which would someday strike his country the severest blow ever dealt to Spanish rule.

Twenty-two years before, Piñeda had discovered the delta and noted the vast volume of fresh water poured into the Gulf. Later de Vaca crossed one of the mouths of the river. One hundred and thirty-two years after de Soto, the undaunted Jesuit Marquette, with his companion Joliet, floated down from far Illinois in a frail birch canoe, past the very bluff upon which the Spaniard stood and upon which he had erected a huge cross, taking possession of the country in the name of Spain. Ten years after Marquette's day, the intrepid La Salle traversed the entire length of the "Father of Waters"; and, fascinated by its majesty, had returned hoping to colonize it, only to die by assassination on the Texas shore.

In 1699, Iberville and Bienville built a fort at the mouth of the delta on the sun-bleached sands of Biloxi and claimed the country in the name of France. Years after, while floating down this great stream, Aaron Burr dreamed of empires in the West, and on its banks Philip Nolan cursed the United States! It was to be a track alike for the palatial steamer, the lumber craft and the flatboat of primitive traders, one of whom was named Abraham Lincoln. Over three hundred years after its discovery Farragut with his storm-beaten prows breasted the rushing current and awakened its quiet shores with the thunder of his guns.

Commerce, trade, history, past and future, these were nothing to the melancholy, desperate de Soto. There was but one talisman to fix his attention, to engage his intelligence, to lead him on—the bright yellow precious metal was still before his imagination.

Moving down the river until he found a place where the ground sloped gently to the water's edge, the Spaniards crossed and took up their weary march. Drawing away from the stream the tired cavalcade plodded on toward the northwest. They discovered no gold but on the banks of the White River in Arkansas, they found something more precious to them in their extremity, and for which they had longed ever since they began their wanderings, and that was salt.

"If I could only have a morsel of fresh meat and a handful of salt," had been the plaint of many dying men, "I think I could live."

Some of them ate it so greedily that they died of it. By and by in despair the wretched army turned to the southward and dragged its way down to the Mississippi. Was the iron will of the conquistador at last broken? Had he repented the decision which led him away from safety after Mauvila? Was the natural longing to see Donna Isabella, to return to civilization at all hazards, strong enough to move him? No, for after passing the third winter in the province of Utiangue, where Juan Ortiz died—a great loss—in the spring time they kept on still exploring, fighting, hoping, though ever moving to the south. Finally they struck the banks of the great river again and followed its winding course until they reached the village of Guachoya, at the mouth of the Red River.

As they had been suffering dreadful hardships, and fighting frequent battles, they were glad to find in Guachoya a friend. Across the river rose the great town of the famous Natchez. De Soto would have liked much to cross the river and recuperate his men within its walls, but the chief of the Natchez would have none of him. When the Spaniard, resorting to diplomacy instead of force on account of the condition of his men, announced himself as the "Child of the Sun," the old chief told him to dry up the river and come over and he would believe him. Alas, the end of all things for the Child of the Sun was approaching.

5. THE MELANCHOLY END

Halting here uncertainly, de Soto was seized with a wasting fever which never left him. In spite of his resolute will he was forced to take to his rude couch, where he grew speedily worse. There is something manly and attractive in the way in which he met his death. His life had been hard, stern, cruel, and merciless. Ruthless and treacherous, he had partaken of all the vices of his age and nation, but there had been in him a magnificent courage, a cool hardihood, forethought for his men, an open-hearted generosity. Here and there were sparks of justice in his dealings with the Indians; once in a while touches of mercy, standing out bright before the black background against which they were exhibited.

These have half redeemed his fame. He had been the noblest, the highest, and the best of the great explorers, and was now the poorest and most miserable. He had everything to live for when he set sail from San Lucar and nothing was left of his possessions now, except the rude hut on the banks of the Mississippi, two slaves, three horses, and a few swine. Disappointment and despair had broken even his resolute soul. All his toil, labour, sacrifice, devotion, courage, had come to naught. It all ended here on the banks of the Mississippi.

He made his final preparations for death like a good Christian, writing his will and testament in cipher on a scrap of paper, confessing his sins and making his peace with Heaven. With prudent forethought he called his followers about him before he died. He had been a stern master but they loved him. Many of them had followed him over the mountain passes of Peru, they had ruffled it with him at the court of Spain, they had fought shoulder to shoulder in the everglades of Florida, charged with him in the flames of Mauvila. Some like de

Tobar and Moscoso had felt the weight of his stern displeasure. These things were forgotten now. They remembered him as the indomitable, heroic, courageous, far-seeing captain. If there was a lack of other comforts, there were tears and affection about his deathbed. In quaint words, which have a genuine ring read today after a lapse of centuries, Balthazar de Gallegos, acting as spokesman for the rest, delivered a homily, words of condolence and comfort, which wire agreeable to the ears of the dying man.

Wishing to avoid dissension, de Soto bade them choose a successor, to whom he could commit the command. With one accord, they left the determination to him, and his eyes turned to Moscoso, his early friend, a decision in which the others cheerfully acquiesced. At de Soto's request, the officers and principal men of the depleted army swore allegiance to the new commander in his hut, and then all the Spaniards in groups of twenty passed beside the bed of the dying commander and bade him farewell.

He died next day, the 21st of May, 1542, having been ill but seven days. The fever of the body, which with increasing virulence burned up his life, was typical of the fever of his soul, which had led him to this untimely end. His death came in the delirium of fever in which his mind reverted to Peru, to Spain, and to Havana, where the lonely Donna Isabella stood waiting on the strand.

Concealing the death of the "Child of the Sun" from the Indians, lest their prestige should diminish, Moscoso caused the corpse to be hidden for three days, while the soldiers were compelled to dissemble their grief by outward manifestations of joy and cheer. At the end of that time, at the dead of night, they buried their great commander in a deep grave outside the village; but the shrewd Indians suspected something, and, in great fear lest they should dig up the plain and find the body, Moscoso determined to disinter it and sink it in the river.

D'Añasco and four other captains soon found a place over a hundred feet deep, which they thought would suit. The next night the body was exhumed, and as there were no stones to weight it, it was wrapped in mantles which were filled with sand and carefully secured. At midnight a little party rowed softly out to midstream, and there, with a muttered prayer from the priests, the cavaliers gently lowered the body over the side of the boat, and with a sullen splash it sank beneath the surface. The mighty mass of water rushed silently on over the iron heart, now so still, which had once beat so fiercely in his breast The night wind in the trees sang his requiem as they rowed back to the shore and left him. Surely earth knows no grander sepulchre and the hand of man cannot rear so noble a monument as the great river which was the one and the other to the soldier now at rest.

What need to dwell upon the melancholy story further?

He had charged upon the survivors to convert the natives of the country to the Roman faith, and add all they could to the crown of Spain, and he advised them to live in peace and love with one another. These things they mainly forgot. There was but one thought in every mind, one desire in every heart, when the leader died—to get home! There were two ways open: one overland to Mexico, and the other down to the sea by way of the river. Ignorant of the distance and imagining themselves to be much nearer the country of Cortez, they decided to go overland.

For five weary months the survivors struggled westward until they came to the great deserts of Arizona. There they halted, and after exploring in various direc-ions, in despair they turned back toward the river, which they reached in December, 1542.

They wintered near the village of Guachoya again and set to work building boats. Fortunately for them, through all their wanderings they preserved one saw. It proved to be their most priceless possession. The enterprise and ingenuity of the Spaniards were astonishing. Every bit of iron they possessed except swords was forged into nails. The winter was a severe one and they only sustained life while they worked, by ruthlessly appropriating every grain of corn from the surrounding villages. So great were their exactions that the helpless Indians died of starvation in scores. Here, too, died the gallant de Tobar. Poor little Isabella and the baby, a sad ending to their love story!

At the expiration of five months they had succeeded in building crazy boats in which they embarked and floated down the river pursued by a great fleet of war canoes of the Natchez. One of the boats was captured with its crew, the horses reduced to twelve in number were abandoned, and finally, on the 18th of July, the flotilla reached the sea. There was divided counsel again. Some of them, led by d'Añasco, who had retained a rude jackstaff through all his wanderings and who had some pretensions to the art of navigation, were for sailing away toward Havana. They tried it for a day or two, but were driven westward by a storm and abandoned the attempt, running along the shore toward Mexico. On the 10th of September, 1543, four years and four months from the day they left Havana, they reached the Panuco River in Mexico, and were soon safe among their own people.

Three hundred gaunt, haggard, starving, broken men, naked, shoe-less, hatless, with neither equipment nor weapon, save here and there a dulled sword which their feeble arms could scarcely lift, were all that were left of the proudest, gayest, and most splendid little army that had ever debarked upon our shores.

Donna Isabella had sent out several expeditions from Havana in all directions to seek for traces of her missing lord, but they secured no tidings of de Soto. Three years' silence had broken her spirit. When the word did come from Mexico of the unfortunate end of the ex-pedition and the death of her husband, like a true and loving woman, having nothing left to live for, she quietly folded her hands and died of a broken heart

2
The Revenge of de Gourgues

1. THE HUGUENOT COLONIES

Of all the passions which have raged in human beasts those engendered in the holy name of religion have been the worst, and the wars of the most implacable ferocity have been waged between clashing creeds. The ordinary method of enforcing particular interpretations of the will of God has been at the point of the sword, and the attempt to propagate a new faith, or uphold an old one, has usually resulted in the development of the most hellish passions. 'Twas religious bigotry writ the word "deicide" in human vocabulary and stamped forever upon the world's face the sign of the cross. Since the hillock of Golgotha, so far had men strayed from the teaching of the Gentle Master in whose Name they perpetrated the most atrocious cruelties, that the rack and the fagot went hand in hand with the Bible and the priest, and the ecclesiastic became the most potent factor in building the kingdom of God upon a foundation of hatred and force. "Kill them all!" answered the fierce abbot to the soldier who asked him before storming a town, how, in the confusion of the sack, he could distinguish the saints and the heretics. "Kill them all! God will know His own!"

On the 12th of July, 1555, fifty years before John Smith landed at Jamestown and sixty years before the *Mayflower* dropped anchor on the bleak coast of Cape Cod, a little party of French Calvinists, backed by Coligny, and under the command of Durand de Villegagnon, a Knight of Malta, who had broken his monastic vows and was coquetting with the Huguenots, landed in the bay of Rio Janeiro, Brazil.

The answer of France to the famous bull of the Vicegerent of Heaven, dividing the new world between the great maritime powers, Spain and Portugal, was the advent of this little band of Protestants to found a state called Antarctic France! For several years they dragged on a wearisome, dreary, precarious existence, as did other colonists of whatsoever degree at that period of the sixteenth century. Re-enforcements came to them in 1557, containing among others two Calvinist ministers from Geneva, the first Protestant clergymen to set foot on the western hemisphere. On the island of Villegagnon in the bay of Rio Janeiro, was preached the first Protestant sermon ever heard on this half of the world, from the fourth verse of the twenty-seventh Psalm. Quarrels arose in the little colony, singularly enough at first about matters of ritual—they have been going on ever since in the Church world, by the way. Villegagnon proved to be a scoundrel and pitched three of the Calvinists into the sea—they gravely call him the Cain of America—despatched many of the others home, and finally followed himself, leaving a miserable remnant to drag out a wretched existence until they were slaughtered to a man, by the Portuguese, after an heroic defence.

Undaunted by this failure, Coligny and the other Huguenot leaders, with the royal sanction, dreaming of the establishment of a great empire on the one hand, a place of refuge for the children of the Reformed faith on the other, sent out another expedition of two ships under the command of Jean François Ribaut in 1562. On April 30th, the expedition reached the coast of Florida. On May 1st, sailing northward, they entered the great river St, Johns, which they called the river of May, and there with much ceremony, the French landed and erected a column of stone bearing the arms of the king.

It was not an unknown world at the time, short as had been the period which had elapsed since its discovery. Within its confines Ponce de Leon had searched in vain for the fountain of youth; its gloomy boundaries had received the expedition of de Narvaez, which struggled with privation and fever and savage attack, until but four of them were left; through its everglades and swamps had toiled the proud little army of de Soto, the unhappy discoverer of the Mississippi. No colony had been established upon its shores, but the monarch who sat upon the throne of Spain, the wily Philip II., confirmed therein by the Pope, claimed the territory as his own.

The ships of Ribaut again sailed northward until they rounded Hilton Head, and anchored in the quiet waters which awakened to the thunder of the guns of Dupont, three hundred years after. There they established the first actual settlement on the coast of North America and named the place Port Royal. Leaving thirty of his men to hold possession, the only Christians in the wilderness extending from the

Arctic Circle to the Caribbean, Ribaut returned to France. The cruelty and the ruthlessness of the captain, a disinclination to work, an ignorance of the humbler and more useful arts, soon plunged the colony into the direst distress. The commander was murdered, the affections of the Indians alienated, and finally, in utter despair, they built themselves an unseaworthy, wretched little boat and set forth upon a return voyage to France; considering the paucity of their resources, it was an appalling undertaking. The hardships they endured on that memorable voyage were frightful. Supplies of every sort gave out, and in their extremity they resorted to cannibalism. The lot fell upon one of their number and he was killed and eaten. When they had abandoned hope they were rescued by a wandering English ship.

Undaunted by these failures, the leaders of the Huguenots persisted in their plans, and on June 25th, 1564, a third expedition, consisting of three ships, the largest of 120 tons and the smallest of 60 tons, under the command of the distinguished navigator René de Laudonnièere, again entered the St. Johns. They found intact the pillar which had been erected by Ribaut. Ascending the shallow marshy-shored river, at a distance of about eight miles from the ocean, they came to a high bluff which descended inland into a verdant meadow bordered by a clear stream and surrounded at some distance by primeval forests growing in tropic luxuriance. There the delighted voyagers at once set to erect a fortification, which they called Fort Caroline, after Charles IX. It was built in the form of a triangle with bastions at each point On the land side there was a ditch and rampart, and on the river, a palisade. Inside were quarters for the men and houses for the officers. Two of the ships returned to France, the other was left with the colonists.

The Indians were friendly and conceived a great liking for the gay debonair Frenchmen. It was summer, and in that land of plenty everyone had enough. They were halcyon days for all. The colonists were composed mainly of gentlemen, adventurers and soldiers, with a sprinkling of criminals—it was common practice to fill the ranks of a colony by resorting to the prisons and offering liberty in the new land to those who would undertake the voyage. There were few artisans and no tillers of the soil. With reckless improvidence, they made no provision for the winter. Policy dictated a strict neutrality between warring tribes of Indians, but they soon became involved in the local savage quarrels, and in their time of need the natives refused to furnish them with further provisions. Labour of any kind was distasteful to most of them.

In similar stress John Smith had remarked sternly, paraphrasing an older saying, *"He that will not work, neither shall he eat."* When he said that, he more than promulgated a rule of local application, he laid down the great principle of national existence. Upon the soil and the tiller of it depend, as upon nothing else, the prosperity, the existence even, of a people. No great nation has ever been founded solely upon the ingot. The dream of the Frenchmen was for another Peru, and their eyes were constantly turned toward the fabled gold mines in the distant Appalachians.

Laudonnière seems to have been a well-meaning man and he did the best he could under the circumstances, but he finally fell very ill, and when his iron hand relaxed its grasp of the situation the discontent came to a head. A number of colonists combined and seized one of the vessels in the harbour, and at the muzzle of an *arquebuse*, with the threat of instant death in case of refusal, wrung a reluctant permission from the helpless commander, to leave the rest and go on a little buccaneering cruise of their own.

The pirates were lucky enough to capture a Spanish *brigantine*, and in several successful raids in the Antilles, amassed much booty; but they were finally overcome off Jamaica by the Spaniards by stratagem; many were killed or captured and only twenty-six of them succeeded in escaping from the island. There was nothing for them to do but to return to Fort Caroline. When the little vessel reached St. Johns, all their supplies had been used except two barrels of wine. To fortify themselves against the consequences of their misdeeds and the righteous indignation of Laudonnière, they proceeded to get drunk, when they were easily apprehended by the faithful soldiers of the garrison, and carried before their commander. Four of them were promptly sentenced to be hanged. "Comrades," said one as the sentence was about to be carried out, "will you stand by and see us hanged like dogs?"

"These," said Laudonnière grimly, "are not comrades of murderers and traitors." However, in obedience to the requests of the others, the ringleaders were shot instead of hanged. The colony was destined to hear from this expedition later, it was a curse that came awfully home.

The situation of the colonists, while it was outwardly peaceful, had become more and more desperate. They were starving and dying when on August 3rd, 1565, the watchman on the bluff, frantic with joy, announced the arrival of a great ship flying the English flag. It proved to be the *Jesus* of seven hundred tons, a very large vessel for the time, and was followed by three smaller ships all under the command of Sir John Hawkins, who was the pioneer Englishman to engage in the detestable slave trade—then considered a proper avocation for a gentleman! Hawkins, who had put into the river because he was short of water, was kindly disposed toward the French Protestants and offered to take them back to France in his squadron.

Laudonnière, however, preferred to purchase from him one of the smallest of his ships, which Hawkins very willingly sold to him, and with mutual expressions of esteem they separated. The colonists immediately began to fit out the ship for their return voyage, when on the 28th of August, seven other ships were seen off the mouth of the river. Ignorant of their character, the colonists sought shelter in the fort, and on the following day, when several boat loads of heavily armed men came cautiously up the river, the cannon of the fort were trained upon them. It was soon discovered that the newcomers were some three hundred Frenchmen, under the command of Ribaut, who had been sent, as before, by Coligny. Among them was Robert, the first Protestant minister to set foot on the continent of North America.

There was great rejoicing among the colonists at this unlooked-for re-enforcement, and many discussions were had between Ribaut, Laudonnière and the other officers, while the ships were discharging their cargoes, as to what was best to be done. They were still dreaming of the gold mines of the mythical Appalache, when on the 4th of September, about midnight, the watchers on the ships, which were still anchored outside the bar at the mouth of the river, became aware of the presence of a huge vessel-of-war, followed by several other formidable craft, which silently drifted down upon them in the stillness of the autumn night. Hails passed at once, and the French were informed that the first ship was the *San Pelayo*, the flagship of a Spanish Armada under the command of Pedro Menendez de Avilés, one of the most distinguished admirals in the navy of Spain. He calmly announced his intention of extirpating the heretics in the morning and when taunted by the French to attempt it immediately, he endeavoured to do so. The ships opened fire upon each other, but the more mobile, though undermanned, French ships slipped away in the darkness and got to sea, followed by the Spaniards.

The day following, the people on shore, who had heard the firing in great perturbation of spirit, were astonished to find their own ships gone and a stranger flying the yellow flag of Spain, the *San Pelayo*, alone, a great ship of one thousand tons, in the offing! They made such sturdy preparations to meet her with the smaller vessels, that, after looking at the fortifications, Menendez turned the prow of his ship to the southward and soon disappeared from view. A few days afterward an Indian war party informed them that the Spaniards had landed a short distance down the coast and were engaged in building a fortification, which they called St. Augustine, and that the *Pelayo* had been joined by many other ships. The news was confirmed, on their return, by the four French ships which had run to sea to escape the Spanish attack. There was thus developed a situation full of menace and danger for the French, and Ribaut, Laudonnière, and the officers engaged in earnest counsel.

Several plans were proposed. One was for them to remain where they were and receive the attack; the other to leave Fort Caroline and march boldly upon the Spaniards before they had time to fortify themselves; and a third was for every available man to go aboard the ships and make a sudden dash upon the Spanish vessels in the harbour, and after surprising and destroying them, complete the annihilation of the land force. Ribaut, in spite of unanimous opposition, resolved upon the latter plan; which seems, after all, to have promised more success than the others.

In truth, their situation was well-nigh desperate, Menendez was at the head of a fleet of thirty-four vessels, carrying twenty-six hundred men; many of his ships were galleons of large size, and among his forces were veteran companies from the Low Countries, of the famous Spanish infantry, at that day an unsurpassed soldiery. Menendez, himself, was well worthy, on the score of ability, of the great trust which had been reposed in him and the honours which had been heaped upon him by his king.

Of a noble Asturian family, like many boys past, present, and to come, at an early age he ran away to sea. He had fought against the Barbary pirates, the French and the English, and early attained high rank in the service. He had made several voyages to the Indies and had amassed great wealth. Though he had at one time fallen into disrepute with his capricious master, he had lately been restored to favour and given command of the whole continent from Florida north, with the title of Marquis and the rank of *Adelantando*. He was a daring and skilful sailor, a distinguished and intrepid captain.

In addition, however, to the usual obligations of his command, he had been intrusted with the duty of driving out the Huguenots who had impiously presumed to sully the soil of New Spain with their heretical presence. The prospect enkindled in his iron breast the feelings of an ancient warrior of the Cross. Some of the Frenchmen from Fort Caroline, who had been captured on that fatal pirating excursion, had saved their lives by betraying the location of the French colony. Some of the members of the Catholic party in the court of France lie under grave suspicion of having sent word to Philip of the plans of the Huguenots.

In the eye of the Spanish king their presence was an offence to God. It was the fond hope of Menendez not only to serve his country and king but his God by extirpating these heretics. Fiske calls him, and justly, the last of the Crusaders. Like himself, his followers were also imbued with mixed ideas; they too dreamed of serving God by killing Lutherans and converting savages; of finding a new empire, perhaps another Mexico; and, incidentally, of turning an honest penny. They set forth upon their expedition with that intensity of purpose which has ever characterized the Spanish zealot. So important was the matter deemed by Philip, that a re-enforcement of fifteen hundred men was despatched after the first expedition started.

The voyage was an extremely stormy one and the ships were scattered and several of them lost. Menendez, however, made a stop at San Juan, Porto Rico, and after collecting five or six of the larger ships containing some seven hundred men and leaving instructions for the rest to follow, pursued his course, until, as we have seen, he fell foul of the French at the mouth of the St. Johns, and thereafter established St. Augustine.

On the 10th of September, Ribaut and his men with five ships set forth upon their daring undertaking. On the 11th one of the fiercest gales ever recorded blew up on the coast. The sailors of Menendez toiling on the ramparts saw the weather-beaten French ships tossing to and fro in the fierce wind and rain on the gray sky line. For several days the tempest continued with unabated violence. The pious Spaniard thought he detected the hand of God interfering in his behalf. All danger from the French was at an end while the storm raged.

2 THE MASSACRE OF FORT CAROLINE

But the genius of Menendez immediately determined upon his plan. While the French ships were beating up against the storm and endeavouring to claw off the dreaded lee shore, he would fall on Fort Caroline.

Five hundred of his best men were mustered and on the 17th of September set forth upon their journey. The rain beat upon them unceasingly as they toiled along under prodigious difficulties. Sometimes waist-deep in water, sometimes sinking into treacherous quagmires, picking their precarious way over morasses, cutting down great trees to bridge the swollen streams, with incredible labours they slowly advanced. The little army was in a chronic state of mutiny from its hardships, and nothing but the iron hand and indomitable resolution of the leader controlled it. Finally on the evening of Wednesday, the 19th of September, they arrived in the vicinity of the fort.

Menendez assembled his men and in the drenching rain he made them one of the fiery speeches which he could so well deliver. They had made their march and achieved their goal. The rest of the task he assured them would be easy and the soul of the man who was killed in the attack might be sure of a swift passage into Heaven by the favour of God, since it was in His cause they were imperilling their lives. He managed to infuse into his drooping band something of his own resolute spirit and during the night the stragglers came up and the men ranged themselves in orderly ranks ready to be led against the hated foe. It had been impossible to keep lighted, or to light, the matches of the *arquebuses*, and they were discarded; their sole reliance was upon the sword.

The dawn was beginning to break through the rain-laden atmosphere when two officers cautiously descended to the meadow and captured a straggling Frenchman. Confident that no danger was to be apprehended from any foe in such weather, the officer of the guard. La Vigne, had retired to his quarters and most of the sentries had followed his example. The two officers dragged the soldier back to Menendez, who was sheltered behind a hillock, and after extorting information from him as to the situation he was instantly killed. The men clamoured to be led forward. Menendez gave the word of command and silently the band came out from the shelter of the trees and debouched in the open. A trumpeter who happened to be awake in the fort saw them and instantly sounded the alarm.

"At them!" cried Menendez. "Santiago. God is with us. Victory!" The Spanish took up the cries and sprang over the ramparts or through the breaches. A few soldiers who had run from their quarters at the call of the watchman made a short but brave resistance. Laudonnière sprang from his bed, seized his sword and shield and threw himself, half naked, against the approaching Spaniards. There was a fierce *mêlée* within the walls in the gray rain of that ghastly morning, but the French were cut down almost to a man. Seeing resistance was useless, Laudonnière turned and fled. The pursuers, unfamiliar with the way, entangled themselves in the tents and Laudonnière leaped the palisade and gained the woods. A number of others were successful in escaping with him, among them the minister.

Fifty of the women and children under fifteen years of age were spared by the orders of Menendez, the rest of the people in the fort were put to death, a number of them being hanged instead of stabbed. Of those who had escaped to the woods, six, ignorant of the excesses of the Spaniards, chose to go back and give themselves up. Their comrades who watched them from the cover of the trees saw them cut down ere they had time to make a remonstrance. The assailants drunken with blood lust, behaved with the most frightful barbarity. It is of record that they plucked out the eyes of the dead and impaling them on the points of their swords and daggers jerked them across the river with cursings and imprecations at the three remaining ships of Ribaut's squadron, one of which was commanded by his son, who seems to have been unworthy of his great father.

When the rain stopped the Spaniards opened fire on these ships; one was sunk and the others fled. Twenty-six of the fugitives under Laudonnière succeeded in gaining these two ships and after great hardships reached the coast of France. The number of killed in the attack amounted to about one hundred and sixty and the Spanish gained a great booty by the sacking of the fort. Above the heads of those he had hanged, the Spaniard caused to be fastened a huge board bearing this inscription: "I do this not as to Frenchmen but as to Lutherans and heretics!" At the close of the day, the pious Menendez wept tears of joy at having been permitted to promote the cause of the true Church in this happy manner, and almost the worst feature of the whole affair lies in the fact that his tears were undoubtedly genuine!

3. THE LINE IN THE SAND

Pass we to the next scene in this trilogy of horror. On the afternoon of the 29th of September two hundred starving Frenchmen were standing bound and defenceless before the implacable Menendez. All of Ribaut's ships had been wrecked at different places on the coast. This particular company had been endeavouring to make Fort

Caroline, of whose fate they were ignorant until informed by the Spanish, who had intercepted them at an inlet henceforth known as Matanzas, which means "slaughterings." Weakened by privation, exposure and hunger, they had placed themselves at the mercy of the Spanish admiral—they little knew its quality! After the French had yielded their arms they had been ferried across the river in groups of ten, and after being well fed—singular act of complaisance on the part of their captors—they were marched behind the sand hills and their hands securely bound. It was evening before the last Frenchman was brought over.

With Menendez was Mendoza the priest, and at his suggestion inquiry was made as to whether any of the captives were Christians (that is to say Catholics). Twelve sailors answered in the affirmative. These with four ship carpenters were released and sent by boat to St. Augustine. The rest were ordered to take up their march over the sand dunes. Menendez and Mendoza walked silently in the lead followed by a platoon of soldiery and then the bound, dejected prisoners, closely guarded. The thoughtful Spaniards stopped in a lonely hollow, deep among the tree-clad hills. Where they stopped Menendez drew a long line in the sand with the cane he carried.

The day was drawing to a close. The sun had set, and as the shades of night descended the first group of the Huguenots reached the line. Without a word of command the Spanish guards fell upon them with sword and halberd and hatchet, and bound as they were, cut them down. As each party came doggedly on it met a like fate. Did they front death with the courage of the warrior, the fortitude of the martyr, the calmness of the philosopher? Did they beg life in anguish, in despair? Did they mingle curses with groanings, or did they suffer in silence? We know not. Not a Frenchman survived to tell the story and the Spaniards have not said. Mendoza the priest stood by thanking God—exulting! *Te Deum Laudamus*. "In religion, what damned error did ever lack a sober brow to bless it and approve it with a text?"

When all was over, Menendez and his band went on their way rejoicing, but not all the waters of Heaven could wash from the shuddering earth that red line!

His work was not yet accomplished however. On the 10th of October, off Anastasia Island, he met Ribaut and the main body of the shipwrecked French—some three hundred and fifty starved, broken men. As before, a river intervened between them and the Spanish. The French were incapable of making any resistance to the force of

Menendez. They resorted to parley and it is believed received some promise from the Spanish captain that their lives would be spared. Ribaut, who seems to have been a man of heroic breed, would scarcely have consented to put himself in the power of the enemy with- out some such assurance.

At any rate, he arranged to surrender. Two hundred of his party, however, refused to be bound by his convention and fled to the southward. The remainder, to the number of one hundred and fifty, were brought across the stream. Ribaut himself gave into the hands of the admiral the royal standard, his commissions and weapons, etc. As before, the French were brought over in groups of ten. While the first party were crossing Ribaut was taken behind a neighbouring sand hill and bound, as were all the others.

There was no marching this time and no red line. The envenomed Spaniards surrounded the bound and helpless prisoners. "Are you Catholics or Lutherans?" they cried. "Will any here go to confession?"

Calmly Ribaut answered: "I and all here are of the Reformed faith." There was a moment's hesitation, followed by bitter murmurs of rage from the Spaniards. The voice of the old man reciting the 132nd Psalm was heard in the tumult: "*Memento Domine.*"

"We are of earth, to earth we must return," he added. "Twenty years more or less can matter little." He turned to Menendez and looked at him. 'Twas such a look as the Gentle Master might have given Peter fifteen centuries before.

Menendez gave the signal. By his direction five youths were spared and the rest were put to the sword. At the last moment Ribaut with dauntless courage reproached Menendez, calling upon him to remember his promise that their lives should be spared. A soldier cut short his denunciations by plunging a dagger into his heart. The head of the brave old Frenchman was cut in four pieces and mounted upon the rain-washed walls of St. Augustine. The two hundred men who had fled were subsequently captured by the Spanish, who, strange to say, kept the promises which were made and spared their lives, though they were treated with ignominy and shame. The total number of killed in the various massacres appears to have been upwards of six hundred persons, most of them cut down in cold blood.

In the gloomy gridiron palace in the mountains of Guadaramas, the indefatigable king of Spain pursued his life of mingled debauchery and despatches. There was great news for him one winter morning.

A letter had arrived from the new world from the trusted Menendez. The king eagerly opened the missive—out of it dropped a blood-stained lock of Ribaut's gray beard! He read with vivid appreciation of the contents, and when he had finished, as was his wont, he seized the royal pen and wrote upon it a few sentences. "Say to him that as to those he has killed he has done well,"—mark the tacit reproof to mercy in the sentence—"and as to those he has saved they shall be sent to the galleys." Is there a more frightful picture in history than the sombre king penning this awful endorsement in the forbidding chambers of the Escurial? The black lines traced by his pen are as damning as the red line of Menendez.

4 THE TERRIBLE EXPIATION

Laudonnière and his fellow fugitives brought the first news of the Spanish conduct to France. Soon afterwards the other atrocities were enumerated. There was peace between the countries of the most Christian and the most Catholic majesties and France was filled with a hue and cry for reparation. Some feeble efforts were made by Charles IX and Catherine de Medici and a correspondence ensued, but nothing was done. After all, they were Huguenots and heretics. What could be expected from a prince who could shoot down his flying and un-armed subjects, who had trusted to his honour, on the dread 24th of August—Saint Bartholomew's day! What could be hoped from a king who could gaze unmoved upon the mortifying body of the betrayed admiral who had not learned in all his study of Scripture the meaning of that text, "*Put not your trust in princes!*" What could be expected from a ruler who said to his fastidious courtiers then, "The body of a dead enemy always smells sweet!"

The court talked, argued, debated— and forgot! But what the power of France could not, or would not effect, was undertaken by a simple gentleman, one of the lesser nobility of the land. Dominique de Gourgues was of that country which gave birth to de Bergerac and d'Artagnan. He was a Gascon and a sailor. He had been captured by the Spaniards and sent to the galleys. He had been a prisoner of the Turks. Liberated by the Knights of Malta, he had made many voyages in distant seas and was a bold, successful navigator. The Spaniards call him a Huguenot and a heretic, but it is more than probable that he was a Roman Catholic. At any rate we fain would think so. If a Catholic he was great enough to rise above his religion. He hated Spain and he loved France. He determined to do what the king and the country dared not attempt.

Selling his patrimony and borrowing from his family, he procured three small ships which he manned with one hundred and eighty chosen men, proven spirits ready for any hazard. With a commission to go on a slave-trading voyage, he set forth in August, 1567, from the Charente. Early in the next spring, after a roundabout voyage, he reached the coast of Florida. Here for the first time de Gourgues revealed to his hardy followers the purpose of his expedition. With persuasive Gascon eloquence he painted the horrible treachery and brutal treatment which had been accorded the colonists. He spoke to them of the lost honour of France, and appealed to them by every quality of their manhood to join with him in wiping out the stain and exacting summary vengeance. Like the bold sailor he was he promised that they should incur no danger he would not share; that they should make no advance he would not lead. With beating hearts they welcomed the bold project, and de Gourgues instantly moved up the coast toward the St. Johns.

The Spaniards had rebuilt the French fort and had renamed it San Mateo. In addition they had thrown up two smaller redoubts at the mouth of the river. So quietly had de Gourgues slipped away from France and so unsuspicious were the Spaniards, that when the watchers in the redoubts saw three ships toiling along in the offing, they gave them a friendly salute, which was returned. De Gourgues landed forty miles north of the river. He was met by bands of Indians in warlike array. There was menace in their appearance, but when they learned that the newcomers were Frenchmen and had come to exact vengeance upon the Spaniards, who had already made themselves hated by their cruelties and excesses, they were welcomed with shouts of joy; and savage voices, filled with indistinct memories, broke forth into fragments of Psalms they had learned from Laudonnière! There was counselling and feasting and preparation. Three days after the landing, de Gourgues, with one hundred and fifty Frenchmen and three hundred Indians, moved down toward the river.

Twenty sailors were left with the ships. The French and their allies, who were led by Satouriona and his nephew Olotoraca, a young chieftain of great prowess, were about to attack over four hundred Spanish soldiers secure in fortifications of their own making. The French descended the coast in boats, several times in imminent danger of shipwreck, until they came to the Indian rendezvous. There they disembarked and marched through the wood. De Gourgues in the full armour of the time, was in the lead; with him was Olotoraca carrying a French half pike. In the afternoon they came to a stream flowing into the St. Johns, on the opposite side of which lay one of the redoubts, and there encamped for the night. There was but little rest for de Gourgues, who, with the Indian guides, spent the long hours in reconnoitring and laying his plans.

In the morning, when the tide was out, they found a sheltered ford behind a clump of trees, and fastening their powder horns to their headpieces and holding their *arquebuses* and swords above their heads, they waded through the water. The oyster shells in the bottom of the river cut and tore their feet but they pressed on. Shortly after noon they drew up in battle array under the trees near the fort.

"Look!" cried the Gascon, pointing at the redoubt. "There are the murderers who have butchered our countrymen! Forward!"

With clenched teeth the men swept on.

The Spaniards had just finished their dinner when one of the artillerymen, who happened to glance over the rampart, in frantic terror gave the alarm. The French were advancing upon them in ordered ranks. A party under Lieutenant Cazenove had been detached to secure the gate. The gunner discharged his cannon at them, but before he could reload, Olotoraca, leaping upon the rampart, drove a pike through his heart. De Gourgues was mounting the glacis when he heard a cry that the Spaniards were escaping by the gate. He led his men toward that point on the run. Cazenove was already hotly engaged and the whole garrison to the number of sixty were caught and killed, except a few who were reserved for a special purpose—there was no mercy in the reservation.

The Spanish redoubt on the other side of the St. Johns had opened fire upon the French. The Indians plunged into the stream and swam across. One of de Gourgues' larger boats had been brought along the shore. Entering it with eighty men he pushed across the river. Terror seized the Spanish and they fled. They were surrounded by Indians, however, and the French fell upon them with determined fury. The utmost efforts of de Gourgues could save but fifteen of them for that special purpose. The next day was Low Sunday, the octave of the Resurrection. The French made no attack on Fort San Mateo that day, though they busied themselves with preparations.

The woods, however, teemed with Indians and the Spaniards dared not leave the fort. One bolder than the rest at last ventured out disguised as an Indian and entered the French line. Olotoraca discovered

45

him at once. From him it was learned that there were two hundred and sixty Spaniards in the fort and that they were mad with terror; they believed the French amounted to over two thousand men.

On Monday night the attack began. The Spaniards opened fire on them with their culverins, but the French remained concealed in the forest, and finally the Spaniards sent out a strong party to reconnoitre. Cazenove, with a detachment, was moved forward to flank the enemy. De Gourgues, himself, kept his men well in hand in the bushes until the head of the Spanish advance was upon them. A deadly fire in front and flank cut them down, and before they could recover themselves, out of the smoke of the battle appeared the steel-clad French. Not a man reached the fort, but in the sight of the rest of the Spanish they were killed or taken.

Those in the fort now lost their heads. They abandoned their fortifications and fled to the woods away from the advancing French. The Indians fell upon them with savage fierceness and held them in check until the French overtook them. Again a few were saved from slaughter. Near the fort were the trees from which had swung the bodies of the Frenchmen whom Menendez had hanged. Thither were dragged the wretched Spaniards whom de Gourgues had saved. They, too, were hanged, and over the mouldering remains of the former inscription a new tablet was nailed bearing these words, which had been traced with a hot iron: "*Not as to Spaniards, but as to traitors, robbers, and murderers!*"

On the 3rd of May de Gourgues set sail for France. The Spaniards from St. Augustine repossessed the land. De Gourgues, broken in fortune and under the disfavour of a king who scarcely knew how to resist the Spanish demand for his head, lived in the utmost obscurity and poverty, but was finally restored to favour, and invited by Elizabeth to enter her service. He chose, however to accept the command of a Portuguese fleet which was preparing to fight against Philip II., when he died at Tours, in 1583.

De Gourgues' revenge had failed in but one point, Menendez, the chief fiend, had escaped, for the Spaniard returned home laden with honours and high in the affections of his king and his countrymen. At the very summit of his career, when about to assume command of a fleet of three hundred sail and twenty thousand men, which was destined to sail against England, he died at Santander, in 1574, in the fifty-fifth year of his age. He had begun at Fort Caroline the work of driving the French from the continent, which was completed by

Wolfe two hundred years after on the Plains of Abraham.

I picture Menendez standing before the Judgement Bar of God, his feet upon a red line in the sand. I see the long indictment read against Philip in the same High Court, bearing these awful words in the king's own hand, "Say to him that he has done well."

The flag of the French was driven from the continent long since by the Anglo-Saxon, and the last vestiges of the great Empire of Spain were wrenched from the trembling hands which vainly strove to retain them by the children of the same proud race, when the hot muzzles of the great guns spoke at Manila and Santiago!

1

Sir Henry Morgan and His Buccaneers

1. PLUNDERING PUERTO BELLO

Woe to the realms which he coasted! for there
Was shedding of blood and rending of hair,
Rape of maiden, and slaughter of priest,
Gathering of ravens and wolves to the feast;
When he hoisted his standard black,
Before him was battle, behind him wrack.
And he burned the churches, that heathen Dane,
To light his band to their barks again.

As in the course of animal growth we pass—embryonically or otherwise—through the various conditions of physical being which mark progressive stages of evolution, so in mental development successive epochs of history are represented. Sooner or later every normal life enters upon an age of chivalry, and the characters upon which we love to dwell are the knights-errant of the past. The words bring before us pictures of courage, generosity, devotion to an ideal and all the chivalric virtues. Rise in our memory the names of Arthur, Lancelot, Galahad, Roland, the Black Prince, Du Guesclin, culminating in that famous knight who was without fear and without reproach.

It is a far cry from Bayard to Morgan the Buccaneer. Yet the latter by the favour of His Gracious Majesty, Charles II of England, was made a belted knight, and henceforth was known as Sir Henry Morgan. A king who could frolic with Rochester and Buckingham, who could sell his honour to the hereditary enemy of his country for French gold, plus Louise de Kerouailles, would thoroughly enjoy Morgan 1

One of the earlier stages of the tempo-mental development re-

48

ferred to is that in which most lads, and some girls perhaps, desire to become—pirates! It precedes, logically enough, the knight-errant phase. (Query: Was the knight a sublimated robber, or was the robber a degenerate knight?) I think it may be on account of the freedom from restraint which a pirate is supposed to enjoy, that his profession is so fascinating to our period of tutelage. Some impressions of youthful days remain—the piratical for instance. We frequently forget to be chivalrous and gentle, but we never altogether lose our appreciation of the ruthless independence of the rovers of the sea, and the story of their lives, with its brutality and bloodshed, grime and horror, fascinates us still.

This is a tale of a few of the exploits of the greatest and worst of the buccaneers. Like "Taffy," Morgan was a Welshman. The parallelism may be carried farther with accuracy, for he was also a thief, but there it stops. "Taffy" was an angel of light beside Morgan. Like the first conspicuous bearer of his name. Sir Henry was a heretic, from the Spanish stand-point. He was born the son of poor but honest parents, farmers in Wales, in 1637. At an early age he ran away to sea, bound himself out as an indentured servant, and sailed for the New World. He faithfully served his time and then cast about to see what fields of action were open for a young gentleman of limited education, entire unscrupulousness, abundant courage and overweening ambition, and decided to join the ancient and successful army of tanners, otherwise buccaneers.

The catching of cattle and the preserving of the meat and hides by the process of "*boucan,*" *i.e.*, drying them over fires of aromatic green twigs, had been a most profitable vocation. Cattle in the West Indies were had for the taking and the life was free, easy, and bold. When the supply of cattle gave out, however, it was a perfectly natural and legitimate transition to turn from tanning the hides of animals to doing a little experimenting in the same direction upon men. The rich and unwieldy Spanish galleons, laden with the treasure of Mexico and Peru, slowly swashing through the Caribbean homeward bound, suggested themselves as objects of profitable attack. There was more sport in their capture, greater reward to be gained therefrom, and there was just as much blood in the human cattle as in the wild beasts that had roamed the hills.

Under the stimulus of this opportunity, into the vortex of the Caribbean were speedily precipitated the vile of all nations. Hereditary national and racial antagonisms were laid aside, or held in abeyance, in the presence of a common hatred. Spain was undoubtedly the most unpopular power that ever dominated the earth. She was also, at that time, the richest. The yellow flag was an invitation to attack which was accepted with murderous avidity. As the buccaneers grew and prospered, from the taking of single ships, or even squadrons, it was an easy step to organize expeditions to seize the principal towns on the Spanish Main and after plundering them, hold them for ransom.

Bartholomew Portuguese, L'Olonnois, and Mansvelt had already made a name for themselves when Morgan rose to unenviable eminence and surpassed them all. He had become widely known through his ruthless boldness and success, and had been chosen as second in command of the great fleet which Mansvelt had assembled with the hope of carving out a buccaneer republic from the Spanish domains, when death put an end to the Dutchman's scheme, scattered the great squadron that had been gathered for the attempt and possibly changed future history to a degree. Morgan attracted to himself some of the bolder spirits and with a force of twelve small vessels he sacked the town of Puerto Principe, Cuba, from which his party gleaned no inconsiderable profit—just enough to whet the appetites of the buccaneers for more! Not that their appetites needed much whetting, for of all the examples of insatiable rapacity the "Brethren of the Coast"—so they called themselves—bear the palm.

After the raid on Puerto Principe a quarrel over the spoil between the French and the English caused the former to abandon his command, and Morgan was left with but nine small vessels, carrying about four hundred and fifty men. Such was the ascendency he had gained over his ruthless followers, that he actually induced them to commit the whole charge of the next expedition to him alone, and the vessels put to sea from Jamaica in the early part of 1668, without the commander communicating his purpose to anyone.

The only information he vouchsafed was that he expected to make their fortunes on this occasion. He knew how to inflame their cupidity and they became eager to follow wherever he chose to lead. They reckoned without the daring of their leader. After a voyage of some days they anchored off Costa Rica; when they made a landfall, Morgan announced to his captains that he intended to sack the town of Puerto Bello. To this proposition there was an instant demur. The boldness of the idea appalled them.

Puerto Bello, although an unhealthy place of residence, was a strong town defended by two large castles and several smaller works garrisoned by three hundred regular soldiers. It contained a resident population of two thousand. The wealthy residents and slave traders lived in the city of Panama and only came to Puerto Bello when the galleons arrived from and departed to Spain. At such times a great fair was held and the ordinary population of the city was largely increased. Morgan had carefully timed his arrival for this propitious season.

The buccaneers hesitated in the face of such tremendous odds, claiming that they were not sufficiently strong to assault so formidable a place; but Morgan, who, with all his badness was a born leader of men, stoutly clung to his plan, pointing out ways and means by which it could be accomplished, heartening and inspiriting the reluctant by his dauntless bearing and confidence, and finally appealed to their ruling passion in this stout phrase:

"If our numbers be small, our hearts are great. The fewer we are the more union among us and the larger shares we shall each have in the spoil." That settled it. They finally agreed to follow him and clamoured to be led to the attack.

Morgan had brought his squadron to a lonely spot some thirty miles to the westward of the town. Favoured by a fair wind they sailed along the shore until they reached a point within a few miles of the city. Leaving a few men in the vessels to work them up to the harbour the next day, the little army landed on the shore at midnight Led by an Englishman who had been a prisoner, in perfect silence they toiled through the dense tropic wood toward the town. As they drew near the outskirts in the gray of the morning, they spied a sentry on the edge of the clearing. The man, not dreaming there was a foe within a thousand miles of him, kept negligent watch over the sleeping town. The buccaneers crept softly through the underbrush, sprang upon him and disarmed him. No alarm was given.

They dragged their captive back to the main body where Morgan questioned him as to the situation and he was menaced with a thousand deaths if he did not tell the truth. Led by their terrified prisoner they took up their march again and soon reached the castle of Triana. They were not discovered until they had completely invested the fortification and demanded its surrender, under pain of no quarter. Disdaining this astonishing request the garrison sprang to arms and opened fire, but the capture of the sentry, the negligent watch kept and the celerity of their movements had enabled Morgan's men to gain the outworks and they presently succeeded in storming the castle.

They had threatened to give no quarter, and they were men who always kept promises of that kind religiously. They had some virtues, these buccaneers. They were usually loyal to each other, obedient to their officers, warred only on Spaniards and frequently had prayers before battle! When they captured the castle, therefore, they forced all the soldiers and officers into the great hall under which they collected all the powder they found in the magazine. Reserving the women and children for a worse fate they barred the outlet of the hall, touched off the powder and then withdrew. The tower was blown up and the garrison killed to a man.

These happenings had given the alarm to the town, the inhabitants of which endeavoured to conceal their treasures and fly to the depths of the forest. Meanwhile the governor of the place and the remainder of the garrison had thrown themselves into the other castle and prepared to make a stout defence. Detaching a body of men to secure the town, Morgan advanced toward the fort. There was no possibility of a surprise of course and how to take the castle was a problem. The buccaneers who were all expert marksmen concealed themselves about the walls and by brilliant feats of sharpshooting kept down the Spanish fire. If anyone appeared in the embrasures he was sure to be hit.

Finally a brilliant idea occurred to the chief fiend. Morgan directed that the monks and nuns from the monasteries and convents which had been seized, should be brought forward. He also caused a number of great ladders to be prepared large enough for three men to mount abreast. When the terrified monks and nuns appeared he ordered them to take up the ladders and place them against the walls. They begged and entreated, but their captor was pitiless and the helpless men and women finally seized the ladders and advanced toward the castle imploring the governor not to fire upon them.

The man who kept that castle was an heroic soldier. He intended to hold the fort at whatever sacrifice, so in spite of the adjurations and anathemas of the priests and the shrieks and prayers of the nuns, he opened fire upon them. It was impossible for the poor men and women to retreat—behind them were the buccaneers. In utter despair they rushed forward and set the ladders, many of them being killed or wounded in the attempt. The pirates carrying fire-balls and grenades scrambled up the ladders and poured over the walls.

All the members of the garrison who did not surrender instantly were put to the sword. The brave governor made an heroic resistance. Deserted by his men, several of whom he had killed with his own hands for their pusillanimity, he fought on alone. In spite of the entreaties of his wife and children, who had been taken, he continued to fight until he was killed, saying when asked to surrender, "I had rather die as a soldier than be hanged as a coward." The other works made but a feeble resistance and the town was soon at the mercy of the buccaneers—a misnomer that, they had no mercy in them.

The pirates forced the prisoners, wounded and unwounded, into one of the rooms of the castle where they were left to their own devices without food or attention of any sort. The women were removed for unmentionable purposes, and the company spread over the town to plunder and destroy. They gave way to the most frightful excesses and debaucheries. Such was the confusion, disorder, and drunkenness, that fifty resolute men could have captured the whole pirate band. Unfortunately they were not there.

For fifteen days the ruthless murderers lorded it over the hapless town, until even their merciless natures were sated with debauchery and crime. Having pillaged the warehouses of the merchants and provisioned their ships for the return voyage, they arranged to depart. Before they left, however, Morgan determined on a final *coup*. He informed the wretched prisoners that unless he received a ransom of one hundred thousand pieces of eight (Spanish silver dollars), he would burn the town and raze the fortifications to the ground. Two prisoners were sent to de Guzman, the governor of Panama, with this message. In reply the governor put a large force of men in motion to take the pirates before their retreat.

Being informed of this expedition by a runaway slave, Morgan prepared a cunning ambush in a defile through which the Spaniards must march and with one hundred men threw the advance into confusion, and after killing a large number forced a retreat. The governor refused, in spite of his defeat, to pay any ransom. He contented himself with promising Morgan no quarter when he should be taken—futile threat.

The miserable inhabitants, however, managed to scrape up the ransom demanded and brought it to the pirates, who, having secured all they could from the town, kept their faith with them and sailed away to Jamaica, leaving the houses unburned.

Before he left, however, Morgan promised de Guzman that he would return in a twelvemonth and pay him a visit! The governor warned him off, but with extraordinary complaisance at the same time made him a present of a beautiful emerald ring!

2. THE RAID ON MARACAIBO

The ill-got gains of the pirates soon vanished and they were ripe for another undertaking. The news was passed among the islands that Morgan was organizing another expedition and men flocked to join him at the appointed rendezvous, a little island south of Hispaniola. The English governor of Jamaica, desirous of taking a hand in the successful and profitable enterprise of the pirate, contributed a large and formidable war vessel from New England, called the *Oxford*, carrying thirty-six guns.

Our thrifty ancestors frequently furnished contingents for such expeditions. While they were provisioning the squadron a splendid French ship from St. Malo, called the *Flying Stag*, carrying thirty-six guns also, joined them.

Morgan cast covetous eyes upon this vessel, which agreed to sail in his company though not under his command. Under pretence of hospitality he inveigled the French officers on board the *Oxford*, where they were arrested on some flimsy pretext and Morgan took possession of their ship. Elated by their success, the buccaneers held a great carouse on the *Oxford*, during which her powder magazine exploded and she blew up. Some thirty officers in the after cabin, removed from the vicinity of the explosion, escaped with their lives; the rest of the crew of three hundred and fifty men were nearly all killed or drowned. The bay was covered with floating corpses for days. Morgan had them stripped of their clothing and jewellery and then allowed them to float uncared for. It was believed that the *Oxford* and her Yankee crew had been blown up by the French prisoners below. I hope so. The French ship was sent back to Jamaica and the governor confiscated her.

In spite of the loss of the *Oxford*, Morgan set sail with fifteen vessels and eight hundred men, the largest ship carrying only fourteen small guns. Eight of his vessels parted company on the voyage and never rejoined him. He pressed on, however, with seven small ships and three hundred men to attack the wealthy and important city of Maracaibo, situated on the lake of that name in Venezuela. The expedition met with little opposition and found the castle which guarded the strait and town suspiciously deserted when they swarmed over the walls. A hasty inspection revealed that the Spaniards had prepared a trap for them by igniting a fuse leading to the magazine. In a few seconds they would have been blown to pieces, and the world would have been thereby the gainer, if Morgan had not gallantly cut the fuse and prevented the danger. The town fell almost without resistance, and the same scenes of torture and outrage ensued.

Having got what they could from the town they made predatory excursions into the surrounding country, which was filled with fugitives, and among other devil doings they sacked the smaller town of Gibraltar. By these expeditions they collected an immense booty and a great number of prisoners. Having been five weeks in possession after exacting an immense ransom for the release of the unfortunate prisoners and for not burning the town, Morgan determined to depart.

Lake Maracaibo is connected with the sea by a narrow strait guarded by a large fort which commands the opening. Toward the latter part of April, 1669, a squadron of three formidable Spanish men-of-war of forty, thirty and twenty guns respectively, arrived off the strait and anchored right in the entrance. The Spaniards occupied the fort upon which they mounted some heavy guns. The squadron easily overmatched Morgan's force. After some bombastic correspondence between the buccaneer and the Spanish admiral, in which the latter offered the pirate free passage home with his men if he would give up his booty and his prisoners and refrain from burning the town, which terms were indignantly refused by the buccaneer, Morgan determined to force the passage by means of a fire ship. The fire ship was rigged with dummy guns and logs of wood dressed in uniforms to give the impression that she was a war vessel. She was filled to the deck with powder, tar, brimstone and other combustibles. Twelve of the most daring of the buccaneers agreed to man her.

On April 30th, the squadron set sail, the fire ship in the lead, heading straight for the huge galleon of the Spanish admiral. The Spaniards believing it to be Morgan's flagship, withheld their fire, intending to crush it with a broadside. They had not reckoned on the swiftness of the fire ship and the activity of the buccaneers. Before they realized it the infernal machine had run them aboard and grappled with them, without receiving a shot. She instantly burst into flames. The buccaneer captain and his crew leaped overboard. The galleon, dry from her cruise in the tropics, caught fire and in spite of every effort was soon burning furiously. In the midst of the confusion while the crew was striving to put out the fire, Morgan came up with the rest of his fleet and opened with his guns upon the galleon. The second ship, terrified by the fate of the flagship, was boarded and captured almost without resistance and the third vessel in attempting to escape got ashore and was burned by an attacking party. The flagship meanwhile burned to the water line and sank.

The admiral and a few of his crew succeeded in reaching the castle, the garrison of which was under arms. The rest of the men were burned or slaughtered. No quarter was the word again. Elated by their success, Morgan landed and attempted to storm the castle, but he met with such a stout resistance that he was driven back with a loss of some sixty killed and wounded. Abandoning the attack for the present, the buccaneers returned to Maracaibo.

The captured ship was fitted out for Morgan's own use and the ransom he had seen fit to demand for the town was increased by five hundred cows for victualling his fleet. By great exertion they were provided and having taken some ten thousand pieces of eight from the wreck of the Spanish flagship, all they could secure out of a total of forty thousand she had on board when she sank, Morgan again made for the sea. It was useless to think of attacking the fort, and while the Spaniards held it, the narrow channel between the lake and the ocean was closed. In this dilemma, Morgan resorted to strategy.

He anchored his ships just out of gunshot range and in full view of the castle. Boats were called away and filled with men who rowed to the shore behind a clump of trees which hid them from the garrison. The men then concealed themselves by lying in the bottom of the boats, which, apparently empty, were rowed back to the ship by a few men. This performance went on all day, giving those in the fort the impression that the buccaneers were landing in force to attack them from the land side. During the afternoon, therefore, the Spaniards busied themselves with shifting their guns to the land side of the fort in preparation for the expected attack.

As the night fell, Morgan weighed anchor and his squadron drifted quietly down the river with the ebb tide. Though it was moonlight he was not discovered until the vessels were right under the walls of the castle. When the alarm was given, every sail was at once spread with ready quickness, and favoured by a strong land breeze the vessels rushed for the open sea. The Spaniards reshifted their battery, but before they could get the long eighteen pounders to their embrasures again, the buccaneers were out of range. The Spaniards fired upon them, but beyond killing and wounding a few men, did little damage. They had scarcely made an offing when they ran into the teeth of a tremendous gale. It was only by the exercise of the most superb seamanship that their boats were kept afloat on the perilous lee shore. After four days of tempest, six heavy armed vessels gave them chase in the midst of the storm. Fortunately for the pirates they turned out to be a French naval force under the command of d'Estrées. When the storm abated, generously assisted by the French admiral, the pirates finally reached Jamaica without losing a ship. The booty was even greater than that taken from Puerto Bello, and every man was loaded with plunder—money, jewels, silks, raiment, liquors, women, slaves, everything which helps to make up the hellish paradise of the rover of the seal

3. The Storming of Fort St Lawrence

Encouraged by this success Morgan organized another expedition, which, from its magnitude and audacity threw his other adventures into the background. He was the king of the buccaneers now, and he had only to lift his hand to find himself surrounded by the cream of the ferocious society. Word was swiftly passed from mouth to mouth in every drinking place, brothel, and purlieu of the wicked cities of the Caribbean, that he was about to take the sea once more, and that there would be rich pickings for bold men under his command. Morgan himself wrote letters to the principal scoundrels of his acquaintance from Tortuga to St. Kitts. A rendezvous was appointed at Port Couillon, on the south side of Hispaniola as usual.

His previous successes and the glowing accounts of the royal times they had enjoyed, which had been spread about by all the swaggering rogues among their detestable kinfolk and acquaintances, caused the greatest numbers to flock to the rendezvous.

Some of them came in ships, others in canoes and small boats, and many with incredible hardships came overland on foot. So great was the number of applicants that it became difficult for strangers to secure a place in the fleet.

Morgan carefully scrutinized the various applicants, and by a process of natural selection secured such a body of desperate, hardened, ferocious, courageous ruffians as probably had never been assembled before or since.

The flagship was the *Flying Stag*, the French ship of thirty-six guns, which had been sent by the governor of Jamaica. It was gravely alleged that Morgan issued commissions to his principal officers in the name of the governor and King Charles II, guaranteeing them from all effects of Spanish hostility. On October 24th, 1670, twenty-four vessels had assembled at the rendezvous. After some predatory expeditions to secure supplies, the squadron set sail for Cape Tiburon, to take in food and water. Here Morgan was joined by several ships from the thrifty coasts of New England, which had been refitted and commissioned at Jamaica. The combined fleet now numbered thirty-seven vessels of various sizes, manned by twenty-two hundred human tigers.

The *armada* was divided into two squadrons under a vice-admiral and other subordinates. The first squadron sailed under the royal English flag, and no more disgraceful band ever served under that noble emblem. The second squadron was under a white ensign, probably French, and Morgan's ship flew a red banner with a white cross and at the bowsprit a red, white and blue flag—singular precursor of our national colours.

Contrary to custom he took counsel with his principal officers to consider the best point of attack. They wavered between Panama, Carthagena and Vera Cruz; the determinating factor being not so much which was the easiest but which was the richest. The decision finally fell upon Panama. I have no doubt that de Guzman's emerald, which he still wore, influenced Morgan to this decision.

We can imagine how the hearts of these buccaneers beat with anticipation, how their eyes gleamed with lust and cupidity, as in the cabin of the *Flying Stag*, with strange oaths and deep potations, they drank success to their enterprise, the most difficult thing ever attempted before or after by the famous brethren of the coast. In order to procure a guide and establish a base of supplies, the expedition first captured the fortified island of St. Catherine. A *mulatto* slave among the captives, who is described as a rogue, a thief, and an assassin, who deserved breaking on the wheel, agreed to guide them. He was promised liberty and a full share of the booty for his pilotage.

Before they could proceed to Panama it was necessary to capture the fort at the mouth of the Chagres River. Morgan and the bulk of his command remained at St. Catherine's, employed in preparation for their enterprise, while five ships and four hundred men under the command of Bradley, a famous buccaneer, were sent forward to seize the castle. Morgan was to follow with the rest after eight days.

The castle of St. Lawrence was built on a high mountain of the same name at the mouth of the river. It was surrounded by strong wooden palisades banked on the inside with mounds of earth. There were four bastions toward the land and two toward the sea. The land side sloped down to a gentle valley, the sea face was precipitous and unscalable. The top of the mountain was divided in two parts by a ditch thirty feet deep. At the foot of the hill was an eight-gun fort and two batteries of six guns all commanding the river. As usual the buccaneers landed some distance away from the point of attack and marched through a wood which was so thick that they had to hew out a way with axes and cutlasses. They finally reached a hill which commanded the castle, but as they were without cannon and beyond musket range their position was of no value.

They finally descended the hill, avoiding the river forts, crawled across the open on their hands and knees to escape the dreadful fire which the Spaniards and their Indian auxiliaries poured upon them, which killed and wounded many of them, and then sword in hand, swarmed up the steep sides of the hill and strove to climb the palisades. Many were shot down before they reached the rampart, where they enjoyed a certain immunity, for the most expert shots among the pirates who had been stationed under cover picked off every Spaniard who showed his head in an embrasure.

The fight dragged on until evening, when the buccaneers, having in vain tried to fire the palisades, retreated down the hill in the dusk in great disorder, having lost heavily. They carried their wounded with them. Bradley had both legs broken by a cannon shot, but his spirit was still undaunted. A steady exchange of musketry was kept up during the evening until night fell, when they made another assault.

Taking advantage of the darkness a strong party crept up to the palisades. At the same time a body of French were detailed to climb the path upon another side and make a diversion. One of the Frenchmen was pierced in the shoulder with an arrow. Hastily tearing the dart from his quivering flesh, he took a handful of wild cotton which he kept in his pouch for lint, wound it around the arrow and then extracting the bullet from his musket substituted the arrow for it. He took careful aim at the castle roof and discharged his piece. The arrow alighted on some dry thatch. The cotton caught fire from the discharge. It smouldered a moment or two upon the thatch and then broke into a bright flame. There was soon a roaring blaze on the roof of the castle. Other buccaneers picked up the Indian arrows and repeated the experiment. Flames broke out on every side and finally a barrel of powder blew up in a bastion, causing great damage.

With fierce cries of victory, the buccaneers rushed to the attack. The poor Spaniards were in a dreadful dilemma. Their situation was indeed desperate. Their forts and houses were burning behind them and their foes were clamouring at the palisades. If they left the ramparts for a moment they would be slaughtered by the foe; if they could not check the flames they would be equally lost. They fought on, however, with the gallantry of their proud race. Their bodies outlined against the bright light presented a fair target for the pirate sharp-shooters, while the latter were invisible in the darkness. While the palisades held, the Spaniards made good their defence, but as the night wore on the buccaneers succeeded in setting fire to the palisades.

When morning broke, the wooden walls had been burned down and the earthen ramparts had fallen in great heaps. Pouring a tremendous musketry fire upon the now undefended place, shooting down man after man at the guns which stood in the open, about noon they advanced to the storm. They passed the ditch by climbing on one another's shoulders. The Spaniards rallied around their governor and defended themselves with the courage of despair. It was a hand to hand struggle of the most dreadful description. Rampart after rampart was taken by the resistless valour of the pirates, and the defenders finally fought from room to room in the castle, making a last stand in the guard room, when the governor, sternly refusing to surrender, was shot dead.

When the buccaneers finally overbore resistance and broke down the last brave defence by sheer weight of numbers, they captured but fourteen men, whom they rendered helpless by tearing their weapons from their hands. Many of the Spaniards disdaining to surrender leaped over the cliff into the sea. The fourteen captives and nine or ten too desperately wounded to move, were all that were left of some three hundred and fifty men in the garrison, not counting Indians. Over two hundred of the buccaneers had been killed or wounded. It was as bold an attack and as desperate a defence as was ever made.

The courage of the buccaneers was beyond description. One of the surgeons has left on record an incident which shows the fortitude and fury of these pirates. A man who had been pierced in the eye by an Indian arrow came to the doctor to have it taken out. The surgeon shrank from the operation, knowing the intense pain it would involve. As he hesitated, with a curse the man tore it out of his eye with his own hand, and binding around his head a piece of rag ripped from his shirt, he rushed forward to the assault once more.

A few days after, Morgan arrived with the main body. Great was the joy of the buccaneers when they saw the royal flag of England floating over the ruined fort. In their eagerness to make the harbour several ships were wrecked on the rocky reef at the mouth of the river, including the famous *Flying Stag*. The crews and provisions were saved, and but for a "norther" which swooped down upon them, the ships might have been saved. The remainder of the ships safely entered the harbour and the fort was rebuilt and garrisoned

4. THE MARCH TO THE PACIFIC

On January 18, 1669, the buccaneers set out with thirteen hundred men in canoes and small boats toward Panama. The great loss at the mouth of the Chagres and the wreck of the ships filled some of the superstitious sailors with foreboding, but they were jeered and laughed at by the majority of the ruffians, and under the threat of being left behind they fell in with the rest. This was the cheer with which they began their march: "Long live the King of England and long live Harry Morgan." A nice collocation that!

For four days they toiled along the river, some in canoes and boats and some on the banks. Their provisions speedily gave out and their hardships began. The country was a wilderness. They met no one. The villages they passed through had been denuded of everything edible and abandoned. They were forced to subsist upon roots, leaves, and grasses. In the absence of any proper equipment for any land campaigning they were compelled to sleep on the ground in the damp, chilly, unhealthy tropic nights, consequently many fell ill. Their clothing was soon torn to rags by the impenetrable forests through which they were forced to make their toilsome way.

On the fourth day they came upon an intrenchment at which they rushed to the attack, sword in hand, but when they climbed over the ramparts they found it had been abandoned like the rest. There was a large number of old leather bags in the place. They cut them into pieces, soaked them in water, beat them soft between two stones, scraped the hair off with their knives, and toasted them by the fire. When cooked sufficiently, they cut each piece into small cubes and swallowed them. A poor substitute for food they found it.

On the fifth day, at a plantation at Barbacoa, they found several bags of flour, some jars of wine and bunches of plantains in a cave, which by Morgan's orders were divided among the most exhausted of the men. Some of them were nearly dead from famine, fatigue, exposure, and illness. The weaker men were placed in the canoes and they resumed the march.

On the sixth day they rested and sent out foraging parties to gather berries and roots until noon when they again started forward. One party wandering from the way came to a plantation and a barn filled with corn. They broke down the crib and fell upon the maize ravenously, eating it raw in their desperate hunger. The rest of the army was notified, and forgetting discipline and order swarmed about the great barn like ants on a hill. Each man received a small portion. They had a skirmish that afternoon with some Indians which was of no importance except that the men, thinking they were at last in touch with the Spaniards, with plenty of food in sight, threw away the maize they had saved. The Indians fled, and the buccaneers crossed the river and struggled on. They were in a state of utter despair, and only the heroic determination of Morgan kept them up. The admiral inspirited them by bribing the guides to tell them that they would soon be at their goal.

On the seventh day they arrived at a town called Cruz. As they approached it they saw, through the thick wood, columns of smoke rising from every side. Imagining that this betokened fires from the village kitchens, they rushed forward with the eagerness of starvation, only to find that the Spaniards had evacuated the place, taking everything eatable with them, and then had set fire to the town. There were a few stray cats and dogs prowling around the deserted streets; the hungry pirates fell upon them and they were soon killed and eaten.

In the only building at Cruz which had not been burned, they found fifteen jars of Peruvian wine. Though Morgan spread a report that the wine was poisoned, the starving and desperate men could not refrain from drinking it. Many of them became violently ill from their excesses. The canoes with the sick were now sent back to join the other boats.

On the morning of the eighth day, Morgan passed his ragged tatterdemalions in review. He found his force was reduced to eleven hundred men. From this number he selected one hundred of the strongest to lead the advance, and then took up the march again. Late in the evening while traversing a rocky pass, they were ambushed by Indians who killed or wounded some twenty men by a flight of arrows. The buccaneers fired blindly into the woods and two or three Indians fell from the heights into the road. One of them was evidently the chieftain of the party; a brave man, for as he lay wounded on the rocks and one of the buccaneers made toward him offering him quarter, he savagely tried to stab his whiter—but no less savage—foe. He was instantly shot down. The Indians broke and fled after the loss of their leader, and though the buccaneers pursued them and killed several, they could not capture any of them. However, a way had been made through the pass, which a hundred resolute men could have held against an army. The rain beat down upon them all that night as they lay in the open without shelter.

The ninth day was a repetition of the others, a day of hunger, of labour, of despair. That day they saw some Spaniards for the first time, and although Morgan offered a reward of three hundred crowns for every prisoner brought in, they did not succeed in catching any. They still toiled on, however, heading ever to the southward, and in the afternoon they climbed a mountain, called to this day, (as at time of first publication), *El Cerro de los Bucaneros,* or the hill of the buccaneers, from the top of which they saw spread before them the heaving waters of the great Pacific Ocean. The sight had meant much to Balboa, more to Sir Francis Drake, it meant still more to Morgan and his men. I have no doubt that the old "*Thalatta,*" which had risen to the lips of the ten thousand on a similar occasion, mingled with the shouts and cries of that triumphant hour. Your most ruthless and dangerous buccaneer was your broken-known gentleman. They were a desperate, ragged band, half-naked, half-starved; animals with scarcely a semblance of humanity left to them, but they knew that they could get all they needed in the city near at hand.

They descended the mountain that afternoon and came to a valley filled with horses, mules, and cows. The ravenous buccaneers fell upon them like beasts of prey. They tore huge lumps of flesh from their quivering bodies while the animals were still alive and scarcely waited to scorch them by the fire in their frantic hunger. Says a contemporary observer; "Covered with blood of the animals they had slain, they resembled cannibals rather than Christians." Having satisfied their appetites with the first full meal they had enjoyed in ten days, they took up their march toward the shore. Ascending a little eminence just at nightfall they saw the church steeples of Panama bright in the light of the setting sun. Salvoes of musketry and wild cheering rang in the air. The red flag under which they fought was unfurled and saluted with blasts of trumpets. The camp was then pitched for the night, the sentries posted with care and then, lying on their arms, they sought much needed rest, in preparation for the demands of the morrow.

5. THE SACK OF PANAMA

When the buccaneers put themselves in motion the next morning, the tenth day, they marched for two hours through pleasant valleys magnificently wooded and diversified by running brooks and lakes of fresh water. At last they halted upon the top of a small hill. Beneath them spread the fairest prospect their eyes had ever looked upon. If Cuba is the Pearl of the Antilles, certainly Panama was the Gem of the Pacific. The white city lay before them embowered in foliage like a "handful of pearls in a goblet of emerald." Broad and fertile *savannas* extended between them and the town. A large part of the plain was under cultivation and the beach was fringed with plantations shaded by groves of orange and lemon trees mingled with tall clusters of cocoanut palms. Beyond the city stretched the broad expanse of the beautiful Pacific. It was a picture of peace and contentment, soon to be replaced by a simulacrum of hell.

The houses and shops of the city were built chiefly of cedar and stone. There were at least seven thousand buildings in the town and the population numbered about thirty thousand. The city was laid out in a handsome and imposing manner with broad streets and plazas. Within its walls eight monasteries, a lofty cathedral, many churches and a splendid hospital attested the piety and generosity of the sons of Castile. The largest buildings, however, were the great warehouses of the Genoese company, which were tenanted from time to time by thousands of wretched human beings torn from their African homes to be sold into slavery. Out in the harbour far away rose the beautiful islands of Tavoga and Tavogilla.

Here, at stated times, arrived the great plate fleet laden with treasure from the mines of Peru, which was exchanged for the negro slaves and for the produce and manufacture of the world, for Panama was the *entrepôt* for all the trade with the South Seas. More than two thousand mules were annually employed transferring gold and silver alone to Puerto Bello. It was the strongest, richest, most magnificent city in the New World.

It was protected by walls and forts, one on the Vera Cruz road mounting no less than fifty guns. There were six hundred soldiers held in reserve in the city and the streets were barricaded. On the plain between the buccaneers and the town an army was drawn up. It comprised four regiments of regular Spanish infantry, a brigade of splendid cavalry, two thousand armed citizens, sixty Indians and some negroes. This formidable array of over five thousand men, nearly fifteen hundred of whom were horsemen, was augmented by a strange auxiliary, consisting of two hundred wild and furious Spanish bulls, which were with difficulty controlled by Indians, negroes and mounted *picadors*.

The Spanish soldiers were all brilliantly uniformed and caparisoned and made a brave show in the morning, advancing steadfastly under the great yellow silken flags of Spain. The hearts of the buccaneers sank at the sight of this army before them. The task seemed beyond their capacity. If they succeeded in defeating this force they still would have to deal with the city.

Morgan by one of his brief, fiery speeches succeeded in infusing some of his own energy into the ranks of his ragged, sullen men, numbering now scarcely more than a thousand blades. He divided them into three battalions, sending two hundred picked marksmen in advance as a forlorn hope. When all of his dispositions had been completed, he pointed out that they had no option, they must fight or die. The buccaneers giving three cheers desperately moved down the hill against the enemy. If ever an army fought with a halter around its neck, it was this. It was a struggle not merely for booty and lust, but life. The thought nerved their arms.

The Spaniards advanced gallantly, the horsemen leading. Morgan sent his forlorn hope against them. As the Spanish cavalry charged, the buccaneers halted in a bit of marshy ground into which the horsemen galloped recklessly, only to find themselves mired, checked and thrown into confusion. The little party poured volley after volley into the cavalry, who made the most strenuous efforts to extricate themselves and advance.

Meanwhile the Spanish infantry and the main body of the buccaneers opened fire upon each other. There was no comparison between the marksmanship of the rival forces. The Spaniards were mowed down in scores but kept on bravely. At this juncture the men in charge of the bulls endeavoured to drive them upon the English flank. The men on Morgan's right hand had not hunted cattle for nothing in days gone by. By clever manoeuvring they succeeded in heading them off, and the maddened animals rushed through the ranks of the Spanish infantry, trampling them and throwing them into terrible confusion. A valuable auxiliary they proved to the pirates.

After two hours of fighting, Morgan so manoeuvred his men that a gap was opened in the Spanish line between the cavalry and the infantry. Into this gap, with the quickness of a born soldier, he threw a small body which he had held in reserve, at the same time ordering a general advance which he led in person. The Spanish line was pierced and broken. The pirates poured through the gap and extended themselves on either side. Taken in reverse the horsemen were cut to pieces. Over six hundred of them were killed outright, a large number

STORMING OF THE FORT AT CHAGRES.

BATTLE AT PANAMA.

wounded, and the remainder were driven in headlong flight from the field. The forlorn hope, which had done such effectual shooting, now turned its attention to the disheartened Spanish infantry. It had been beaten out of all semblance of organization and assailed on two sides after a few more volleys and some desultory firing, the men broke and fled. The buccaneers pursued them unrelentingly, giving no quarter. The field became a scene of indiscriminate slaughter. The Spaniards were completely broken and scattered. Morgan had meanwhile adroitly interposed between the Spaniards and the city, so that only a few fugitives gained the walls.

Allowing his men, who were tired out from hacking, hewing, and slaughtering, but a short time for rest, for he appreciated the necessity of giving the Spaniards no time to recover themselves, Morgan took up his march for the city. Like a good soldier he avoided the fort on the Vera Cruz road and approached from the direction of Puerto Bello. The pirates were met by a smart fire from the ramparts, but their blood was up now, and they recked little of works or fortifications. They carried the outer works by storm and poured into the terror stricken city in a resistless horde. The Spaniards left there made an heroic defence, fighting from street to street and from house to house, until they were cut to pieces, but nothing could stay the onslaught of these human tigers. Ere sunset they were in complete possession of the city.

Ample warning had been given of the approach of the buccaneers and many of the wealthy citizens, including a large number of women and children, had fled to the islands and the surrounding country. They had taken much treasure with them and concealed much more. In spite of this, however, the conquerors found themselves in possession of a vast booty. The Spanish officials had been confident that the pirates would be unable to capture the city. They had trusted in the numbers and valour of their army and they had therefore not destroyed and concealed everything and they had not entirely depopulated the town. Indeed it would have been impossible. Morgan, fearful lest his men should get entirely out of band, enjoined them, under the severest penalties, to drink no wine. They had lost heavily in their tremendous battle, probably not more than six hundred able bodied men remained to him, and there were many wounded needing attention. He was fearful lest the Spaniards, who still greatly outnumbered him, should rally and overwhelm his little force. The men were restrained with the greatest difficulty.

They had struggled, fought, marched and suffered so dreadfully they could scarcely be made to understand the necessity for further restraint in the presence of wine, women, and treasure lying under their grimy, bloodstained, lustful, covetous hands. Unable to defend the town with his little force, Morgan resorted to a desperate expedient. He himself set fire to a number of the principal buildings of the city, to placate his men spreading the report that the Spaniards had done it. The night was dry and windy and the fire got beyond control, burning down the greater part of the town before it could be checked.

That night the buccaneers camped under arms outside the walls. When the fire finally burned itself out, Morgan despatched a strong party to the Chagres River to announce the victory, and see that all went well with the garrison, and then the victors entered the trembling city. They fortified the Church of the Trinity, raised earthworks about it, and mounted all the guns they could crowd in the plaza. The remainder of the guns on the walls and the forts were spiked.

Then began the search for treasure. That night the passions of hell pent up in their bosoms, and, burning more fiercely from their unaccustomed restraint, were let loose. The bright moon from the clear heaven looked down in all its tender tropic splendour upon such a carnival of crime and debauchery as possibly the world had never seen. The sacking of a town is a most frightful event, even when it is done by regular soldiery, but when the army is made up of men like the buccaneers, there are added to the scene touches of horror and atrocities which no pen can describe. The lust and greed of the conquerors was proportioned to the difficulties they had undergone in achieving the conquest.

Rapine, murder, plunder, outrage, drunkenness, excesses of every kind, filled the night with misery. Neither old age nor youth, beauty nor innocence, wisdom nor folly, good nor evil, were spared. It is impossible to depict the horrors of the period. The wounded and the prisoners were crowded into the churches where they had so often worshipped and were left to starve or die. Tortures of every kind which their rude ingenuity could suggest were inflicted upon helpless victims to make them disclose the hiding place of their treasures. Women killed themselves, happy if they could deliver the blow which ended their lives before they were forced to submit to their conquerors. Others less fortunate, struggling in the arms of these demons in human shape besought piteously and in vain for that death they would have so gladly welcomed.

For days these practices continued. They hung the prisoners up by their beards and the hair of their heads, or by a single arm or leg, and let them swing. They drew them as tight as they could with tackles on their arms and legs and then beat them with rattans. They tied slow matches beneath their fingers and toes, lighted them and let them burn. They improvised racks which tore off limb after limb, they broke them upon wheels, suspended them in the air and loaded them with timbers and stones until their arms pulled out. But their favourite method of torture, favourite because it was so easy and efficacious, consisted in tying a stout cord around the head of the victim, inserting the barrel of a pistol between the forehead and the cord and twisting the cord until the eyes sprang from their sockets! The only mercy they exhibited was sometimes to kill those whom they had tortured. The Spaniards were completely broken, and though small bodies of men were seen from time to time hovering about the city they never made any attack or rallied in sufficient numbers to become formidable.

Parties of buccaneers daily scoured the country in all directions, going out in the morning with light hearts and high hopes and returning in the evening loaded with spoil and driving before them parties of wretched men and women whom they had routed from their fastnesses. Morgan manned a small boat in the harbour with twenty-five men and sent it after a great ship which was loaded with church plate and other treasure, and contained over four hundred women, which had been sent away the morning of the capture of the city. It was a prize which appealed to the buccaneers from every standpoint. The party located the galleon at evening and determined, under the stimulus of the wine they had taken and the pleasant prospect presented by a score of unfortunate women they captured, to defer taking her until the morning. When the next morning came she was gone with all her precious freight. The escape is the one bright incident in this chronicle of horror. The little party returned after capturing a Spanish *brigantine* carrying twenty thousand pieces of eight.

Morgan now set forth with three hundred and fifty men to scour the country far and wide, raiding every plantation, torturing every master and outraging every mistress they came across. When he returned he found that a shipload of Spaniards had arrived from the south, ignorant of the capture of the fort. Among them was a woman of surpassing beauty and heroic soul, the young wife of a rich merchant in Peru. The buccaneer fell in love with her. The ogre washed his bloodstained hands, clothed himself in the rich vestments of his captives, paid his court to her, and laid the treasure of his heart at her feet. He caused her to be comfortably lodged and respectfully treated while he prosecuted his attentions. She repulsed him with disdain. When, inflamed by her resistance, he would have outraged her, she snatched his own dagger from his side and swore that if he laid hand upon her she would *poniard* herself before his eyes. The brute must have been really in love with her, for he spared her life in spite of her refusal. Though he treated her to the greatest indignities, she succeeded in preserving her honour in spite of all. She was the one woman who came forth unharmed from the hands of the buccaneers.

The magnitude of their capture, the quantity of their booty, the terrible license which had prevailed, created dissension and distrust between the men and their officers, which especially vented itself upon Morgan. The most solemn oath of buccaneering was that the spoil should be fairly apportioned and that there should be no individual concealment. This was violated, Morgan himself, it was more than suspected, doing the most of it. One hundred of the buccaneers conspired to seize a boat and make for the South Seas. Morgan discovered the conspiracy, burnt the boat and punished the malcontents severely. His position was a difficult one. If he had not played off the different bands of adventurers divided into jealous nationalities, against one another, he would probably have been deposed. As it was, he held the command in an iron grasp.

Finally, after utterly ruining what was left of the town, the buccaneers took their departure on February 24, 1671. They had a vast amount of precious merchandise, one hundred and seventy-five beasts of burden laden with gold, silver and jewels alone, and six hundred prisoners held for ransom.

The pirates were divided into a van and rear guard, with the prisoners between them. They marched circumspectly under arms. The unfortunate captives, especially the women and children, suffered horribly, but they were driven forward relentlessly. Those who fainted and died on the roadside were counted happy by those who survived. Those who had been young and beautiful before they fell into the hands of the buccaneers, fared the worst.

The Spanish woman who had so bravely held her honour against Morgan's advances, was taken with the rest. She sent two priests to friends of her husband to get her ransom money—fifteen thousand pieces of eight! They had betrayed their trust and had used the money to rescue some of their own friends. When Morgan learned of this fact he released the woman without ransom, and treated the messengers with the utmost rigor. It is the one solitary act of clemency and mercy which appears in his whole history. When the party reached the village of Cruz, Morgan halted until all but a few of the poor prisoners were redeemed. The false messengers, by the payment of a prodigious sum of money, escaped a just retribution for their treachery. The treasure was unloaded and embarked in boats and sent down the river to Barbacoa. There, a muster of the buccaneers was held, and everyone was searched for concealed booty, Morgan himself setting an example by submitting to the search. The search was most thoroughly done, but in a way which greatly infuriated the sated, covetous pirates. The men were even compelled to discharge their firearms lest they had concealed jewels in the gun barrels.

The band, now almost in a state of revolt, took up the march and finally reached the Chagres once more. Morgan and a body of his favourites, mainly English, were in terror of their lives. They put a bold front upon the situation, however, and the day after their arrival they divided the booty, which amounted to over two million dollars, or pieces of eight, in cash, not counting the value of silk, cloth of gold, arms and merchandise. The jewels were sold unfairly, the admiral and his friends buying the greater part for a mere song; besides which, in spite of the search, Morgan had found means to conceal an immense treasure in small compass. The buccaneers were disgusted and infuriated at the small sum which they individually received, and they even proposed to seize Morgan and compel him to disgorge and redivide. He got wind of their intention, however, and treacherously abandoned the main body by stealing out of the harbour in his own ship followed by four English vessels, whose captains and crews had been in his confidence.

6. THE END OF THE BUCCANEER

Morgan returned to Jamaica, and, contrary to his custom, invested his money, foreswore pirating and married the daughter of one of the principal men of the island. His position was an uneasy one, however, and it was rumoured among the buccaneers who escaped from the Chagres in small detachments, wandering to various parts of the Caribbean and never apparently assembling in great force again, that Morgan, fearing for his life, had determined to take possession, with a party of congenial spirits, of the famous island of St. Catherine, and take up the old trade again. The men, whose former affection for him was now turned to bitterest hatred, determined to waylay him on his voyage and capture him with his wife, children, and treasure. But before Morgan could get away a new governor arrived at Jamaica with a royal order to send Morgan to England to answer to the complaints of the king of Spain.

Undoubtedly the reformed pirate did not find this a hard matter; possibly some of the gold, silver and jewels of Panama found their way, beside the French crowns, into the coffers of the needy English king, for Charles II disgraced knighthood by giving this dishonoured adventurer the royal accolade! Sir Henry Morgan returned to Jamaica in triumph where he continued his respectable career and rose to positions of prominence. In 1680, the Earl of Carlisle, the then governor of the island, returned to England on account of ill health, and left Morgan as the deputy governor! The old buccaneer had his hour. He remembered his old comrades and the threats they had made against him, and he used his new found authority to apprehend them and hang them without mercy until the arrival of a new governor put a stop to his revenge. When his royal protector, Charles II, died, he was thrown into prison, and of his further fate nothing is known.

If any man ever earned a place in hell Morgan did, and when we read of his atrocities in the rude chronicles of the past, we can easily be unchristian enough to hope that he got it.

There is another thought which rises in the mind in connection with the story of the sufferings of the Spaniards in Central America, and it is a thought of retribution. The chronicles of their own people and the testimony of impartial observers show that in their period of domination they had treated the unfortunate aborigines of the land with a cruelty and rapacity which would have made an Aztec warrior blush and put even a buccaneer to shame. When they suffered under the expeditions of the buccaneers they might look back upon the peaceful populations they had exterminated, the wretched women they had debauched, and the smiling land they had destroyed in their lust for gold, and remember that text of Scripture, which says:

"With what Measure Ye Mete, it shall be Measured to You Again."

2
Under the "Jolly Roger"

The year 1701 which marked the accession of Philip V, a Bourbon Prince, to the throne of Spain, and saw the entrance of Louis XIV of France into the field of Spanish colonial power, also marked the end of the buccaneer. It was one thing for the English "Brethren of the coast," the "gentlemen adventurers" of the Spanish Main to make war upon the weak and neglected outlying dependencies of a decadent power like Spain, and quite another to attempt to continue the practice when the Spanish colonies were protected by the white flag of France. Their careers were dosed forthwith.

The situation threw the buccaneers into consternation. What could gentlemen of the sword who had been accustomed to plunder where they listed, to rob and murder at their own sweet will, do to make a living under such circumstances? Honest labour, industrious toil were not to be thought of. What happened? A few—a very few—of them reformed; many of them died of excesses and dissipation, or ended their careers in the common gaols for a wide variety of crimes; most of them, however, became—should I say degenerated into?—out and out pirates and in a spirit of universal hostility warred against everybody.

The "Jolly Roger" with its ghastly "death's head and crossbones" on a black field, supplanted the various ensigns of the buccaneers. In greatly diminished companies the ruffians—and others inspired by their successes, including two women pirates!—undertook plundering and murdering expeditions thereafter in ships and vessels of various sizes, as they could compass them, sweeping the ocean in every direction and generally confining their undertakings to the high seas. It was not until 1730 that they were completely put down by the combined efforts of everybody who was respectable, and peaceful ships were allowed to sail the ocean with a minimum of anxiety and a maximum of safety from, these rapacious and bloodthirsty plunderers.

The buccaneer had a few virtues usually—as bravery and fidelity to his associates—just enough to throw into high relief the hideous agglomeration of his vices. The pirate had no good qualities whatsoever, even his courage was fitful as a rule, and usually failed him in the end. I have chosen two as typical illustrations of the brood and because they were captured by two gallant gentlemen after two as pretty fights of the kind as ever took place.

Drummond, Teach, Thatch, "Blackbeard," so the catalogue of aliases and descriptive titles runs, was originally a sailor—an "indifferent honest" man, I take it—of Bristol, England. In the long war of the Spanish Succession he had been at various times an officer, part owner, and commander of a privateer. He had suffered financial losses and met with galling personal indignities from the French in his several cruises. On one occasion having been taken prisoner he had been woefully treated during his confinement, undergoing great hardships before he escaped from captivity. When peace was declared in 1715, and he was forced to return some of the prizes he had taken, he found himself practically a ruined man. In company with a Mr. Benjamin Hornigold—a singularly appropriate name for a pirate—he proceeded to make individual war on his own account against the French. The right of private vengeance of this character not being recognized by the law of nations he speedily found himself an outlaw and promptly degenerated into a professional pirate. In this day he would probably have been sent to a lunatic asylum, where he belonged.

The much frequented and carefully patrolled waters of Europe soon became exceedingly dangerous places for the indulgence of his piratical proclivities, so he hoisted the black flag and bore away for that halcyon section of men of like ilk, the American coast. Of all those who cruised up and down in our waters—and they were a choice lot of scoundrels, certainly—he became preeminent for cruelty, brutality, depravity, and success. Blackbeard, his name, or his pseudonym rather, became painfully known from one end of the coast to the other. He was so styled from an immense black beard with which he was endowed, which he was accustomed to plait in two long braids and tie them up behind his ears with delicate blue ribbons—a nice combination, that!

When he went into action it was his practice to stick lighted matches[1] under his hat to give his face a terrifying appearance. In addition to the usual belt studded with weapons he habitually wore another one across his breast from which depended as many pistols as he could hang on it.

He was a man of huge proportions and of herculean strength, but ineffably base and cruel, yet he knew how to control the ruthless bands of human hyenas and wolves which he assembled from time to time. He used to shoot one of them every once in a while to keep his hand in and make the rest feel that he was master! One of his men, whose name Stevenson has appropriated to the coxswain in his immortal romance *Treasure Island*, was called Israel Hands. For some reason Hands was not executed when the usual fate befell Blackbeard and the rest and he told a story of how the pirate chief— query; why chief, I wonder?—entertaining some of his men at dinner one night in his cabin suddenly blew out the light and began to shoot at the legs of the men under the table, just to let them know he was there! It was a wonder—and a pity—someone did not kill him.

On one occasion, the weather being mild and the ship needing no attention, he called all hands into the hold, closed the hatches, and set fire to a barrel of sulphur with the truthful remark that since they were all devils and the ship was a perfect hell, he intended to see how much of the real thing in the way of popular accessories they could stand. He remained there until his men were almost choked to death, although he himself did not appear to be seriously affected—possibly because he was more of a devil than the rest. I quote from a quaint old book a portion of his journal. He was a semi-literary pirate, it seems.

Such a Day. Rum all out:—Our company somewhat sober;—A damned confusion amongst us!—Rogues a plotting;—great talk of separation.—So I looked sharp for a prize:—Such a day, took one with a great deal of liquor on board, so kept the company hot, damned hot;—then all things went well again.

It was his habit after a profitable cruise to turn his ill-got plunder into cash at the first convenient town, then get rid of his crew either by dismissing them or marooning them on desolate islands where they might starve or die for all he cared, while he spent his money on shore and deluded himself with the idea that he was having a good time and enjoying life! The pirates were exceedingly good customers

1. Slow matches, of course, which were used for igniting the priming of the cannon.

of the townspeople along the shore—those who owned no ships, that is—from Massachusetts to Carolina, and by confining their preying strictly to the sea were in high favour with landlubbers.

Among other things, Blackbeard was accustomed to indulge himself in marriage, which he did to the extent of fourteen wives in different places! What sort of a woman could she be who would marry him, I wonder? He would linger on shore until his money was gone, then he would beg, borrow, or steal—more often the latter—a small boat, desert his latest wife, assemble another crew and proceed upon his nefarious way once more. If he captured a better ship than his own he appropriated it By this means he once had under his command a large ship mounting forty guns which he called *Queen Anne's Revenge*, though what that gentle and rather stupid princess could have to revenge, and why she was connected even thus innocently with piracy is hard to understand.

On this vessel he performed two notable exploits. He beat off His Majesty's ship-of-war *Scarborough*, of twenty guns, after a long and severe engagement and then taking his station off the harbour of Charles Town, South Carolina, he captured all the outgoing and incoming merchant ships for several days. One of them contained a number of important personages who were returning to England. After sinking the ship and plundering the passengers, being in need of medicine, spirits, and other things, the audacious pirate sent a demand to Governor Johnson for these necessaries and stated that if his request were not complied with at once he would proceed to murder his prisoners!

His emissary's boat was wrecked and the time set for his return having elapsed Blackbeard cold-bloodedly set about carrying out his threat. Fortunately for them, however, just as they were to be executed, a messenger came off to the ship explaining the cause of the delay and they were respited for another day, at the end of which time the humiliating terms were complied with. It was hard on Johnson and the Carolinians, but they had to do it. Blackbeard set the prisoners on shore far from Charles Town, as it was called then, which they finally reached after many hardships.

On the occasion of his marriage to his fourteenth wife after he had marooned most of his company, he had gone to Bath, North Carolina, on the Pamlico River, where he had taken advantage of the king's amnesty and abjured and renounced his former practices. Governor Eden was present at the marriage. He was also present at the distribution of the plunder which took place shortly after when Blackbeard resumed his former avocation, the gubernatorial share in one capture being some sixty barrels of sugar. It was lucrative partnership for His Majesty's representative.

Emboldened by this connection the pirate's rapacity passed all bounds. He began to plunder the ships of those who had hitherto tolerated his existence and practices for commercial reasons. The governor still protected him and complaints proved unavailing. Indeed, the complicity of Governor Eden was so apparent to the merchants of North Carolina, whose ships had suffered severely from this red scourge, that in their desperation they appealed to the famous Alexander Spotswood, governor of Virginia, to rid them of Blackbeard's presence. Virginia had suffered with the rest and the governor acted promptly, and with the concurrence of the burgesses determined to settle Blackbeard forever.

There happened to be two of His Majesty's ships-of-war lying in the Chesapeake at the time, the *Pearl* and the *Lyme*. Robert Maynard, a dashing young officer, was a lieutenant on the *Pearl* He volunteered to lead an expedition to destroy the pirate. Two small sloops were hastily procured and manned and word having been received that Blackbeard with a new schooner lay at Ocracoke Inlet, Maynard at once made his way thither. Blackbeard's schooner mounted eight guns and was a heavy overmatch for the two sloops, although as they each carried upwards of thirty men they had nearly twice as many fighters as the pirates.

Maynard came within sight of the pirate late on the evening of the 21st of November, 1718. Placing his ships so that they barred the exit he waited until morning to make the attack. Blackbeard, whose vessel was aground in the shallow water, also prepared for the expected battle. In the morning by lightening his vessels and using sweeps, the Englishman approached the pirate. One of the chroniclers records a quaint dialogue which purports to have taken place between the two commanders ere the battle was joined.

Blackbeard in all his awe-inspiring paraphernalia, which was so terrifying to women and children and peaceful traders, but rather amusing to men of war, mounted on the rail and called out:

"Damn you for villains, who are you? And from whence come you?"

"You may see from our colours we are no pirates," replied Maynard.

"Send a boat aboard!" roared the other.

"I cannot spare my boat, but I will come aboard of you as I can with my sloop," answered Maynard, urging his men to redoubled efforts at the oars.

Blackbeard sprang to the rail of his schooner and seizing a bottle of whiskey drank from it and then shouted the following toast:

"Damnation seize my soul if I give you quarters or take any from you!"

"I neither ask for, nor will I give you any quarters," replied Maynard.

At this juncture the second sloop got aground, but Maynard dashed on alone. Having come within range of the small cannon on the pirate schooner Blackbeard opened fire with a heavy broadside of "langridge"—a hideous and death-dealing charge of nails, balls, old iron, scraps, etc.—a discharge which did great execution. As Maynard's men were entirely exposed no less than twenty of them were killed or wounded. Fortunately a breeze having sprung up which rendered the use of sweeps unnecessary, Maynard directed the remainder of his crew to go below and conceal themselves in the hold. He made the man at the helm who steered the sloop lie down on the deck while he himself stood up alone on the deck covered with the dead. The pirates poured furious discharges upon him but in the smoke and confusion fortunately he remained untouched.

Presently the little sloop fell aboard the pirate still aground. As the two vessels came together the pirates hurled a lot of improvised hand grenades on the deck of the sloop which exploded without doing much damage, and seeing no one in the smoke, Blackbeard at the head of fourteen of his men sprang aboard of it. As the boarders gained the decks the wind caught the sloop and drove her clear of the schooner, which still contained about as many men as had reached the sloop.

The separation was unlucky for the pirate. Maynard calling his men from below at once sprang forward and engaged the enemy. There were but thirteen Englishmen to meet fifteen pirates. The conflict was extremely severe. The two commanders at once crossed swords, but the pirate had at last met his match in the honest man. After eight of his men had been killed and he himself had received—so the veracious chroniclers state—no less than twenty-five wounds, his throat was pierced by the sword of the gallant Maynard, who had himself been severely wounded. Blackbeard's pirate days were over. The seven pirates remaining, all wounded, were captured. Most of Maynard's twelve had been wounded and several were killed. The decks of the little sloop were deluged with blood.

Meanwhile, the other sloop had floated with the rising tide and had engaged and captured the pirate schooner and the balance of the crew after a stout but unavailing resistance. The pirates' papers showed conclusively that Governor Eden had been associated with them. Maynard acted promptly. He sailed up to Bath, North Carolina, broke open the governor's storehouse and carried off everything which the books showed had been received from the pirates, including the sugar. Taking his prisoners and bringing the body of Blackbeard he then sailed back to Virginia. He entered the Chesapeake with the head of the decapitated ruffian swinging by his long hair from the bowsprit end. The body of the pirate was hung in chains in a place known thereafter as "Blackbeard's Island." He was surrounded by the undecapitated bodies of his crew, with the exception of Israel Hands mentioned above. For a long time the more reckless spirits among the hard-drinking squires who were wont to assemble at Williamsburg, the Dominion capital, were accustomed to drink rum punch out of a huge silver-mounted bowl, the bottom of which was composed of the skull of the infamous pirate. The curious bowl, like the custom, has happily been lost.

It was a most gallant and heroic expedition and brilliantly carried out on the part of young Maynard. It apparently elicited no particular attention from the home authorities at the time, however, and Maynard received no especial reward for his services, for the records show that he did not receive his commission as captain until twenty years after this exploit. In modern days the recognition of such a successful enterprise would have been prompt and adequate.

2. Colonel Rhett and Major Bonnet

That these military titles should appertain to a ferocious pirate and his gallant captor is a thing which might at first be thought strange. Soldiers often have piratical instincts, to be sure, but they do not usually exhibit them on the sea. Circumstances, however, bring about strange results and, contrary to the rule in the case of poets, pirates seem to be made rather than born.

Early in the eighteenth century there lived at Bridgetown, in the island of Barbados, a retired officer of the English army whose name was Stede Bonnet. He was a man of good birth, independent fortune, and no little education. He was prosperous and respected by his neighbours, and apparently there was no reason why he should not have continued to hold their respect while he pursued the even tenor of his way until the end. In the spring of the year 1717, however, he lightly took it into his head to become a pirate!

The cause of this determination has always been more or less of a mystery. What could have induced an elderly man who had been a professional soldier and who knew absolutely nothing about the sea, to become a pirate, especially as he was not driven by the pressure of want or by the consciousness of injury, or by any other assignable cause to undertake this nefarious profession? Only one reason has ever been alleged and that but tentatively. Mankind, since the days of Adam, has been accustomed to lay everything disastrous that happens to a woman. Bonnet had a wife. She seems to have partaken rather of the character of Xantippe than of that of Griselda. Bonnet, it is stated, was not endowed with Socratic patience, and to escape his wife's temper he turned to piracy. Frankly, I do not believe the story at all. I think he was insane.

At any rate, from whatever cause, the decision having been arrived at, he set about carrying out his purpose. His money and his respectability made it easy. He purchased a swift handy schooner which he called the *Revenge*—favourite name for piratical craft, I presume because their owners tried to delude themselves into the belief that they had been injured by society and had therefore a quasi-right to prey upon it. Lavishly providing this vessel with everything necessary and manning it with a choice and select body of scoundrels. Bonnet bade farewell to Barbados and his wife, and set forth ostensibly upon a trading voyage.

As soon as he got off soundings he hoisted the black flag and announced to his surprised crew that he was now a pirate. The statement did not worry them a bit. They were more than willing to go pirating. If there were any who were not willing they kept discreetly quiet and nothing marred the unanimity with which the crew embraced the opportunity. It was evident to everyone that Bonnet knew nothing about seamanship or navigation and in fact, except in one particular, was about as unfit a person to command a pirate ship as could be imagined. The one exception to his disabilities lay in his bloodthirsty courage. The subordinate officers among his crew would have gladly seized the ship, deposed him and gone pirating on their own account, but Bonnet, who was possessed of ferocious determination which went to the length of killing two or three of his ruffians, finally succeeded in establishing his ascendancy over them.

The world was before him and he proceeded to open his oyster. From Massachusetts to the Carolinas he roved along the coast at his own sweet will, plundering and destroying. In all the atrocious customs and habits of pirates he speedily became a past master. This once respectable English gentleman and churchman could look with as utter an indifference upon the suffering of the poor hapless wretches whom he captured and forced to walk the plank, as if he had been bred among buccaneers. Murder, robbery, rapine, outrages of every kind he perpetrated upon the high seas.

On one occasion he fell in with Blackbeard and the two pirates cruised in company with doubly damnable results. Blackbeard soon found that Bonnet knew nothing about ships. Inviting him to dine, therefore, and having by this means got him on board his own ship, he coolly deposed him from his command. Bonnet protested vehemently, but as he was surrounded by Blackbeard's men and as his own men were lukewarm in his cause, he could do nothing but protest. Blackbeard did not kill him, he made him a clerk! It was intensely galling to the bold spirit of the soldier-sailor, but there was no help for it. He was with Blackbeard when he made his famous raid on Charles Town, and when the *Queen Anne's Revenge* was wrecked in Topsail Inlet, North Carolina, and Blackbeard got rid of the troublesome members of his crew by marooning them while he went off to get a pardon and enjoy his plunder, he gave Bonnet back his sloop.

Bonnet had learned something, and choosing a time when Blackbeard was absent he also went off to Governor Eden, surrendered himself and received a pardon under the king's amnesty proclamation. Armed with this and with a few bold spirits in his company he set forth on the *Revenge*, announcing that he was bound for St. Thomas. There he stated that he intended to get a commission as a privateer to prey upon the French and Spanish ships, the war then being in full blast.

All he needed was a crew. He knew where to find it. He ran down to the desolate island off Topsail Inlet, where Blackbeard had marooned the men. The sometime pirates were in desperate straits. Bonnet took them on the *Revenge*, revived and fed them, and then announced his intention of resuming his former vocation and incidentally of his purpose of hunting for Blackbeard. The marooned men were only too willing. It speaks well for the courage of Bonnet that with a handful of men he was desirous of engaging so redoubtable a villain as his old captor, but it does not speak well for his discretion or his sanity. At any rate, although Bonnet hunted for him assiduously he did not find him, and at last, despairing of success, he bore away for northern waters for metal more easy, if less attractive.

On this cruise he changed the name of the *Revenge* to the *Royal James*, which was the title of the young Pretender. I suppose Bonnet deluded himself again with the idea that having now become an adherent of the house of Stuart he was at liberty to work his will upon the high seas. He also changed his name to Captain Thomas—for the good of his health.

He had a royal time, from the pirate point of view, off New York and Philadelphia, and finally with his hull full of plunder and with two captured vessels he turned to southern waters once more. Having been injured somewhat in a storm and being tired with the long cruise, he entered the Cape Fear River with his prizes. Grown bold and reckless, instead of purchasing the things he required for the repair of his ship and the comforts of his men, he landed bodies of men and took what he wanted wherever he found it.

The South Carolinians and their hot-headed but able governor, Johnson, were still chafing under the humiliating tribute which Blackbeard had enforced. When the settlers about the Cape Fear River informed the authorities by expresses of the arrival of Bonnet, and of his actions, Johnson determined to do something.

Among the principal settlers of South Carolina was one William Rhett. This gentleman was born in London in 1666, and he had come to Carolina in 1694. By profession he was a gentleman sailor. Circumstances, to wit, the colonial need and his own force of character, had made him a colonel of the Carolina militia. When a French and Spanish squadron made a descent upon Charles Town in 1708, he had been appointed "vice admiral" of the colonial naval force, and had driven the invaders away from the coast after capturing one of their ships.

He was a high-tempered, passionate and irascible man, but endowed with undaunted courage and undoubted ability. For the rest, he was a warden of St. Philip's Episcopal Church and the agent for the distribution of the stipends of the Society for the Propagation of the Gospel in Foreign Parts. Colonel Rhett immediately offered to lead an expedition against Bonnet. Two small trading sloops, the *Henry* and the *Sea Nymph*, commanded by Captains Martin and Hall, and mounting eight small guns each, were both filled with volunteers. The contingent on the *Henry* was seventy men, that on the *Sea Nymph*

83

sixty.

"Colonel-Vice-Admiral" Rhett hoisted his broad pennant upon the *Henry* and set sail. Some time was wasted in chasing another pirate who had ventured to take a look in at Charles Town harbour, but on the 20th of September, 1718, the cruise against Bonnet, who was still carrying things with a high hand in the Cape Fear River, was begun. On the evening of the 26th Colonel Rhett arrived off the bar at the mouth of the river. The tide was out and his pilots were not sufficiently acquainted with the river to allow him to move up to attack the pirates, the topmasts of whose vessels could be seen above the trees around an adjacent headland. Rhett therefore anchored for the night in a position to command the river.

As soon as he became aware of the approach of the Carolina cruisers Bonnet manned his boats and under the supposition that the vessels at the mouth of the river were traders, organized an expedition for their capture. A nearer approach disclosed the true state of affairs, however, and Bonnet found himself in a quandary. While the *Royal James* mounted ten guns and was manned by a crew of sixty men and while she was larger than either of Rhett's vessels, and her guns heavier than those the cruisers mounted, yet she was an indifferent match for the two of them. Besides, your genuine pirate always avoided a fight as long as he could help it.

Bonnet, therefore, determined to make a run for it, hoping to beat off the sloops and gain the open sea. The *Royal James* was in no condition to do this that evening or he would have tried it at once. All night long, however, his men worked indefatigably to fit her for cruising and with much success, for as the day broke, abandoning his prizes, he stood toward the sea. Rhett was ready for him. Expecting just such a manoeuvre he had kept his men at their guns all night, and as they saw the *Royal James* come flying down the river before a strong offshore breeze, with every sail set, Rhett ordered his two sloops to beat toward her.

As Bonnet came tearing down the stream the approach of the *Henry* and the *Sea Nymph* forced him to hug the shore more closely than he intended. In fact so skilfully did Rhett handle his two ships that Bonnet had to choose between running him down and thus bringing on a hand to hand fight with both of them, or leaving the channel. He left the channel and went aground. Rhett, in hot pursuit of him, had no time to check the way of the *Henry* before he, too, took ground, within pistol shot distance of the *Royal James*. The *Sea Nymph* also ran on one of the sand bars with which the mouth of the river abounds, but unfortunately too far away from the pirate to be of much service to Rhett.

The *Henry* and the *Royal James* immediately opened fire upon each other. The tide was ebbing and such were the relative positions of the two ships that, as the water shallowed and they careened on the sand bars, the deck of the *Royal James* was turned away from the deck of the *Henry* which her own inclination left entirely exposed. This gave Bonnet a decided advantage, for his men could shoot at the king's men without being exposed themselves, while the helpless Carolinians on the slanting deck had absolutely no protection from the pirate's discharges.

Farragut's famous maxim about the best protection from the enemy's fire being a well-directed fire from your own guns, had not been enunciated, yet Rhett knew the principle thoroughly. Animated by their commander, who, some accounts say, was wounded in the fight, his men stood to their guns manfully and poured a perfect stream of shot from their weapons upon the pirate, which was returned with equal resolution and much greater effect, for no less than forty per cent, of the Carolinians were either killed or wounded. For five long hours they kept up the conflict, the *Sea Nymph* joining in at long range.

It was evident that whichever vessel would be first floated by the tide when it reached its flood, would be able to terminate the conflict out of hand. The pirates were in high glee over the situation. One of the old tellers of the tale relates how they mocked and jeered at the unfortunate Carolinians and how they made a "whiff with their bloody flag" as indicative of their contempt; but their joy was turned to despair when, as the tide came rolling in, they saw the *Henry* gently rising to an even keel and the *Sea Nymph* following suit while their larger vessel still lay aground.

Calling up the *Sea Nymph* Rhett now made for the pirate. But the spirit had gone out of the men on the helpless *Royal James* and they clamoured to surrender. Bonnet, pistol in hand, swore that he would never yield and attempted to fire the magazine, but his men overpowered him and, just as the two attacking ships took position to rake them, flung out the white flag.

The total loss on the little squadron of Rhett was twelve killed and twenty-eight wounded, which was very heavy indeed considering that the *Sea Nymph* had been but slightly engaged. The pirate's loss is not definitely stated, but it was believed to be over thirty. The *Henry* and the *Royal James* were so shot-torn and shattered that they could with difficulty be kept afloat. Rhett, however, patched them up and taking the two prizes returned to Charles Town. He had a warm reception when he arrived with his little flotilla with the royal standard floating above the black flag on the pirate's schooner.

Bonnet and his men to the number of thirty were at once put on trial for piracy. Chief Justice Trott, himself an arrant scoundrel, but a man of great ability, presided at the trial. They were all found guilty and sentenced to be hanged Trott was a man mighty in the Scriptures, in the letter that is, though not in the spirit —so for that matter was Bonnet—and a few paragraphs from his address to Bonnet on his conviction are curiously interesting.

"You being a gentleman that have had the advantage of *liberal education* and being generally esteemed a man of letters I believe it will be needless for me to explain to you the nature of *repentance* and *faith* in Christ they being so fully and so often explained in the Scriptures that you cannot but know them. And therefore perhaps for that reason it might be thought by some improper for me to have said so much to you as I have already upon this occasion; Neither should I have done it, but that considering the course of your life and actions, I have just reason to fear that the principles of religion that had been instilled into you by your *education* have been at least corrupted if not entirely defaced by the *scepticism* and *infidelity* of this wicked age; and that what time you allowed for study was rather applied to polite literature; and the vain *philosophy* of the times than to a serious search after the *law* and *will* of God, as revealed to us in the Holy *Scriptures*. For *had your delight been in the law of the Lord, and that you had meditated therein day and night* Psal. 1-2 you would then have found that God's *word was a lamp unto your feet, and a light to your path* Psal; 1 19-105, and that you would account all other knowledge but loss in comparison of *the excellency of the knowledge of Christ Je*sus Phil. 3-8 *who to them that are called is the power of God and the wisdom of God* 1 Cor: 1-24, *even as the hidden wisdom which God ordained before the world.* Chap: 2-7."

And so on in the same strain.

Bonnet had behaved with much personal dignity and courage under Trott's disgraceful brow-beating during the trial, and some sympathy had been elicited for him therefore, but when the issue was determined and his hideous fate was realized, he broke down, and played the coward. He overwhelmed everybody, including Colonel

Rhett and the governor, with the most abject, pusillanimous, disgraceful pleas for mercy; and because he had been born a gentleman and was of a different social stamp from the ordinary pirate, he actually moved some of the persons to whom he addressed himself—a curious state of affairs. The fact that he had been born to better things really made his wickedness more reprehensible. Johnson sturdily refused to commute his sentence or to grant him a reprieve to go to England or anywhere else. He was even deaf to such appeals as this which Bonnet in his despair finally addressed to him.

> I heartily beseech you'll permit me to live, and I'll voluntarily put it ever out of my power by separating all my limbs from my body, only reserving the use of my tongue to call continually on, and pray to the Lord, my God and mourn all my days in sackcloth and ashes to work out confident hopes of my salvation, at that great and dreadful day when all righteous souls shall receive their just rewards. And to render your honour a further assurance of my being incapable to prejudice any of my fellow Christians, if I was so wickedly bent I humbly beg you will (as a punishment of my sins for my poor soul's sake) indent me as a menial servant to your honour, and this Government during my life, and send me to the fartherest inland garrison or settlement in the country or in any other ways you'll be pleased to dispose of me.
>
> Now the God of Peace that brought again from the dead our Lord Jesus, that great Shepherd of the Sheep, through the blood of the everlasting covenant make you perfect in every good work to do his will, working in you, that which is pleasing in his sight through Jesus Christ to whom be glory forever and ever is the hearty prayer of
>
> Your Honour's most miserable and afflicted servant
>
> Stede Bonnet.

The concluding paragraph was worthy of the religious Trott.

Before he could be executed Bonnet with four companions escaped from confinement and attempted to get to sea in an open boat. Contrary winds drove them ashore upon Sullivan's Island. Colonel Rhett headed an expedition to capture him and his company, which was easily done after two of the pirates had been killed. Bonnet and his men were hanged at Execution Dock on the 24th of November, 1718. Sharp and summary had been that administration of Carolina justice and the surviving pirates began to feel that it would be well for them to keep away from the Carolina coasts hereafter.

What became of the wife who appeared in shadowy outline at the beginning of this sketch, is not known; but if she actually existed we seem to find in Bonnet's character, as he exhibited it in his piratical expeditions, sufficient excuse to justify her for everything of which she was even remotely accused. If she ever lived she should have been glad that he was hanged, but being a woman who probably loved him some time, I suppose she was sorry for his end. This statement I consider a handsome amendment for having set down the vague story of the suspicions about her character.

1

Some of Frontenac's Exploits

1. THE MASSACRE AT LA CHINE

A few miles above the city of Montreal the St. Lawrence pours its mighty flood of water in mad turmoil over those jutting points of rock, the passage of which is the most exciting experience in the descent of the great river. Upon the banks of the stream, just above the rapids, where the low-lying land permits it to widen into a vast expanse of water known as Lac St. Louis, one Robert Cavelier, Sieur de la Salle, by permission of the Sulpicians, whose influence was paramount in Montreal, had built himself a manor and established there a village, which, in the year 1689, contained some four hundred inhabitants. To this place, with fanciful anticipation that the great river if pursued far enough would afford a convenient passage to China, the long-sought-for and mysterious East, had been given the name of La Chine. The name is still preserved in the whirling rapids.

On the night of the 4th of August, 1689, in the midst of a furious storm of rain and wind, hundreds of birch-bark canoes were launched upon Lac St. Louis, and silently paddling across the river, some fifteen hundred ferocious Iroquois landed upon the shore and without a sound surrounded the village. A failure to invest Fort Frontenac had left these Children of the Longhouse, as the savage confederates of the Five Nations were called, free to attack this unprotected and unsuspicious point. At a given signal the blood-curdling war whoop was raised, the doors of the houses were burst open and the startled inhabitants were killed or captured before they realized what had happened. Many of them, awakened from sleep by the touch of a rude hand, opened their eyes to see a hideous painted face bending over them and before their lips could form a cry a tomahawk would be sunk into their brains—a happy fate which those who were spared for the moment would fain have preferred.

After the settlement had been plundered by the rapacious Indians the torch was applied to the houses, which, in spite of the rain, burned furiously, the bright glare warning the scattered inhabitants far and near that the threatening war with the Iroquois had at last begun. The Indians completely devastated the village. Added to their natural ferocity were the passions engendered by the captured liquor of which they freely partook, and under the double stimulus, they committed acts of indescribable horror.

Two or three palisaded forts in the vicinity of La Chine were garrisoned with soldiers and militiamen in small numbers, but for the most part they remained in their intrenchments paralyzed with terror and did nothing. Subercase, a gallant officer in command of the troops in the field, was at Montreal when the news of the massacre was brought by a frightened fugitive the next morning. Some two hundred soldiers lay encamped midway Montreal and La Chine. They had been apprised of the massacre by fugitives and had been ordered under arms, but had not dared to advance. Subercase, riding full speed, found them hesitating. Rallying to their support about a hundred inhabitants, he put himself at their head and moved forward. The ruins of La Chine, the dead men, women, and children smouldering in the embers or hanging to stakes, filled their hearts with rage and revenge.

Word was brought to them that the Indians were encamped a few miles farther on. Although few in numbers they were eager to attack, and Subercase, sword in hand, led them into the forest glades. His victory would have been certain, and his vengeance complete, for the Indians, it was afterward learned, were so overcome with liquor that they could have made but little resistance. As he approached their encampment, however, he was overtaken by the Chevalier de Vaudreuil, who bore peremptory orders from Denonville, the governor of Canada, for the party to return at once. To his bitter disappointment, Subercase was compelled to obey and the whole detachment retreated to Fort Roland. Montreal was wild with terror and Denonville had recalled the troops to protect the town from the supposed inevitable attack.

The Indians, recovering from their debauch, ravaged the country about the city for miles, but made no effort to attack the town—everything outside of its walls and the forts, however, was plundered and destroyed. Among other things the savages succeeded in cutting off a detachment of some eighty soldiers trying to reach Fort Roland from Fort St. Remy. They massacred them almost to a man. Having sated themselves with plunder in their long sojourn, one afternoon they took their hapless captives across the river, and that night, after torturing their victims with diabolical ingenuity, ended their revel by an awful cannibal feast. The wretched, impotent French stood in little groups on the strand at La Chine and Montreal, and with sickening hearts watched the flickering lights at Chateauguay which hovered over the place of death, dishonour, and horror to those they loved.

This appalling incident was the result of the incapacity of the governors of New France, the culmination of years of treachery, duplicity and oppression, and was the beginning of a series of frightful episodes, which did not terminate until the power of the Five Nations was broken, some eight years after. The people of the land cried out for a man to extricate them from their awful situation, and King Louis XIV sent them one in the person of old Frontenac.

2. THE BURNING OF SCHENECTADY

Louis de Buade, Comte de Palluau et de Frontenac, sprang from an ancient and honourable Basque family, cradled in the shadow of the Pyrenees. His grandfather had been advanced to high station by Henry the Fourth. His father had been maintained in the same degree of eminence by a continuance of the favour of that merry monarch. The melancholy Louis XIII had consented to stand godfather for the baby born in the year 1620, who was to be the future governor, and he vouchsafed to him the signal honour of giving him the royal name. By his ardent, fiery Gascon nature, Frontenac was marked out for the profession of a soldier, and in 1635, at the age of fifteen, he entered the French army as a gentleman-volunteer under Maurice of Nassau, rising, when twenty-three years of age, by successive acts of hardihood and audacity to the rank of colonel of the Normandy regiment. He took part in many of the sieges and battles in Flanders, and commanded his regiment with brilliant success in Italy, earning a reputation for desperate gallantry and headlong valour which made him the darling of the court of Louis XIV.

He was wounded again and again, but nothing seems to have dampened his military ardour. Rapidly passing through the different grades he was made a lieutenant general in 1669 and sent by the great Turenne, the first soldier of his day in Europe, as his especial choice to command the forces of Venice in a life and death struggle the Republic was then waging in Candia against the Turks. It was a most arduous and difficult position, but Frontenac accepted it gladly. From causes which he could not control, ultimate success did not attend his endeavours, but the price which he made the Turks pay before they conquered the island—their loss being reputed at one hundred and eighty thousand men—taken in conjunction with the insufficient means at his disposal, raised him to a very high place among the soldiers of the world.

Long before this campaign, in 1648, with his usual audacity he had made a love match with one of the beauties of the court, Anne de la Grange-Trianon, aged sixteen at the time; capturing that lady as it were by storm, and whisking her off to the church under the noses of her violently opposing guardians! The match was not a happy one, for if Frontenac was flint, Anne was steel, and they disagreed violently and quarrelled from the beginning. They therefore lived apart, each apparently retaining the highest respect for the other!

It is more than surmised that the first appointment of her fiery, hot-tempered husband to the governorship of Canada, was largely the result of his wife's influence. Singular to state she was not immoral, which is saying much for a woman so circumstanced in that court, and she appears to have remained faithful to her titular lord. She simply wished to be rid of him. Another cause, however, has been assigned for sending this brilliant soldier and courtier to New France, and perhaps with better reason, for he is reputed to have promised to become a rival of the Royal Sun in the affections of the famous Marquise de Montespan.

However that may be, for ten years, from 1672 to 1682, he had enjoyed a tempestuous and stormy career as governor of Canada. During this time he quarrelled with everything and everybody, but in spite of his rancorous difficulties with the Jesuits and Bishop Laval, and the Intendants Talon and Duchesneau, he showed such executive ability and general capacity, as had been manifested by no previous governor since the days of Champlain. During his term of office he sent forth Joliet and Marquette to discover the Mississippi. It is interesting to note that when Joliet saw for the first time the mighty "Father of Waters," he called it the River de Buade, and although Marquette named it La Concepcion, De Buade it remained for some time. Frontenac was the patron and friend of that other heroic spirit La Salle, who was assassinated in the swamps of the Gulf of Mexico vainly endeavouring to found an empire for France.

The royal governor was so far in advance of his time as to actually constitute and summon in New France a sort of States-General, or

Parliament, for the government of the country—under him, of course. This was much to the disgust of that most absolute of monarchs, Louis XIV, who hated Parliaments and made himself the States-General of his kingdom, and the king severely rebuked him for his action and countermanded his Parliament. It was a singular thing for the old noble to do for he was by nature one of the most aristocratic of men.

The quarrels in Quebec became so fierce finally that Frontenac and the *intendant* were relieved and ordered home. The two succeeding administrations of La Barre and de Denonville, culminated, as we have seen, in the awful massacre at La Chine. Before the news reached France, Louis had decided to replace Frontenac on the great rock of Quebec, and after he heard the tidings he determined to maintain him there.

The French king was then in the zenith of his power, the peace of Nimwegen had left him the undisputed primacy in Europe. The years of extravagant excesses which followed, coupled with the tremendous strains involved by his previous campaigns, had, however, undermined his resources, and France was never so vulnerable as at this moment of her triumph. The desire of Louis to replace James II upon the throne of England, and his inveterate hatred of William of Orange, caused war to break out again in 1688, and Frontenac was charged with carrying it on in the New World. To him was allotted the task of exterminating the English colonists on the seaboard and bringing the whole continent of North America into the power of New France. To bring about this magnificent result, he was provided with his brains and his hands by Providence, and re-enforced by the good will and the orders of the king, who was so busily occupied in other directions as to be able to spare him but little in the way of troops and supplies.

On the 12th of October, 1689, the governor reached Quebec and found New France at the last gasp. Instead of conquering the English it was necessary to struggle for life. In his magnificent planning Louis had given no thought to the Iroquois, and even the news from La Chine scarcely enlightened him. The Indians, undoubtedly inspired by the English, had given evidence of their intentions toward Canada in the massacre, and it was rumoured that preparations were already under way on the part of the English vigorously to follow up the inroads of their savage allies. With characteristic energy Frontenac endeavoured to relieve the situation, and rehabilitate the country. Striving by diplomacy and cajolery to propitiate the Indians for the time being, in spite of the awful blot left upon the colony by the unpunished foray, he sent three expeditions to strike the English border settlements, to restore French prestige in the savage mind, and to make at least a beginning toward overwhelming that thin line of humanity on the seaboard.

It was winter before the three expeditions got away under the command of different members of that young Canadian noblesse, who showed themselves men of distinguished capacity and courage in all the campaigns on this continent. One party under the command of de Mantet, and three of the sons of the celebrated Le Moyne, of whom d'Iberville was chief, comprised something over two hundred and fifty men, half of them French, the others Christianized Hurons. Having marched twenty-two days in midwinter, in which they suffered incredible hardships, on the 4th of February, 1690, they arrived near the little Dutch village of Schenectady, the northernmost settlement in New York. Albany had been their destination, but Schenectady lay nearer to them and exhausted human nature could do no more.

The people of Schenectady had laughed at the warnings of Governor Leisler. That night the ten militiamen who garrisoned the town mounted snow sentinels at the two gates of the stockade, which they left open, and under this secure wardship, retired to their barracks. The unsuspicious inhabitants were all asleep. The French and Indians lay concealed until nightfall and then in the midst of a furious snow storm they softly entered the town, encircled the houses, made all preparations and awakened the inhabitants with the usual war cry. Some sixty were killed, including twenty-two women and children, and ninety persons were made prisoners. The killing was attended by frightful barbarities, perpetrated by the Indians as usual. The town was looted and burned, and taking some thirty prisoners with them, having turned adrift the balance, the French, laden with plunder, retraced their steps to Canada with light hearts. A party of warriors from the Long-house overtook them and in a fierce battle killed some eighteen of them, but otherwise they got back safely with their prisoners and their plunder.

Another expedition numbering fifty-two persons, under de Rouville, surprised the settlement at Salmon Falls on the Piscataqua River, on the night of March 27th, and re-enacted the butchery at Schenectady. As they were retracing their steps with fifty-four prisoners they fell in with the third French party, and early in June the combined force moved against the settlement on Casco Bay, called Fort Loyal, which is now Portland, Maine.

This place was garrisoned and was regularly besieged. After six days of gallant defence, the officer in command, Captain Sylvanus Davis, surrendered under promises of protection, which were basely forgotten, and the usual massacre ensued. All these predatory excursions had been most brutally and ruthlessly carried out to complete success by the infuriated French and their savage allies. The effect upon popular opinion, and especially on the Indians, was immediate and decided. There was some fight left in the French after all, it appeared.

Meanwhile, for the first time in many years, the savages from the northwest had been able to transport their furs and peltries to Montreal. Frontenac's vigorous policy had opened a way for them and a constantly increasing stream of wealth and trade poured through the colonies. There was a great meeting of the chiefs and braves at Montreal in July, and it is gravely related that the spirited old governor general actually seized a *tomahawk* and personally joined in the war dance, by which an alliance offensive and defensive was celebrated.

A curious picture is presented by this *habitué* of the court of the proudest, most punctilious, and best dressed of monarchs, abandoning himself to wild Indian revelry; whooping, yelling, brandishing his *tomahawk* with all the fervour of the most savage of his allies. But one of the secrets of his success lay in his intuitive knowledge of the savage character and his ability to control the Indians. He was half Indian in spirit himself, this fierce old warrior, and his actions they could understand and appreciate. Even those who warred against him, cherished for him an instinctive respect and went softly in his presence.

3. Phips' Failure at Quebec

But the sturdy English colonists did not submit tamely to the inroads of Frontenac's partisans. The sluggish Dutch blood of New York was stirred by the dreadful news that came down the river, and a certain Captain John Schuyler, raised a force to attack Montreal by land; Massachusetts came to his assistance. A party of several hundred colonists, under Winthrop and Schuyler, were assembled in the spring to march up to the attack by the familiar route along Lake Champlain, which was the inevitable war path of the different contending nationalities on this continent until the victory of MacDonough finally shut the gate.

Meanwhile, Massachusetts, bankrupt in treasury and exhausted in credit, boldly undertook an enterprise of even greater magnitude, no less than the capture of Quebec itself. Massachusetts bore the same relation to the provinces that South Carolina, later on, did to the Southern States. She was always spoiling for a fight and generally found people ready to accommodate her. Appealing to England for help, and when her appeals were unnoticed falling back upon her own limited and over-strained resources, she assembled some thirty-four vessels, only four of which were of respectable size and the rest small and of trifling force. In these vessels were embarked twenty-two hundred men under the command of Sir William Phips.

Phips was a plain, rough sailor, originally a ship-carpenter, grossly ignorant and obstinate, who had captured Port Royal in Nova Scotia without striking a blow. He was honest, according to his lights, and he was brave. Other qualifications for leadership he had none. Earlier in life he had located a sunken galleon in the West Indies and had recovered from it the treasure it had contained. He had put down a mutiny on the king's ship he commanded on that occasion by the force of his vigorous personality and had been knighted for these exploits. He was chosen to the command of this expedition, and the soldiers, who were, of course, militiamen, were under the direction of John Walley, a Barnstable mechanic. He, too, was brave, but untrained, ignorant and inexperienced.

The ships were scantily provisioned and inadequately provided with ammunition. A more capable commander would never have dreamed of attempting so stupendous a feat of arms with so feeble a force. Encouraged, however, by his easy success at Port Royal, Phips blithely set forth upon his impossible expedition. His departure was much delayed, waiting for re-enforcements from England which never came, and it was not until October, near the commencement of the closed season, that the fleet dropped anchor in the basin of Quebec.

The land expedition up Lake Champlain, badly conducted, having effected nothing whatever, decided to return. Before doing so, Schuyler pushed forward with an advance party and had a severe engagement with a larger force of French and Indians in which the honours remained with the Dutch-Americans, but the mind of Frontenac was set at rest by the news of the prompt and final retreat of the party.

His calmness was speedily broken by the arrival of a courier at Montreal with the startling news that the English were coming up the river! Leaving Callières, governor of Montreal, to bring up the garrison to Quebec, with all speed Frontenac made his way down the river. By his orders fortifications had been commenced on the landward side of the town. He had caused a stockade with a ditch and earth wall to be built from the St. Charles River to the St. Lawrence. The work was not entirely completed when he arrived, but with his usual vigour he infused so much of his own spirit into the population that during one night they finished the palisade. Cannon were planted on the walls of the city and upon the *plateau* of Cape Diamond, to command the shipping in the basin, and two batteries were erected near the water's edge in front of the lower town. The country was scoured for the hardy Canadian militia, and the regular garrisons of the nearby posts on the river were concentrated in the town.

Early in the morning of October 16th, 1690, the fleet of Phips came slowly trailing past the Isle of Orleans and dropped anchor just out of gunshot of the city. Phips had not displayed his usual energy. He had lingered three weeks at Tadoussac and then had proceeded leisurely up the river, touching at several places, in most of which he met with a warm reception from Canadians and Indians, who, from the cover of the thick woods, on the shore, inflicted great loss upon his men. The first sight of the city and the natural strength of the position, apparent even to his dull mind, possibly for the first time convinced him that the task was not the easy one which his experience at Port Royal had led him confidently to expect

Putting a bold face upon the matter, however, he sent an *aide* ashore under a flag of truce. The officer was blindfolded by the orders of Frontenac and led by a roundabout road over barricade after barricade into the town. Then, still blindfolded, he was conducted to the great hall of the Chateau St. Louis, the residence of the governor, and the bandage was taken from his eyes. He found himself standing before a tall, thin old man of commanding presence, with a nose like an eagle's beak, who looked at him sternly out of a pair of fierce gray eyes, deep set under great tufted brows, a weather-beaten, age-lined face, which, better than the upright figure and the easy grace of movement, bespoke years of campaigning on the field. It was Frontenac.

He was surrounded by a brilliant group of the young noblesse of the colonies, attired in all the bravery which the French have ever managed to assume however hard their circumstances or however desperate their situation. To him the rude young provincial officer presented an impudent summons from Phips to surrender. The letter was read aloud, and was received with bursts of indignation by the officers and men present. Frontenac, however, restrained their passion and dismissed the officer, refusing to give him any letter for his commander,

THE MASSACRE AT LA CHINE

ANNOUNCING THE ARRIVAL OF THE ENGLISH.

saying that he could get his reply from the mouths of the cannon. He remarked incidentally, that a man of his station and reputation should not be approached in the rude and brusque manner in which Phips had addressed him.

In spite of Phips' bold demand, his situation was well-nigh hopeless. But there were two or three things which he might have done which would have presented a faint possibility of success. He was advised to attack the landward side of the town and was informed that there was a practicable path farther up the river affording access to the *plateau*. It was the same path by which Wolfe made his famous ascent of the cliff seventy years later. Phips rejected this offer and decided to land his men on the side of the Charles River opposite Quebec, cross the river at a ford and capture the town by storm, while he, himself, engaged the different batteries with his ships! While these preparations were going on, the garrison of the town was re-enforced by the arrival of Callières and his men from Montreal; that was the end of Phips' last hope if he had known it, which, of course, he did not.

In pursuance of his foolhardy plan, after some delays Walley and fifteen hundred men were debarked at Charlesbourg. They were met by a warm fire from parties of French on the Quebec side of the Charles River, who proceeded to annoy and harass them greatly, inflicting severe loss upon them. The New Englanders fought bravely, charging their concealed foes in the thickets again and again, but to no avail. Before Walley could properly make such disposition as his untutored mind permitted, with culpable impatience Phips moved over to attack the town with his ships. It was perfectly practicable for him to enter the Charles River and cover the passage of his troops by his ships, instead of which, he threw away the only remaining chance of success and proceeded to bombard the upper and lower town and the rocky heights of Cape Diamond.

Frontenac was ready for him, and the ships and the town engaged in a hot fire for two days. No harm was done the city; the gunnery of the English was execrable, their powder supply was finally exhausted and they accomplished nothing beyond battering up the face of the rock. On the other hand Frontenac dismasted the flagship, seriously damaged many other vessels, and finally drove the whole fleet out of action, Phips' flag which floated over to the strand was picked up by the French as a trophy.

Meanwhile, smallpox broke out among the men on shore. When Phips heard of this news he practically gave up the game. Although he blustered somewhat, the spirit was gone out of him. He had still to extricate Walley's troops from their now precarious situation. Manifesting at last some little evidence of military aptitude, he moved some of his vessels near the shore to protect Walley's wretched men, who had suffered greatly from rain, exposure, and sickness, and from parties of French skirmishers and Indian raiders, until the weather permitted to re-embark the party on the fleet.

Having done this successfully, on the 21st of October, after wasting two aimless days, he turned tail and, followed by his disorganized and scattered ships, went helter-skelter down the river. Stopping below Isle Orleans to careen his shattered ships and repair damages, he finally reached Boston with but few of his vessels in company, and while many of them finally arrived at different ports, a number of the vessels were lost with all on board. As the result of this disastrous expedition, the credit of impoverished Massachusetts was lower and her treasury a little more empty than before. The prestige of Frontenac was greatly enhanced by this gallant defence, and his most Christian Majesty at Versailles even went so far as to strike a medal in honour of the event, which, like all the medals he struck, bore the image of his own royal physiognomy.

During the remainder of Frontenac's term of office in Canada, neither party being able to muster an army formidable enough to undertake a conquest on a large scale, the French, English, and Indians confronted one another with an implacable hatred, which found no outlet save in predatory excursions and forays. A trail of blood and terror extended over all the frontier. The torch and the scalping-knife were busy in every direction. Success inclined sometimes to one side and sometimes to the other, but on the whole, the balance of advantage was with the French.

In 1691, Peter Schuyler, ancestor of General Philip Schuyler of Revolutionary fame, had an encounter with Valrenne near Chambly on the Richelieu River, which Frontenac characterizes as the hottest fight which had yet taken place in Canada. The honours appear to have been equally distributed in the barren but desperate engagement. By Frontenac's orders and inspired by the Jesuit priests from 1691 to 1695 the Abenakis broke up the English settlements on the coast of Maine by repeated raids of the same terrible character. Indeed the Christianized Indians were quite as ferocious as their heathen brethren. In the end the French were entirely successful and the English were pushed down to the sea-board settlements and compelled to stand on the defensive. But little could be done for the support of the English colonists in this war by the Home Government, which, at the time, had troubles of its own on its hands. The Iroquois, too, suffered severely and after the defeats of the English they never took the field in force as they had done at La Chine.

4. D'Iberville in Hudson's Bay

In 1696 an expedition comprising three ships under the famous d'Iberville, captured the fort at Pemaquid. After this adventure d'Iberville sailed for Newfoundland, captured St. John's, and ravaged the island. The next year among other attacks which Frontenac planned was one upon the English trading posts on Hudson's Bay. To drive the English from this section, which he considered particularly his own, had been a favourite project of the king. Therefore, by Frontenac's orders, in 1697, d'Iberville turned the prows of his little squadron of five ships to the northward and skirted along the coast of Labrador. Picking his way through the ice floes which came floating down from the frozen north, in August he finally entered that gloomy gray inland sea named after the unfortunate Henry Hudson.

At the entrance of the bay the supply ship was caught in the ice-pack and lost. A few days later a violent storm arose which separated d'Iberville from his three remaining ships. As he sailed down the bay in his frigate the *Pelican*, forty-four guns, one morning the lookouts sighted three large vessels coming toward them. Supposing that they were his missing ships he immediately headed for them, but to his great surprise presently discovered that they were three large English vessels—the *Hampshire*, a man-of-war of fifty-two guns (in bad condition); and two armed merchantmen—the *Daring*, of thirty-six, and the *Hudson's Bay*, of thirty-two. The three ships greatly outclassed his own single frigate, but with the usual dauntless gallantry of his race, d'Iberville immediately engaged them.

It was about nine o'clock in the morning. The battle that ensued was an exceeding hot one. During the combat, by his brilliant seamanship, however, d'Iberville so manoeuvred his frigate that he succeeded in raking his opponents in succession. About one o'clock he managed to take such an advantageous position off the quarter of the dismasted *Hampshire* that she literally sank with all on board under his furious broadsides. He then closed with the *Hudson's Bay*, which presently struck her flag in a sinking condition, upon which the *Daring* fled and was seen no more. The *Pelican* was too much cut up to pursue.

Flushed with victory d'Iberville stood on down toward Fort Nelson, which it was necessary to capture. Another fierce gale blew up and his ship ran ashore and was wrecked. She had been badly shattered in hull, masts, and rigging, and was in no condition to weather the storm. By herculean efforts he succeeded in landing his men and prisoners and saving his arms and ammunition. The *Hudson's Bay* was also lost. Undaunted by this misfortune he marched overland to the fort and invested it. Fortunately, however, his missing ships arrived at this time. The fort was vigorously bombarded and after three days surrendered, the garrison receiving honourable terms. The French spent the winter there and when the spring came they returned to Quebec, having utterly broken up the English trade. It was a glorious exploit and well worthy the genius of the colonizer of Louisiana. "He had triumphed over the storms, the icebergs, and the English." Yet the brilliant adventure is scarcely referred to in history.

5. Striking the Iroquois

New France was now exceedingly prosperous. The fur trade, upon which it depended, had recommenced and there remained no enemy to be dealt with except the Iroquois. The spirit of this wonderful confederation of savage tribes was as high as ever, but their power had greatly diminished. Continued warfare with enemies constantly growing more powerful, as the French, and with foes to whom an inveterate hatred superadded an unwonted bitterness in combat, like the Huron and the Illinois, had greatly depleted the ranks of their fighting men. With sullen defiance, however, though they were in the main abandoned by their English allies, they refused to make peace, which Frontenac so earnestly sought of them, and whenever opportunity presented they continued their savage forays against New France.

In the year 1696 the governor general determined finally to break their opposition. By great exertions he assembled at Fort Frontenac on Lake Ontario, the largest army which had ever set forth upon a land expedition in Canada. In a vast fleet of *bateaux* and canoes some twenty-two hundred men under the leadership of the indomitable old count himself, then seventy-six years of age, crossed the lake and entered the Oswego River. Transporting their boats by portage around the falls and overland they embarked on Lake Onondaga and presently reached the land of the Long-house.

As the army debarked upon the shore they saw in the distance dense columns of smoke and as they advanced in martial array through the forest, with drums beating and trumpets sounding, they found that the Onondagas had burned their town and fled rather than risk a battle. Frontenac sent his men to complete the destruction of the crops in the fields and the villages nearby, which they did with merciless severity. They made captive several fugitives who had failed to make good their escape and these they put to death with an exquisite refinement of torture, which would not have shamed an Iroquois. Then, having marched through the country in a high-handed manner and demonstrated their power in such a way that even the unthinking Indian realized it, they returned to Fort Frontenac, and the Indians soon thereafter sued for peace. Perhaps they were further moved to this design by the signing of the treaty of Ryswyck, September 20th, 1697, which brought about peace between England and the French and deprived the Iroquois of their strongest ally.

The news of the peace also nipped in the bud some brilliant schemes of the aged count, which he was preparing to put into operation, in spite of the fact that he was not only an old but a broken man. He had become in fact so worn out by his strenuous life, that in the last campaign against the Iroquois, it had been necessary to carry him about in a chair. The eagle spirit with which he had fought through so many battles had at last worn away the bars of the cage and was about to take its flight. His end was peaceful. The *intendant* Champigny, with whom he had been continually at odds, forgot their differences and did his best to cheer the declining hours of the lonely old governor. He kept up his haughty spirit to the last, hurling defiance at Lord Bellemont, the royal governor of New York, in a spirited correspondence, until the end of all his struggles came quietly and peacefully on the afternoon of the 28th of November, 1698. It is interesting to note that he bequeathed his property to the wife of his youth, who survived him. I wonder if she remembered the romance of her girlhood.

Frontenac left the colony at the very height of its fortunes; not before, nor after, was it in the enjoyment of such prosperity. Though in the idea of absolutism in rule which it represented was enshrined the inevitable cause of its downfall, when Opposed to the idea of independence exhibited by its English rival, yet Frontenac endued it with such vitality, that through him it lasted for sixty years longer, until it died with Montcalm.[1]

Frontenac had all the vices of his age. He was high-tempered, pas-

---

1. *Montcalm at the Battle of Carillon (Ticonderoga) (July 8th, 1758* by Maurice Sautai also published by Leonaur.

sionate, haughty and unyielding. Conciliation was an element entirely foreign to his character. He quarrelled always, everywhere and with everyone. He contended for his personal prerogatives with as much zeal as he fought for his king. He cannot be held guiltless of inaugurating the ruthless reprisals which devastated the border. It is not on record that he took any steps to prevent the calamities and mitigate the horrors attendant upon the raids which he planned and which were carried out by his partisans, wood rangers and Indians. He was a good hater and an unsparing combatant, but his faults were more than counter-balanced by his good qualities and his virtues.

He was loyal to his friends, generous in his appreciation of the merit and achievements of those beneath him. Petty jealousy of his officers had no place in his large mind. He was a man of splendid executive ability, unwearied persistence and the highest courage, a trained and brilliant soldier of wide experience, and a devoted servant of his king and his country. Between Champlain and Montcalm he stands the most splendid representative of the power of France in America. He succeeded where others failed, and few men who have lived have so far impressed upon the keen judgement of the red men—who with all their faults, were seldom deceived in their estimate of a man and a soldier—such evidence of power and capacity and courage, as this grim soldier from the battle fields of the Old World, this gay courtier from the parks of Versailles, who finished his course, like the eagle in his aerie, on the gray old rock of Cape Diamond.

2
Oglethorpe on St Simon's Island

1. THE SPANISH EXPEDITION

It is perhaps not generally known that the Spanish-American War of 1898 had a precursor on this continent in the War of the Austrian Succession, sometimes called locally "King George's War." During this conflict the Spanish invaded the province of Georgia in great force, and but for the skill and courage of James Edward Oglethorpe would probably have carried their arms successfully up the coast for an indefinite distance. Save in the largest histories the defence of St. Simon's Island, which was the principal and most picturesque episode of the war, is passed by with scarcely more than a mention, yet it was as pretty a feat of arms on the part of the colonists and as brilliantly successful in its outcome as any campaign ever fought on the continent.

Oglethorpe, the founder of Georgia, was one of the most interesting characters in the whole range of colonial record. Our personal knowledge of him is probably greater than that we possess of any of his contemporaries, for he lived to a great age, being ninety years old when he died; and as he was of good birth, ample fortune, a man of affairs who had risen to high station, he mingled with the best society in his long life, and many interesting anecdotes of him have been recorded. He and the great Dr. Johnson were warm friends, for instance, and the industrious and ever delightful Boswell has set down much about him, with that discriminating eye for interesting personal gossip which he possessed.

Oglethorpe was born in London near the close of the seventeenth century, probably in 1696.[1] He early entered the military service and

---

1. There is much uncertainty about the date of Oglethorpe's birth, and the authorities differ widely The latest and most authoritative work on the subject, *The Dictionary of National Biography*, gives it as 1696.

in the Austro-Turkish War served as an *aide* to the celebrated Prince Eugene, and was present doing good service at the famous siege of Belgrade. While scarcely more than a boy, dining with a prince of Würtemberg and other officers, the prince rudely filliped a few drops of wine from his glass into the face of the young ensign.

In Boswell's words:

Here was a nice dilemma. To have challenged him instantly might have fixed a quarrelsome character upon the young soldier; to have taken no notice of it might have been considered as cowardice. Oglethorpe, therefore, keeping his eye upon the prince, and smiling all the time as if he took what his highness had done in jest, said, 'My prince, that is a good joke; but we do it much better in England,' and then threw a whole glass of wine in the prince's face! An old general who sat by, said, 'That was well done, my prince, you began it.'

Oglethorpe had chosen a remarkably neat and effective way of getting out of the difficulty, and one which would not have occurred to many boys of his age. Under the circumstances there was nothing the prince could do; what he thought of it all has not been recorded.

After leaving the army, in which his service had been exceptionally brilliant, Oglethorpe entered Parliament and, his attention being turned by service on a committee of investigation to the situation of insolvent debtors of England, he determined to relieve their hard condition. With the sanction of the king a company was formed and a grant of land obtained south of the Carolinas, which was to be constituted "a place of refuge for the distressed people of Britain, and the persecuted Protestants of Europe."

The prospective settlers therein were all scrupulously examined by the agents of the company and no one was allowed to embark for the colony whose character and ability could not pass the scrutiny successfully. In this respect the colony of Georgia was unique. The only debtors, too, who were allowed to go there were those who had become involved in difficulties and were languishing in prisons through misfortune, and fraudulent debtors were rigorously excluded,

Oglethorpe was a stanch Protestant and he debarred from his colony all Papists. He was liberal enough, however, to welcome Jews if any should desire to come. The first settlement was formed at Savannah in 1733 and by Oglethorpe in person, and thereafter a steady stream of immigrants of the very highest class poured into the colony and settlements were made at different points. Among those who sought refuge in the new land were sturdy and industrious Lutherans from Salzburg, fleeing from the persecutions of their prince-bishop; frugal and pious Moravians under the leadership of the cultured, able, and learned Spangenberg; and a small body of bold and warlike Highlanders from Scotland. The colony grew and prospered in spite of the fact that rum and negro slavery were both equally prohibited. Among its inhabitants at different times were John and Charles Wesley and George Whitefield.

When the European War began, which Carlyle calls "Jenkins' ear war," from the act of the Spaniards in cutting off the ear of a certain English sea captain of unsavoury reputation named Jenkins—who lied about the incident atrociously, by the way—the southern American colonists, of course, were involved in the struggle. Oglethorpe, who had gone back to England in the interim, was appointed brigadier general, with supreme command of all the military forces of Georgia and the Carolinas. He returned to the province he had founded and so ably administered at the head of a trained, disciplined regiment of six hundred men, which had been raised and equipped in England.

In the summer of 1740 he undertook an unsuccessful and ill-advised campaign against St. Augustine, with a motley force of two thousand colonists and Indians and a squadron of six English ships. The invaders effected nothing. They had no siege guns, the Spaniards were re-enforced from Havana, and after exhibiting a high degree of forbearance for the inoffensive inhabitants of the land, whom they had treated with unusual courtesy, they gave over the attempt and withdrew from Florida.

The commander of Fort Augustine, Don Manuel de Monteano, who had successfully repulsed Oglethorpe's attack, conceived the design of delivering a return stroke which would be decisive. Summoning to his aid all the forces of Cuba, great preparations were made for the coming campaign. The Spaniards hoped to sweep the whole southern seaboard, overwhelm the weak colony of Georgia, take the wealthy and populous Carolina provinces, and carry the war at least as far as Virginia. The result of the campaign would probably make them masters of all the territory south of the afterward Mason and Dixon's line, and add an empire to the Spanish colonial dominion.

Over fifty ships of various sizes were assembled between the two ports, Havana and St. Augustine, upon which were embarked between five and six thousand men, many of them veterans of the celebrated

Spanish infantry which had often proved itself among the best soldiery of Europe. The expedition was provided with every necessary equipment including an unusually fine artillery train.

The Georgia seaboard, even more than that of the Carolinas, is covered with large islands and shoals, access to the main land being had through numerous sounds between the islands. On several of these islands Oglethorpe had erected fortifications, notably Fort William on Cumberland Island, commanding Amelia Sound; but the principal defensive works were on St. Simon's Island, off the mouth of the Altamaha River.

Here some six years before had been established the military settlement of Frederica. As he had named the province Georgia in honour of George II., so he had called the town Frederica, after the worthless and dissipated Frederick, Prince of Wales, who is known to fame as the father of George III., and is the man for whose dog Pope wrote the following verse:

I am his highness' dog at Kew.
Good reader, pray, whose dog are you?

These are the principal things for which Frederick is noted.

Georgia was of necessity what we would now call a "buffer" State, between the older northerly colonies and the Spanish settlements in Florida. Oglethorpe had chosen the location on St. Simon's Island with an eye single to its defensive possibilities. On a high bluff surrounded by thick and impenetrable forests, about midway on the western shore of the island, he had built a fort protected on the land side by a tidewater ditch, and on the riverside by a water battery and by another battery of twelve heavy guns so mounted as to command the channel of a navigable river which gave access to the place, for three quarters of a mile. Any attacking ships would be forced to subject themselves to a rating fire for that distance as they came in. In addition they would be compelled to endure an oblique fire from the fort itself.

The intrenchments were strongly built of a material called "tabby," a compound of lime, sand, and shells, which hardened upon exposure into stone-like cement of impenetrable consistency. The fort and the batteries were amply provided with artillery. On one side of the fort before the forests began was an open place used as a parade ground, which was completely commanded by its guns. Back of the fort, the town, surrounded by a rampart, was built. No access to Frederica, built upon the landward or the river shore, was possible from the seaward

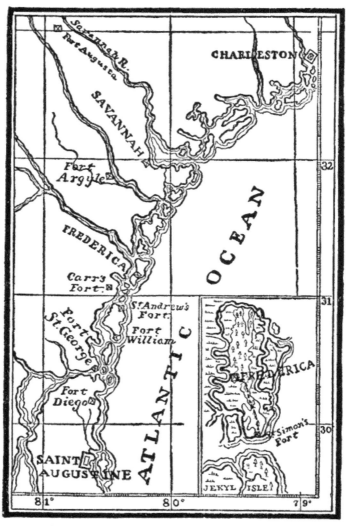

EARLY SETTLEMENTS IN GEORGIA, AND MAP OF ST. SIMON'S
ISLAND AND FREDERICA

shore of the island, on account of the character of the beach and certain pathless morasses beyond it. At the lower part of the island and commanding St. Simon's, or Jekyl, Sound, several batteries had been erected and a well-built road laid out connecting Frederica with these works. The road wound about in devious course between impenetrable forests and dangerous marshes. Sometimes it would widen into a meadow or *savanna* where would be a clearing spacious enough in which to pitch a camp, but presently the forest and the marsh would approach each other once more and the road resume its character of a narrow pass.

To garrison Frederica, Oglethorpe had his own regiment, which was an efficient body of men, well officered, several companies of Rangers, and a small body of Highlanders from the settlement at Darien, full of warlike courage and zeal as became the children of the fighting Scottish race. In all they amounted to less than eight hundred men. To supplement this force he had his own schooner of fourteen guns and eighty men, two sloops of about the same size and armament, a large merchant ship called the *Success*, which mounted twenty-two guns, and several smaller craft.

Before attempting any enterprise against the upper coast cities to the northward, it was necessary for the invaders to dispose of this force. It would be dangerous to leave such a post to menace the rear of the Spanish expedition and possibly destroy its communications. Monteano therefore intended to sweep the little English and colonial force off the coast in short order and proceed on his way rejoicing. He thought it would be an easy task. He reckoned without his host, as we shall see.

On the 22nd of June, 1743, the commanding officer of Fort William found means to inform Oglethorpe that fourteen Spanish ships had appeared off Amelia Sound. It was the advance of the expected attack. After a smart engagement with the fort they were driven off with some loss and entered Cumberland Sound north of the island and out of range of Fort William, but within easy shooting distance of Fort Andrew. The two forts on Cumberland Island were both small and not provided with large garrisons. Their situation was critical. Oglethorpe acted promptly; he always did. Embarking two companies of his regiment on his own schooner and the two sloops and taking advantage of a favourable wind, he at once put to sea.

On the evening of the 23rd of June he came in sight of the Spanish squadron riding quietly at anchor. Giving them no time to get under way or to make any other preparation for battle, with bold yet calculated courage he dashed at them. Although one of his captains, named Tolson, became panic-stricken at the sight of the odds and bore away from the approaching contest seeking safety in ignominious flight, Oglethorpe, followed by the other sloop, kept right on. The Spaniards were taken by surprise by the audacity of his manoeuvres, yet they hurried to their quarters and opened a wild and ineffectual fire upon the approaching English from the guns that bore. Oglethorpe skilfully ran into the smoke banks to leeward and, himself hidden, deliberately poured his broadsides into the huddled mass of the Spanish at short range, with such effect that no less than four of the Spanish vessels afterward foundered in a storm on account of the severe handling they had received.

The two little vessels succeeded in passing the Spanish fleet with little or no loss. Oglethorpe landed immediately on Cumberland Island and, after spiking the guns of Fort St. Andrew, threw some of his soldiers and the garrison of the; abandoned work into Fort William. Leaving a promising young Scotsman named Alexander Stewart in command of that work, the general succeeded in regaining St. Simon's Island with his two remaining vessels without further loss. His arrival was a source of great joy to the soldiers and inhabitants of Frederica, as the boat which had run away had returned bearing the news that Oglethorpe's flotilla had been sunk by the Spaniards and that he had been lost. The cowardly captain was immediately put under arrest for his pusillanimous conduct.

2. The Defence of Frederica

On the 28th of June the united Spanish fleet appeared off St. Simon's Bar. The number of vessels varies in the different accounts, some authorities stating that there were as many as fifty-six. There were at least thirty-six of them, however, the largest being three ships of twenty guns each, although the majority of them were vessels of a sort known as a "half-galley," probably propelled by sweeps as well as sails; some of them were large enough to carry one hundred and twenty men and mount an eighteen-pound gun, although being built for service in inland streams, they drew but five feet of water. The statements as to the number of soldiers on board range from seven to five thousand. On the 5th of July, the Spaniards, taking advantage of a brisk gale and a heavy flood tide, crossed the bar and engaged the forts at the end of the island.

For four hours the battle was severely contested. The *Success* and the small ships also joined in the encounter and the Spanish made four different attempts to board the *Success*, which, from her larger size, was necessarily anchored farthest away from the shore. They were repulsed in each instance with heavy loss. They finally abandoned the contest, but they succeeded in passing the forts and entering the river well up toward Frederica.

Oglethorpe acted promptly as usual. Sending his vessels to sea with orders that they proceed to Savannah, he spiked the guns of the batteries at the lower end of the island and concentrated his forces at Frederica. The Spanish commander, having reconnoitred the water approach to that fort, and after having advanced rather hesitatingly to attack it, which attempt was repulsed with some loss, determined to land his army at Gascoigne's bluff on the island. Some four thousand men, including the Spanish artillery, grenadiers, and dismounted dragoons, and regiments of negroes and mulattoes, took possession of the abandoned forts, erected additional batteries mounting twenty eighteen-pound guns, and made other preparations for the expected conquest.

They had discovered that it was impossible to take the fort by water, and that it was equally impossible to lead an army through the woods. The military road which Oglethorpe had built offered the only practicable mode of access to Frederica. On the 7th of July, Don Manuel sent out a scouting party comprising one hundred and twenty Spaniards, forty Indians and forty negro grenadiers. They came marching gayly up the road and walked blindly into an ambush which had been prepared with consummate skill by the English commander. In the battle that ensued the greater part of them were killed out of hand. A few only of the Indians and negroes escaped to tell the tale. Oglethorpe took a prominent part in the fighting, engaging the Spanish captain hand to hand and finally killing him. He performed several feats of personal prowess in the encounter which greatly endeared him to his men. The English pursued the flying Spanish for several miles until they came to an open meadow on the edge of which Oglethorpe posted them in anticipation of a return attack. He himself returned post-haste to Frederica to bring up the rest of his men.

Don Manuel when he heard of the disastrous defeat immediately sent out a second and much stronger party comprising one hundred grenadiers, two hundred infantry, a small squadron of horse, and a large body of negro troops and Indians, all under the command of

Don Antonio Barba, a veteran and experienced soldier. Throwing out scouts and making use of every precaution, they marched up the road to the place held by the detachment of Oglethorpe's men and a small body of Highlanders. Notwithstanding their previous success, in some way the regulars became panic-stricken as the Spanish advance appeared in the open, and after exchanging a few futile volleys they abandoned the field and withdrew.

The retrograde movement soon became a rapid retreat and they streamed up the road in one of those strange panics which sometimes seizes upon the best of troops. A platoon of the Highlanders under Lieutenant Mackay and a small company of colonial Rangers under Lieutenant Sutherland, brought up the rear. Fortunately they did not share the prevailing fear of their comrades, and after retreating a short distance they resolved to lay an ambuscade for the pursuing Spaniards. They halted, turned about, made a detour, struggled back through the woods until they actually got in the rear of the Spanish force still advancing up the road. They chose a position where the way narrowed to a width of less than twenty yards and bent into a crescent between a morass and the thick wood, and there determined to wait an opportunity of dealing a decisive blow, not doubting that the enemy would soon return.

Having learned something of the dangers of the way by their previous disastrous repulse, the Spanish advance had been halted after a short pursuit, and as they thought they had dispersed the force before them and as they were not strong enough to attack Frederica, they retraced their steps and returned to the open to make a camp. They came back slowly, so that the Georgians had ample time to make proper dispositions. They carefully chose their place and lay concealed in the thick undergrowth awaiting the enemy. Presently the Spaniards came marching along the road. As they reached the spot where the English had been awaiting them and whence the regulars had retreated in terror, imagining that no enemy was anywhere near them, and considering themselves protected by marsh and wood, they entered the defile covered by the guns of the waiting Scots, halted; dismounted, stacked arms and prepared to repose and rest under the shade of the palmetto tree.

The colonists had been cautioned by Mackay, the ranking officer, on no account to fire until he gave the word. It was his desire completely to surround the Spaniards before he began the engagement, but a Spanish horse happening to catch a sight of a Highland bonnet through the trees over the undergrowth—the wearer, in disobedience to orders, having risen to get a better look—shied violently and attracted the attention of his rider and he at once gave the alarm. The Spaniards awoke to the peril of their situation and sprang to their arms.

Concealment was at an end. Instantly the Highlanders and Rangers fired. The Spaniards taken at a great disadvantage and seeing the woods on either side of them ablaze with musketry, after a few feeble and ineffectual discharges by such men as could reach their weapons, turned to fly. The officers bravely tried to check their retreat, but unavailingly. Don Antonio Barba was mortally wounded and many of the officers fell. The Highlanders and Rangers burst out of the woods and charged upon the enemy with bayonet or claymore in hand. This completed the rout. More than two hundred of the Spanish party were killed and wounded on the spot and many captured before they got out of reach of the little party of scarcely more than fifty Highlanders and Rangers.

Back on the road advancing at the head of the rest of his troops, Oglethorpe met the fleeing soldiers of the regiment and heard the story of their disgraceful retreat. Rallying the men and putting an officer in charge of them with instructions to bring them up at full speed, he galloped on ahead down the road at a great pace. He saw of course that the Highlanders and Rangers were not with the rest of the troops, and when he heard the firing he imagined that they had been, or were being, cut down and captured. The Spaniards had openly declared that they would give quarter neither to man nor woman.

In great anxiety Oglethorpe made his way toward the scene of the encounter. What was his joy when he reached the pass to find that not one of his troops had been touched and that over two hundred of the enemy lay dead and dying before him! Of the remainder of the Spanish party but few reached the main camp. So fierce had been the attack and pursuit of the colonists, that most of the Spaniards had forsaken the road in their blind attempts to escape. Those who unwittingly plunged into the hideous marsh of course never succeeded in extricating themselves from its awful depths; while for years afterward hunters ranging the woods would find in lonely spots skeletons which told grim tales of lost Spaniards dying of starvation and exposure in the savage wastes of the forest. The encounter was called the Battle of Bloody Marsh, and Oglethorpe promoted the two young officers who had commanded the Highlanders and Rangers, on the field. It is noteworthy that this battle was gained by the colonists alone after the men of the regiment recruited in England had fled the field.

Meanwhile the situation of the soldiers in the Spanish camp was growing desperate. Fever and dysentery had broken out, hundreds of the men fell ill, and fresh water was scarce. They were unable properly to care for the many wounded and ill. They had lost over five hundred men in the several battles. They made, however, one more attempt to capture the place, this time by a boat expedition. The attack was gallantly made, but they were beaten off with great loss by the forts and the batteries at Frederica. Several of the Spanish boats were sunk and Oglethorpe, commanding the boats of the place, pursued the flying Spaniards until he was within range of the guns of their ships.

Dissensions sprang up between them on account of these repeated failures, and the rivalry between the contingents from Cuba and Florida at last developed a dangerous degree of antagonism and discontent. Learning this situation, Oglethorpe, although the Spaniards still numbered over three thousand effectives, determined to beat up their camp. For the expedition he chose five hundred of his best troops, notably the Highlanders and Rangers, Who had done such valiant work at Bloody Marsh, and with them advanced to the attack on the night of the 12th of July.

A Frenchman in the party, however, gave the alarm to the Spaniards by firing his musket, and before he could be apprehended escaped in the darkness and made his way to the Spanish camp, in which the men immediately stood at their arms. Oglethorpe therefore had to withdraw. But he turned the man's desertion to good account. The traitor revealed to Don Manuel the feebleness of the garrison of Frederica and urged him to attack it in force, when the result would be certain success.

The commander was hesitating when a Spaniard, who had been taken by Oglethorpe and who professed to have escaped from captivity, was brought to him. On his person was found a letter which he confessed to have agreed to deliver to the Frenchman for a sum of money that had been given him. The English general had written this letter to the Frenchman purporting to consider him as his spy; and in it, among other things, urged him to persuade the Spaniards to remain in their camp for three days or more, or until an English fleet with two thousand troops aboard, then on its way, should come down from Charleston. He also stated that Admiral Vernon was about to attack St. Augustine with another fleet. Oglethorpe had bribed the prisoner and the letter fell into the hands of the Spanish command-er—as Oglethorpe knew it would—instead of being delivered to the Frenchman.

The ruse succeeded perfectly. Instead of the friend whose advice was worth having and who would have helped them, the Spanish officers looked upon the Frenchman as an English spy. They would have hanged him in spite of his protestations of the falsity of Oglethorpe's letter, had not Don Manuel, who entertained some doubt as to the reports, interfered to save his life. The situation of the Spaniards, however, was such that when word was brought them that three ships—South Carolina scouting vessels—had been seen in the offing, supposing them to indicate the approach of the English fleet, they were filled with terror. Sick, hungry, thirsty, dispirited, they set fire to the fort and, abandoning large quantities of stores and supplies, including their guns, they piled aboard their ships and sailed away. There was no English fleet anywhere near the scene of action and none was coming; no ships were menacing St. Augustine, either.

Oglethorpe at once surmised that they would stop at Fort William and endeavour to strike one effective blow there. He sent expresses, therefore, to the young commander and bade him hold out at all hazards. For two days Ensign Stewart and sixty men sustained a vigorous attack from the Spaniards, whom they finally repulsed. Oglethorpe had followed in the wake of the retreating ships with his own small vessels and annoyed them as much as he could. Shortly after the middle of July the Spaniards abandoned their expedition and the whole armada left the coast, never to return.

The celebrated Whitefield, who was with Oglethorpe at the time, said of the results of the campaign, "The deliverance of Georgia is such as cannot be paralleled save by some of the incidents of the Old Testament." When the smallness of his force and the overwhelming strength of the Spaniards is considered, the student of history must agree with the theologian. Oglethorpe's defence had been brilliant in the extreme. He had saved the Southern colonies from coming under the evil of Spanish rule. Of the little campaign it is not too much to record, with approval, the phrase which called the narrow road between the wood and the marsh at Frederica "the Thermopylae of America."

Oglethorpe returned to England in 1743. He lived until 1785, having risen to the highest military rank and having survived all his contemporaries. He preserved his physical and mental vigour until the very end. Like the Law-Giver of the Old Testament, his eye was not dimmed nor his natural force abated when he died. Walpole writes of him:

His eyes, ears, articulation, limbs, and memory would suit a boy, if a boy could recollect a century backward. His teeth are gone; he is a shadow and a wrinkled one; but his spirits and his spirit are in full bloom; two years and a half ago he challenged a neighbouring gentleman for trespassing on his manor!

Boswell corroborates this testimony and says that he was "very healthy and vigorous, and was at last carried off by a violent fever."

In his youth and early manhood he was noted for his handsome face and noble bearing. The illustration shows him in his extreme old age. Then he irresistibly reminds us of Holmes's *Last Leaf upon the Tree*.

The mossy marbles rest
On the lips that he has pressed
In their bloom;
And the names he loved to hear
Have been carved for many a year
On the tomb.

But now his nose is thin
And it rests upon his chin
Like a staff:
And a crook is in his back.
And a melancholy crack
In his laugh.

But this was a soldier once who deserved well of his country and whose name and exploits should not be forgotten in the new land his courage and skill preserved from the iron rule of the Spaniard.

3

Pepperrell at Louisburg

1. THE DUNKIRK OF AMERICA

The extreme south-eastern boundary of the mouth of the Gulf of St. Lawrence is marked out by the island of Cape Breton. Huge promontories, beetling cliffs, massive indentations and broken reefs mark the bold shore and make the rocky coast line among the most dangerous in the world. On the south side of the island there is a deep and splendid haven upon the edge of which now nestles a dilapidated fishing village. On the peninsula which juts out toward the east and which, with a continuing line of reefs ending in a rocky islet, encloses the spacious harbour, are the grass-covered mouldering remains of one of the greatest fortresses of the world.

In the year 1744 the massive ramparts, which had been laid out in accordance with those principles of scientific fortification established by the celebrated Vauban, enclosed the town of Louisburg. After twenty-five years of labour and the expenditure of over twenty million *livres* (between five and six million dollars), they were still uncompleted, although even then so formidable in character as to be practically impregnable. It was fondly believed that unfinished as they were, any adequate garrison could successfully hold the works in despite of any force which could be brought against them.[1]

Across the base of the peninsula referred to as extending between sea and harbour, had been built a line of works about twelve hundred yards in length. The glacis sloped gently up from a vast marsh which prevented approach from the landward side. Between it and the walls lay a ditch eighty feet wide and thirty-six feet deep. On the opposite side of this moat a huge rampart of earth from forty to sixty feet thick, rose to a height varying between thirty and forty feet. It was faced

---

1. See maps on page 192 and page 202.

with masonry, defended by three formidable bastions, and surmounted at intervals by cavaliers, or super-imposed works further to enfilade
the wall. The bastions were known as the King's (the citadel) in the
centre and the Queen's and *Dauphin's* at either end. The wall was carried around the seaward and landward edges of the peninsula, enclosing a wide triangle, the apex of which was finished by another huge
bastion called the bastion Maurepas, after the famous prime minister
of King Louis XV.

Beyond this bastion stretched an unprotected piece of low ground
used as a cemetery, which gradually narrowed into a barrier of rocky
and impassable reefs forming an excellent breakwater, extending across
the bay and terminating in a huge rock upon which was erected a
powerful battery of thirty heavy guns. This formidable work which
commanded the entrance to the harbour, which was about a half mile
wide, was called the Island Battery. Commanding the entrance from
the inner shore of the bay another fort had been erected, called the
Grand or Royal Battery, which mounted twenty-eight French thirty-six pounders (equivalent to an English forty-two), and two long
eighteens. Thus an enemy's vessel attempting to enter the harbour
would be subjected to direct fire from the Island and an enfilading fire
from the Grand Battery.

The main works of the town were pierced with one hundred and
forty-eight embrasures, though but ninety guns, many of them of
large calibre including several mortars, were mounted therein. There
were a few breaks in the wall toward the sea where there was no access by land, and an approach for ships so difficult as to be prac- tically
impossible. Even here, however, temporary works afforded sufficient
protection. Opposite the Island Battery a tower of lofty proportions
from whose summit a fire blazed nightly, indicated to approaching
vessels the entrance to the harbour. Access to the town from the land
was had at the northwest corner of the base wall, over a causeway and
bridge which was protected by a circular battery of eighteen cannon
covered by the Dauphin bastion.

The various works were garrisoned by eight companies of regular
soldiers, three of which were Swiss mercenaries. The force was supported by some fourteen hundred Canadian militia. In quality the
defenders were deficient. The commandant and his second were ir-
resolute and vacillating, the troops unpaid and badly treated. They had
been compelled to work on the fortifications without extra compen-
sation, their regular pay was long in arrears, and official peculation, the

curse of New France, had deprived them of their legitimate perquisites and comforts.

A short time before the investment they had broken out in open mutiny and had been persuaded to return to their duties with the greatest difficulty. The spirit of the peasants, traders, and other inhabitants was not much better. The folly of France in allowing such conditions to obtain in the place upon which so much had been lavished, and which was deemed of such importance, is apparent. Aside from the fortifications and harbour, the place had little value; the inhabitants were poor and their dwellings mean.

By the terms of the treaty of Utrecht in 1713, which closed the long wars of Louis XIV, England retained possession of Nova Scotia (Acadia), and France, with a prompt appreciation of its importance under the changed conditions, immediately began fortifying this strategic point on Cape Breton Island. Louisburg was the only naval depot held by the French on the continent of North America. It commanded the St. Lawrence River, afforded a safe harbour of refuge for fleets, an excellent base for future naval operations against the English colonies, and was an advantageous point of departure for possible privateers. For that reason in war times it became known as the Dunkirk of America.

The long peace between England and France was broken in the year 1744 by a war, which may be regarded as a phase of the Second Silesian war. The unscrupulous ambition of Frederick the Great[2] and the resolute determination of Maria Theresa to protest by force of arms against his unjust aggression, which plunged Europe into a quarter of a century of dire conflict, finally involved England and France in a struggle for supremacy lasting many years. Though the long period was marked by intervals of feverish peace, the conflict did not end until France, ruined at sea at Trafalgar, was finally crushed on land at Waterloo.

The two greatest results of these wars from our point of view were, first, the loss to France of all of her American possessions, and, second, the independence of the United States. The first Anglo-French war of the period was terminated by the peace of Aix-la-Chapelle in 1748 and the principal interest of the war centred about this fortified point on the iron-bound shore of Cape Breton; for one of the most audacious conceptions that ever entered the brain of man had resulted in the capture of the tremendous fortress.

---

2. *Frederick the Great & the Seven Years' War* by F. W. Longman also published by Leonaur.

2. An Impossible Proposition

When the news of the declaration of war was received by Du Quesnel, the governor of Louisburg, he immediately despatched a force to capture the fisheries at Canso in Nova Scotia, and having succeeded in the enterprise, he sent forth a larger expedition under Du Vivier, his best subordinate—his only good one by the way—to take Port Royal, or Annapolis, the principal English stronghold in Nova Scotia. The expedition failed in the end. The news of these attacks was at once carried down the coast until it reached the ear of the versatile William Shirley, the governor of Massachusetts. Shirley, a capable English barrister, was an able and ambitious lawyer and administrator, an author of tragedies in a small way, and believed himself to be a born soldier of a high order.

He immediately projected it is said at the instance of William Vaughan of Damariscotta, a return stroke in the capture of the redoubtable fortress of Louisburg. Vaughan was a bold, impetuous man of wealth and prominence, a member of the Massachusetts General Court and interested in the fishing industry, and therefore doubly inimical to Louisburg as a standing menace to the profitable fishing of the Grand Banks. Having with difficulty won over the Massachusetts General Assembly to acquiesce in his scheme, by a majority of one— only obtained it is said by the opportune breaking of a leg of one of the opposition which kept him at home when the final vote was taken—Shirley, with characteristic courage and zeal, prepared to carry out the expedition.

The grotesque audacity of the enterprise is apparent when we reflect that, save for a few old Indian fighters and some inconsequent remnants of the disastrous Cartagena expedition, there was not a single professional soldier in the colonies at the time; that there were no regular troops, no trained officers, no experienced veterans, no naval force, and that Massachusetts was entirely bankrupt, its paper practically worthless.

The prime movers of the expedition had so little idea of the magnitude of their undertakings that it was gravely proposed to advance upon Louisburg in the midst of winter when the depths of the snow which would probably be piled up around the ramparts would enable them to attack at once and, by swarming over the walls, capture the city! When they finally set forth, Shirley's detailed plan for surprising the town when the garrison was asleep, was scarcely less absurd than this winter proposition. However, just because nobody realized the nature of the attempt, everybody entered upon the affair with light-hearted zeal. It is a maxim in war that green troops will attempt that impossibility from which the experienced veteran recoils, and this enterprise evidenced the soundness of the maxim.

Massachusetts sent about thirty-three hundred men, Connecticut five hundred, and New Hampshire the same number, a part of whom were paid by the bankrupt but enthusiastic colony of Massachusetts. New York lent to the expedition some eighteen cannon of assorted sizes and qualities. The other colonies gave their goodwill and their prayers and nothing else. Cautious Rhode Island did enlist a number of men for the purpose, but waiting too long to see which way the "cat would jump" the contingent did not arrive until after the siege was over. Including the guns from New York, the artillery train of the army comprised thirty-four cannon and mortars, the largest being a twenty-two pounder.

With ignorant audacity, they counted upon making up a proper train of siege guns by taking them from the French, and by Shirley's orders they carried with them a large quantity of ammunition and balls for the forty-two pounders. About ninety transports were easily assembled, consisting of fishing and coastwise trading vessels, the war having broken up the fisheries and destroyed trade. These were convoyed by a dozen armed vessels belonging to the navies of the separate colonies, assembled for the purpose.

Shirley placed the naval force under the command of Captain Edward Tyng, of Massachusetts, who had displayed his courage and capacity by recently capturing a French privateer which greatly outclassed his own ship. His flagship was the frigate *Massachusetts*, of twenty-four guns. Captain John Rous, another hardy New England sailor, commanded the *Shirley Galley*, a ship of twenty guns, and the other war-vessels except the *Caesar*, of twenty guns, were of less force.

The army was commanded by one William Pepperrell, a prosperous and enterprising merchant of Kittery, Maine, one of the richest and most influential men in the colonies. The son of a Welsh immigrant who had made a fortune by trade, shipbuilding and fishing, he was a man of great native shrewdness and capacity, who had been reasonably well educated, having gone so far as to study surveying and navigation, though like many other men of his time he seems to have prosecuted these studies to the neglect of the gentle art of spelling. Although a colonel of militia, when appointed lieutenant general of this expedition, he had enjoyed no military experience whatever. Nobody in the army had for that matter. Courage, energy, tact, good nature and good sense he had in plenty, and he was popular with the army, a first requisite under the circumstances. The second in command was Major General Roger Walcott, of Connecticut.

The army was recruited from large numbers of unemployed fishermen in the seacoast towns, who carefully took with them their cod lines in addition to their fire locks, from hardy farmers, substantial mechanics and daring frontiersmen. The most singular contingent, however, was a goodly company of preachers. The famous Whitefield furnished a motto for the flag in the following words, *Nil desperandum Christo duce*, and to the stern Puritans of New England, the fact that their foes were Papists, whom they hated with the proverbial intensity of the children of Plymouth Rock, lent to the whole affair something of the nature of a crusade. It was that religious spirit which lifted the undertaking above the level of the *opéra bouffe*. Not only every regiment, but many companies, enjoyed the services of a chaplain.

Even Shirley himself was sensible that as a military performance the enterprise was more or less of a farce. He proposed, however, to avert all disaster, by giving from his house in Boston, before the departure, such minute directions as would provide for every emergency and suffice for every contingency in order to ensure the success of the enterprise. These orders were actually drawn up and constitute a unique military document, a monument to the industry of the indefatigable governor, if nothing else. As his naval contingent was so insignificant he despatched a swift sailing vessel to Commodore Peter Warren, the commander of the British forces in the West Indies, requesting his cooperation. Warren had married an American woman and owning large tracts of land in the colonies was much interested in promoting their welfare.

On the 24th of March, 1745, the fleet set sail from Nantasket Roads, and after a very hazardous and stormy passage, arrived early in April at the harbour of Canso, which they promptly took possession of. There are numerous interesting contemporary accounts of the expedition in the shape of diaries, letters and sermons, which show that Pepperrell was not alone in the army in his contempt for orthography. One of them refers to the passage in the following terms: "But not haveing a good Pilate suffered verry much att sea." Shade of the Procurator!

Arrived at Canso they found that the harbour of Louisburg and the adjacent shores where they proposed to land were blocked with masses of ice, and they were forced to remain inactive for some three weeks. They passed the time in drilling and drinking, preaching and playing. Meanwhile, Tyng, Rous, and the other colonial captains established a strict blockade of the harbour with the privateers. It required no mean skill and seamanship on the part of these New England privateersmen to maintain an efficient blockade on such a coast and keep off the dangerous lee shore.

On the 18th of the same month, the colonists encamped at Canso, were surprised by the sound of heavy cannonading to seaward. It seems that the French frigate *Renommée*, 32, then commanded by the distinguished Comte de Kersaint, who lost his life and his ship subsequently while heroically fighting against the great Lord Hawke at the famous night battle in the storm at Quiberon Bay, had been sent by the French Government, which had heard of the expedition, with despatches and supplies to Louisburg. The *Renommée* first fell in with the *Shirley Galley*, which promptly engaged her. Captain Rous made so gallant a fight with his little ship that he held the heavy frigate off until the *Massachusetts* and some of the other privateers came within range. The *Renommée* was brilliantly fought and manoeuvred by her able captain, but the delay caused by the superb fighting of the *Shirley Galley* enabled the other ships to close and de Kersaint was forced to abandon his attempt to enter the harbour, and turn back to France. He led the privateers a long chase and by a gallant fight finally escaped from their overwhelming force. A day later he fell in with a belated squadron of transports, convoyed by several small privateers and with them he sustained another severe engagement in which, however, he effected nothing, as the convoy all got in safely.

On the 22nd of April, a heavy frigate flying the English flag came into the harbour. It was the *Elthan*, 40, the first ship of Commodore Warren's squadron. In the absence of orders the commodore had at first refused to leave his station, but having received word from England, after his refusal, that he should cooperate with the colonists, he had gathered such ships as he could and set sail for Boston. Having learned from a Massachusetts schooner he overhauled that the expedition had sailed, he changed his course and came direct to Louisburg. On the 23rd of April, the rest of the squadron, comprising the *Superbe*, 60, *Launceston*, 40, and *Mermaid*, 40, arrived at Canso. After consulting with Pepperrell the commodore immediately sailed to assume charge of the blockade, the colonial ships, by Pepperrell's orders, being put under his command.

Toward the last of April, the ice having broken, and the harbours being open, the weather mild and pleasant, the army embarked on the shipping and beat up toward Louisburg. On the morning of Saturday, the 30th, a landing was effected in Gabarus Bay, which Pepperrell managed with great skill. The privateers ranged along the shore poured a furious fire upon the exposed places to the west of the town. The regiments embarked in the boats of the fleet which were directed toward Flat Rock Point. Du Chambon, who had succeeded to the command of the place on the death of Du Quesnel a short time before, sent Captain Morepain, a French privateersman, with eighty men to oppose the landing.

The boats pulled vigorously toward the shore, but when almost within musket range suddenly turned to the left and dashed toward a little sand-beached bay formed by the mouth of a river, which offered easy access to the shore. Wolfe landed there years after. Morepain and his men made for the same spot, but as they had to traverse the large arc of a circle, while the boats had a much shorter distance to go in a straight line, the advance guard was able to make a landing, before the French party appeared. When they did come in touch, however, they attacked with great spirit, but were beaten off with severe loss by the constantly increasing numbers of the Americans. They thereupon retired to the town. Advance parties were immediately sent out by Pepperrell, to cover the landing of the rest of the army which occupied several days; the troops lying at night upon the ground very much exposed and without cover. Fortunately the weather then and during the whole of the siege continued unusually mild and agreeable.

On the second day after the landing Pepperrell detached the irrepressible Vaughan with some four hundred men to advance through the woods, pass round the town and destroy the valuable storehouses in the rear of the Grand Battery. The expedition met with no opposition and Pepperrell was apprised of its success by vast columns of smoke which rose from the burning buildings.

The next morning, May 3rd, with but thirteen men, Vaughan made a reconnaissance of the Grand, or Royal, Battery. As the little party approached they discovered no. signs of life and it appeared to the Americans that the battery had been abandoned. Unable to credit the testimony of their eyes, they hesitated on the outskirts of the battery for some time, and Vaughan finally bribed an Indian, by the proffer of a whiskey flask which he had in his pocket—possibly for just such emergencies, for he is careful to tell us that he did not drink himself—to enter the fort. The Indian was drunk enough to be reckless and with his courage further stimulated by Vaughan's whiskey, he crawled into the battery and found that it was indeed deserted.

The French in cowardly panic at the sight of the burning buildings, had hauled down their flag and fled to the city after hastily spiking their guns. When the rest of the party entered the fort, William Tufts, an eighteen-year-old Massachusetts boy, climbed up the flagstaff and fastened his red coat to the top in lieu of a British ensign. The French greeted him with a general discharge of artillery which did no damage. Vaughan immediately despatched a messenger to Pepperrell informing him of the capture in the following telling words:

> May it please your Honour to be informed that by the grace of God and the courage of 13 men, I entered the Royal Battery about 9 o'clock, and am waiting for a reinforcement and a flag.

Meanwhile, the French, in four boats, repenting of their panic, returned to reoccupy the fort. The dauntless Vaughan with his thirteen devoted men stood on the open beach in plain view (why they did not occupy the fort is hard to understand), and under the fire of the French guns from the town and Island batteries, and beat back by the accuracy of their fire, the boats filled with Frenchmen. They succeeded in maintaining their ground until re-enforcements arrived, making the capture secure.

This may be considered as the determining event of the siege and it was the one detail of Shirley's astonishing plan which was successfully carried out. The besiegers found themselves in possession of a number of heavy guns of the latest and most approved pattern. The spiking had been done so carelessly that Major Seth Pomeroy, who was a gunsmith by trade, was able to extricate the files from the "tutch holes" without difficulty. A notable man this Pomeroy. Says Parkman:

> On board one of the transports was Seth Pomeroy, gunsmith at Northampton, and now major of Willard's Massachusetts regiment. He had a turn for soldiering, and fought, ten years later, in the battle of Lake George. Again, twenty years later still, when Northampton was astir with rumours of war from Boston, he borrowed a neighbour's horse, rode a hundred miles, reached Cambridge on the morning of the battle of Bunker Hill, left his borrowed horse out of the way of harm, walked over Charles-

town Neck, the scene of action as the British were forming for the attack. When Israel Putman, his comrade in the last war, saw from the rebel breastwork the old man striding, gun in hand, he shouted, 'By God, Pomeroy, you here! A cannon shot would waken you out of your grave!

In their hasty evacuation the French had failed to destroy the munitions of war in the battery and the New Englanders found themselves in possession of what they quaintly describe as "Sume Bums," which the "Bumaneers" of the army put to good use in bombarding the town. A very good attempt at phonetic spelling that, for a man who disguised the familiar word shillings as "She Lins!"

The English forty-two pound balls just fitted the captured guns and they immediately began to play upon the town with great effect. The morass which extended from the landing place to the wall of the fort rendered it impossible to draw the guns, which the army had brought with them and landed from the transports, over the ground in the usual way. Lieutenant Colonel Meserve, who happened to be a carpenter, improvised great flat sledges upon which the cannon were placed. Some two hundred men were attached to each sledge by breast straps and ropes and the guns were dragged over the marshes until they could be mounted in the five batteries which were opened near the town. The guns from the Grand Battery, which had been captured so easily, were distributed among these several batteries, and a furious fire was poured upon and returned from the French works. The diaries are full of the roaring of cannon, the exploding of the "Bums" or "Bumbs" as the word is indifferently spelled!

There was a woeful lack of competent artillerists in the besieging force and Commodore Warren, at the request of Pepperrell, sent several veteran gunners ashore to teach the New Englanders, but in spite of the instruction they received, through their careless and reckless handling of the guns, several of them burst with dire consequences to the amateur cannoneers. The besiegers and the town kept up a continuous fire upon each other, but the effect was felt more by those in the town than by those outside. Every house within the walls was untenable. Many were destroyed and set on fire. To escape from the deadly fire, the miserable inhabitants were forced to take to the casemates, where they dragged out a wretched existence. Provisions became scarce and powder scarcer. Their condition became critical.

The New Englanders steadily advanced their batteries, and although entirely ignorant of the art of making trenches and opening parallels, succeeded in demolishing the circular battery opposite the gate, dismounted many of the guns on the walls and began to make serious breaches therein. Their intrenchments were absurd, but the French made no sortie. Perhaps the commander was afraid to use his mutinous troops outside the walls.

Meanwhile the condition of the besiegers was scarcely more happy. Their powder, so lavishly expended, was running perilously low and the soldiers had suffered great hardships on account of the lack of everything which goes to make up the proper equipment of an army. They kept up their cheerfulness, however, with creditable zeal, and tenaciously clung to their endeavour, amusing themselves by pitching quoits, shooting at a mark, wrestling, and generally having a good time when not actually at work in the batteries. At one period over fifteen hundred men were on the sick list at once, most of whom subsequently recovered. The diaries abound with interesting and amusing incidents of the siege. One of the officers gravely records that "One of ye genls died who went into an house to plunder and killed himself with drink." During the siege a French captain was made prisoner and his death is thus recounted by another chronicler:

> The French capt. died this day that was wounded & taken ye 17 day, he offered ten thousand pounds for a fryar to pardon his sins before he died and I would have done it myself as well as any fryar or priest living for 1-2 ye money.

What a lost opportunity to turn a few honest pounds!

So impressed were Pepperrell's men with their prowess that early in the siege, on the 7th of May, they sent a summons to Du Chambon demanding an unconditional surrender, to which the French commander replied that the only answer he could make to such a demand would be delivered from the mouth of his guns! A council of war held to consider this doughty reply, determined to carry the fortifications by storm and "laders and fa sheene's" (fascines) were prepared for the purpose. The day brought prudence, however, and it was a good thing for the final success of the expedition that at the last moment wiser counsels prevailed, for at that date the attempt certainly would have resulted in disaster, so the cannonade was vigorously resumed.

As a French merchant ship had succeeded in running the blockade and entering the harbour, the mouth of which was commanded by the Island Battery, Pepperrell determined that the next step undertak-

THE DEFEAT OF *LE RENOMMÉE* BY THE MASSACHUSETTS PRIVATEERS

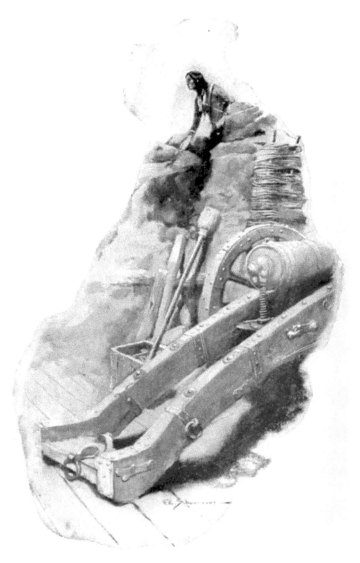

The Capture of the Grand Battery.

en should be the capture of this battery, mounting thirty guns, seven swivels and two mortars and garrisoned by one hundred and eighty men. The dashing Vaughan, elated with his success at the Royal Battery, offered to undertake the capture with a couple of hundred men. Volunteers were called for, but the party which assembled for the purpose, with the democratic notions which prevailed in the army discarded Vaughan and elected one of their own number, named Brooks, to take charge. Several attempts were projected which were hindered by weather conditions, but finally on the 26th of May, some four hundred and fifty men in a number of boats made the attempt.

In order to effect a surprise the boatmen discarded their oars and softly paddled the boats over to the island. The surf was breaking heavily upon the only practicable landing place and it was found impossible to land more than three boats at a time. The landing was effected without hindrance, however, but when about a third of the attacking force had been drawn up on the beach, someone proposed three cheers, which were given with such a will that they awakened the Frenchmen, who sprang to arms and poured a deadly fire upon them, which was promptly returned. Probably the enthusiast who gave the alarm was drunk—the diaries are replete with statements that so and so was drunk—for although the matter had assumed the appearance of a crusade, there was probably as much New England rum in the commissary stores as anything else. Rum, Puritanism, and Religion went hand in hand.

Several more boatloads landed on the Island, but the great guns from the fort sunk some of the remaining boats with their crews and drove off the rest. When the morning broke there was nothing left for the shore party, cut off from its retreat by the defeat of the boats, but to surrender, which they accordingly did. The total loss in killed, wounded, and taken in the expedition amounted to something under two hundred men. This was the only French success and the garrison were much elated thereby.

The undertaking having failed, Pepperrell determined to land a party on Lighthouse Point, erect a battery and thence attack the Island. There was a young civil engineer in the army named Richard Gridley, who undertook the work, though he had no military experience. What he learned in this campaign stood his countrymen in good stead years after, for it was he who traced the line of earthwork for that midnight party under Prescott, which threw up the first American intrenchments on Breed's Hill in 1775. The battery was soon in working order and poured such a concentrated fire upon the Island Battery that its guns were dismounted or destroyed. The condition of the French was now desperate, and Du Chambon at last resolved upon a sortie. He sent the Sieur de Beaubassin with a chosen party of troops who were joined by eighty Indians, to attack the lighthouse battery. They were met by the New Englanders while still in the woods, defeated with heavy loss and driven back to their boats, carrying with them a badly wounded commander.

Meanwhile France had made another effort to relieve the town. The ship-of-the-line *Vigilant*, sixty-four guns, and commanded by the Marquis de la Maisonfort, had been filled with four months' supply of provisions, one thousand barrels of powder, twenty brass guns and three hundred soldiers and despatched to Cape Breton. On the 19th of May the *Vigilant* sighted the blockading squadron. Instead of running directly for the harbour, disregarding everything else, when the chances are that he could have relieved the town, Maisonfort turned aside from his path and attacked the *Shirley Galley*.

That little vessel, as usual, made a stout resistance and by a running fight drew the rash Frenchmen into the midst of the English blockading squadron, where after an heroic defence and loss of eighty killed and a large number wounded, Maisonfort was compelled to strike his flag. The loss of the powder was fatal to French hopes and the capture replenished Pepperrell's depleted magazines. The *Vigilant* was refitted, manned by six hundred New Englanders and added to Warren's fleet, which had been re-enforced from time to time by the arrival of several English ships. By a ruse sometime after, the besieging party found means to acquaint Du Chambon of the capture of this ship and with it perished the last hope of the French. They held on desperately for some time longer, however, hoping for the arrival of a relieving fleet.

Warren was getting very impatient over the slow progress of the siege and finally proposed to enter the harbour with his ships while the army attempted to storm the town. Preparations were made to carry out his bold plan when on June 15th, the French drums were heard from their dismantled works beating a parley. On the 16th of June, 1745, the great fortress actually capitulated to this assemblage of farmers and fishermen, led by a lumber merchant, and Pepperrell had the satisfaction of receiving the keys of Louisburg in his hand. The incredible had happened. The credit of it all was due to Shirley and Pepperrell, though the enterprise which the one planned and the other carried out would not have succeeded had it not been for the efficient blockade maintained by Warren and his ships.

The king was properly grateful. He created Pepperrell a baronet and made him a colonel in the English army. Shirley was also made a colonel of a regiment and Warren was promoted to the rank of admiral. Gallant Captain Rous of the *Shirley Galley* was given a commission of post captain in the Royal Navy. The siege had been a picturesque affair, grotesque and amusing when looked at from a distance, but real and earnest enough to the participants. Pepperrell deserved all he got; he had spent over ten thousand pounds of his own money in the enterprise. Some time afterward Massachusetts was repaid for all her expenditures from the Royal Treasury and the finances of the colony were thereby put on a sound basis.

When the army entered the town after the surrender expecting unlimited plunder, it was very much disgusted at the poverty of the inhabitants and the small booty which awaited it. One diarist records the situation as follows: "A great noys and hubbub amongst ye solders a bout ye plunder; som cursing, som a swarein." I should think so. The wealth of Louisburg was in its walls, and they were battered to pieces and could not be taken away.

Among the preachers was one zealot named Moody, who set forth upon the enterprise armed with an axe, with which he proposed to destroy and break up the idols which were worshipped by the French, and perhaps incidentally convert a few of them! The first thing he did when the colonists entered the town was to proceed to the churches and enter upon the work of demolition. A spiritually minded, gentle Christian crusader, he seems to have been—quite up to the level of his ironclad prototypes!

The French in an endeavour to retake the town prepared a great fleet under Admiral d'Anville, who set forth the following year, but the expedition proved the most unfortunate ever undertaken by France. The ships of the fleet were scattered and wrecked by frightful storms, the men died like sheep from disease, and the expedition, never even sighting an enemy, effected nothing and ended in the most ignominious and heartbreaking disaster. At the peace of Aix-la-Chapelle, however, the work of the brave colonists was rendered of no effect, for by the terms of the treaty, England returned Louisburg to France. The gigantic undertaking had all to be done over by Amherst, Wolfe and Boscawen, thirteen years later. These commanders were supported by a great fleet and a perfectly appointed army of brave soldiers.

This colonial expedition was the maddest enterprise and the most impossible from a military point of view that was ever undertaken. That it succeeded was due to the combination of patient endurance, religious zeal and innate capacity of the New England men, seconded by the shrewdness and ability of Pepperrell, the hearty cooperation of Warren, and the culpable supineness and inefficiency of the garrison. Its importance to the future history of this country was not little. Many of the colonists learned how to fight in this campaign and the drums which rolled in triumph at the head of the hardy colonists as they strode through the sally port at Louisburg were the same which beat the long roll on the slopes of Bunker Hill. When the New Englanders saw the mud walls Gage erected on Boston Neck and compared them to the mighty ramparts of Cape Breton, which they had so gallantly surmounted, they laughed them to scorn.

1

The First Failure

1. WASHINGTON'S EXPEDITION.

The greatest figure of his age here enters the pages of history. On Christmas day, 1753, a little party of white men and Indians took their departure from a rude frontier fort at Venango at the junction of French Creek with the Allegheny River in western Pennsylvania, and plunged southward into the primeval forests extending for leagues in every direction about them. Since the 30th of October they had been prosecuting a difficult and dangerous undertaking in the wilderness of western Virginia and Pennsylvania. Exhausted and worn out from the tremendous hardships they had undergone, depressed by their lack of success—although their mission had not been altogether a failure— their pack horses jaded and feeble, they were in no condition to undertake the terrible journey which intervened between them and the report which would mark the completion of their duty.

The embassy had been sent by the lieutenant governor of Virginia, Robert Dunwoodie, to protest to the French, who, by the direction of Du Quesne, the governor of Canada, a descendant of the great naval commander who defeated de Ruyter, were establishing themselves in the valley of the Ohio—a section of the New World claimed by both England and France for various reasons more or less vague and unsatisfactory. The English, or Americans rather, were also to win over, if they could, the Indian tribes of that section of the country to the cause of England. Dunwoodie's protest was emphasized by the threat of resort to arms in case the French did not heed it.

The sturdy Scottish governor had chosen as the most fit person for this arduous mission a young man, a member of one of the first families in the Commonwealth, who had recently been appointed major and adjutant general of the Virginia militia; his name was George Washington.

On October 30th, the youthful major, then but twenty-one years of age, had set forth from Williamsburg accompanied by a certain old soldier of fortune, a Dutchman named Jacob van Braam, whose acquaintance he had made previously and who had spent the summer at Mt. Vernon, Washington's home, teaching the young planter and would-be soldier what little he knew of the noble art of war. Van Braam was taken on the expedition as an interpreter, for the veteran added to his other doubtful accomplishments a smattering of French. To these two were added subsequently one Christopher Gist, a bold and daring frontiersman, hunter and trader; John Davidson, an Indian interpreter; four other frontiersmen, and several Indians.

The expedition had met with indifferent success. They had managed to gain the partial adherence of the most important Indian in the Ohio valley, quaintly called from his subordination to the Iroquois Confederacy the "Half King," and it was believed that if he did not actually espouse the English cause he would at least remain neutral, but otherwise they had accomplished little. The party had first arrived at Venango on the 4th of December. They were hospitably received by Captain Chabert de Joncaire, the commandant, to whom a visitor in the lonely wilderness about the post was a veritable godsend. They seem to have made a night of it, French, Americans, and the Dutchman, together. Amid the deep potations of the others, however, the young commander, who had partaken but sparingly in the carousing, preserved his wits and heard the boasting betrayal of the French plans for occupying and holding the valley.

Farther up the river—about twenty miles from Presqu' Isle (Erie)—lay the principal post of the French, Fort le Boeuf, then commanded by a brave and accomplished chevalier named Legardeur de St. Pierre, to whom, by Joncaire's direction, the party repaired, as he was the ranking French officer in that region. They were received with courteous and gracious hospitality; Dunwoodie's letter of protest was delivered and after a delay of several days Washington received St. Pierre's reply, which was in effect similar to the famous remark of MacMahon at Sevastopol, "*J'y suis, j'y reste*" ("I am here and here I stay!"). With this not too encouraging missive, for the reply had been committed to writing, having so far completed their mission, they started for home in canoes down the river, and after a brief stay abandoned their boats at Venango and resumed their journey.

For three days they struggled southward through the roadless forest in the midst of blinding storms of snow and sleet which froze as it fell. The poor pack horses proved to be unequal to the demands made upon them, so the men finally gave up their saddle horses to relieve them of some of their burdens and the party pressed on afoot. The Indians, suborned by the French, deserted them, and matters assumed a serious complexion.

Their progress was very slow and the young commander, who was most anxious to deliver his report, finally put the cavalcade under the charge of van Braam with directions to follow on as best he could. Then equipping himself in an Indian hunting suit with a heavy Indian match-coat[1] to protect himself from the cold and the inclemency of the weather, attended by the redoubtable Gist similarly clad, he pressed on ahead of the party.

It was one of the most dangerous journeys ever undertaken. Through trackless forests, over unknown mountains, or crossing icy rivers swollen to raging torrents, in the midst of the furious tempests of a winter of unusual severity, the two men struggled on. The Indian who guided them through the wilderness was in the pay of the French and he led them far from their way. His treachery finally culminated in an open attack. Seizing a favourable opportunity he turned suddenly and fired point-blank at his employer, but George Washington was not destined to die by a savage rifle shot in an unknown wilderness. God had other things for him to do and the bullet missed him. He and Gist were upon the Indian instantly and Gist, with the *lex talionis* of the frontier in his heart, would have killed the traitorous savage out of hand, but Washington humanely interfered to save his life. They disarmed him, drove him from them, and, having kindled two delusive fires, doubled on their trail and escaped from the pursuit which their false guide instituted as soon as he joined his band.

Reaching the banks of the unfordable Ohio one night and finding it not yet frozen over, with one poor hatchet that remained to them they made a wretched raft and attempted to pole themselves across the river amid the swirling cakes of ice. The raft was capsized in midstream and only by the most desperate exertions did they succeed in gaining the bank of an island nearby. There they lay all night in their wet clothes and Gist was badly frozen. The next morning luckily they

1. "A large loose coat formerly worn by American Indians, originally made of fur skins matched and sewed together, and afterward of match-cloth, a kind of coarse woollen cloth, called so, as resembling in texture the fur skins originally used."

found the narrower waters on the other side of the island frozen over, and were thus enabled to cross and proceed on their way. Starving and frozen, after incredible hardships they finally arrived at the rude hut of a trapper named Frazier, on the banks of the Monongahela River. Resting there until the first of January, 1754, they pressed on to Gist's house sixteen miles farther. Here they separated. Washington procured a horse and on the 16th of January placed the defiance of the French in the hand of the governor at Williamsburg. ,

2. THE FATE OF JUMONVILLE

The stout Scotsman immediately took measures to make good his threat. Preparations were at once made to occupy the valley, and a fort was projected at the point where the Monongahela and the Allegheny Rivers unite to form the Ohio. With a soldier's ready eye, as he passed the confluence of these two rivers on his journey, Washington had discerned it to be the proper place for a fortification to command the valley and control its trade. Subsequent generations which have built the great city of Pittsburgh on the same site, have attested the accuracy of his observations and the correctness of his judgement.

Thither Dunwoodie despatched Captain Trent with Lieutenant Frazier and Ensign Ward, together with a hundred men to build the fort. In the meantime, extorting reluctant acquiescence and some small sums of money from the refractory House of Burgesses, he set about raising a regiment for the purpose of prosecuting the campaign on the Ohio. Joshua Fry, an English gentleman of some soldierly experience in the Low Countries, was commissioned colonel with Washington as his lieutenant colonel. Recruiting went on slowly until it was stimulated by the promise of a land bounty, always a useful and effective inducement and one frequently offered in the United States after it came into being.

On the 2nd of April, 1754, matters had so far advanced that Washington started from Alexandria with two companies amounting to one hundred and fifty men. The remainder of the regiment and the artillery were to be brought up by Colonel Fry. At Wills Creek (now Cumberland, Maryland), the Ohio Company, a powerful and influential trading organization, had a large storehouse. There Trent was to meet Washington's party with pack horses and they were to go forward and garrison the fort, which he was supposed to have completed—but which he had not.

They found Trent there on the 20th of April but no pack horses.

Washington immediately sent back to Virginia for them, but on the 25th of April the men of the advance party of fort builders who had been left at the designated spot under Ensign Ward, arrived at Wills Creek. They were a sorry looking lot and they had a sorry tale to tell.

The French had also seen the advantage presented by the location which the English had seized and Monsieur de Contrecoeur, who had succeeded old St. Pierre as chief in command of the valley, when he heard of the advent of the English despatched some five hundred men to dispossess them. They arrived before the unfinished English work and demanded its evacuation. As they were provided with cannon and in overwhelming force, to resist would have been madness. Ward received assurance that he could withdraw unharmed with all his supplies and wisely accepted the terms. The French destroyed the crude English stockade and at once began the erection of a formidable work which they called in honour of their commander, Fort Du Quesne, thereby immortalizing him.

Washington acted promptly; his instinct as a soldier and his impulses as a man always led him to attack. That he subsequently schooled himself into such a great defensive fighter shows the mastery he acquired and maintained over himself. He determined to advance to another storehouse nearer the enemy from which he could threaten him and strike if opportunity arose, while he awaited his re-enforcements. On the 29th of April, therefore, he marched from Wills Creek. His progress was slow and toilsome in the extreme. The creeks were flooded by the spring rains and it was not until the 23rd of May that he reached a place called the Great Meadows. This was an open and level field surrounded by tree-covered mountains. Washington says that he thought it "a charming field for an encounter," and he proceeded to make preparations for one.

He cleared away the bushes and taking advantage of a ravine with a shallow creek brawling through it, he marked out a rude fort. The little army encamped and set to work upon the intrenchments. On the 25th, however, having received news from some friendly Indians that a party of French had been lurking in the vicinity, Washington determined to surprise them. He set forth from the camp in the dead of night with forty men, six of whom straggled from the party in the darkness. Guided by his friend the "Half King," the little band stumbled through the woods in the darkness and came upon the French just before sunrise upon the morning of the 26th of May, 1754. The

French, who were partially surprised, at once sprang to their arms. Washington gave the command to fire. For some fifteen minutes the two parties kept up a fierce fusillade upon each other, at the end of which the French threw down their arms and surrendered.

Washington lost one killed and three wounded. The French had ten killed and twenty-one wounded and captured, but one man escaping. Among the killed was the commander, a young ensign named Coulon de Jumonville. The French chose to regard the death of Jumonville as an assassination, claiming that he was an envoy bearing a peaceful letter of warning, and they wasted a vast quantity of poetry and protest over the matter. The claim is absurd and untenable and was abandoned by everybody but statesmen and romancers—terms not devoid of a certain association. Peaceful envoys who are desirous of delivering letters do not lurk concealed for days in the presence of the enemy.

There, in that obscure skirmish in the backwoods of America, rather than at Lexington, was fired "the shot heard round the world." When the young Virginian gave the word to begin, he precipitated a globe-encircling series of conflicts which did not end until the final defeat of France and Napoleon on the field of Waterloo, sixty years later. Let it be noted, too, that amid all the splendid figures, statesmen, soldiers, patriots, men who shed lustre upon this great period of conflict, the name of no one stands higher in these categories than that of Washington.

The young colonel was greatly elated by his success. The two parties had been about equal in numbers and he had shown no little skill in making his dispositions for the attack. With the enthusiasm of a very young man he wrote to his brother as follows: "I fortunately escaped without any wound; for the right wing, where I stood, was exposed to, and received, all the enemy's fire; and it was the part where the man was killed and the rest wounded. *I heard the bullets whistle, and, believe me, there is something charming in the sound.*" [1]

King George is reported to have said in his dryly humorous way, when this rodomontade, as Walpole called it, was reported to him, "He would not say so if he had been used to hear many." When he was an old man Washington was asked if he had made the statement ascribed to him. He justified it by saying that if he did, it was when he was very young. As to that, although he learned to conceal his feelings in after years, I very much doubt if he ever changed his opinion, for if there

1. Italics mine.—C T. B.

GEORGE WASHINGTON AT THE AGE OF TWENTY-FIVE.

GENERAL BRADDOCK.

was anything on earth he loved, it was a fight.

3. THE FIGHT AT FORT NECESSITY

The prisoners taken were sent back to Dunwoodie and the main body remained in the camp. Provisions were very scarce, in fact the detachment was nearly starved and the name they gave to their intrenchment, Fort Necessity, is grimly indicative of their situation. They were regularly and vigorously drilled, however, and every Sunday in default of a chaplain Washington conducted religious services himself.

Presently the remainder of the regiment came straggling up to the Great Meadows. Colonel Fry had died at Wills Creek and Washington found himself in command of some three hundred men. They were indifferently armed, poorly provided, wretchedly clothed. With them also came an independent company from North Carolina. Mackay, who commanded them, held a king's commission and would receive no orders from Washington who held a colonial rank only. His men regarded themselves as regular soldiers and bore themselves with great arrogance, and indolence as well, toward the Virginians. Therefore, leaving Mackay to garrison Fort Necessity, Washington with high hopes of success, marched forward on the nth of June to attack Fort Du Quesne. Neither he nor any other Englishman was to get a glimpse of it even, for years to come.

On the way thither he received word that the place had been heavily re-enforced and its capture with his force was out of the question. A council of war was called and in accordance with its unanimous decision, he determined to return to Wills Creek; then, after obtaining further re-enforcements, he intended to advance once more. The retiring regiment got no farther than Great Meadows, however, in its retreat. The soldiers were completely exhausted by the labour of carrying the baggage and dragging the artillery, which comprised nine little swivels, and they were forced to stop at Fort Necessity for rest.

Hard on their heels came the French. They were led by Coulon de Villiers, called from his many successful enterprises "Le Grand Villiers," who was burning with desire to avenge the death of his young brother, Jumonville. His party was composed of five hundred regulars and Canadian militia and as many Indians. Washington, who was advised of the approach of the enemy by his scouts .whom he had mounted on wagon horses and sent forward to reconnoitre, finding it impossible to go farther had devoted his time to strengthening Fort Necessity, which was now a rude square stockade with the swivels mounted upon the walls, which afforded little or no protection for the gunners. There was a shallow ditch around the fortification.

On the 3rd of July, early in the morning, the French appeared on the wooded hills. Washington drew up his men in the meadow outside the fort and made ready for battle. It was a bold defiance and the indicated desire for a hand to hand conflict in the open was quite in keeping with the character of the man. The French, however, and especially the Indians, had no mind to play that sort of a game. They remained concealed in the surrounding woods firing on the Americans from the shelter of the trees. Washington thereupon reoccupied the fort and a battle commenced which was maintained with great vigour all day long.

During the afternoon it rained frequently and heavily; so much so, that, at times, the combatants were forced to suspend operations, but whenever there was the slightest intermission in the falling water, the fighting was resumed. Poor and wretchedly equipped as the Virginians were, they were excellent marksmen and they poured a steady fire upon their encircling foes deliberately and coolly discharging their pieces and endeavouring to make every shot tell. The French and Indians were equally good shots with the rifle and the casualties on both sides were severe. It was found impossible for the Americans to make any effective use of their swivels as almost every man who attempted to manipulate them was immediately shot down.

As the evening drew on the condition of the besieged became desperate. Their ammunition was almost gone and nearly one hundred men out of a total of three hundred and fifty had been killed or wounded. The stockade had at last become untenable, for the French had found a position from which they could enfilade it and every corner was being searched by the leaden messengers of death whenever the rain made firing possible. Washington's condition was hopeless. Fortunately for him, however, the French were not in a very much better situation. They had suffered about an equal loss in killed and wounded during the engagement; the Indians, who were not happy in a siege, were threatening to break away; their ammunition was also nearly exhausted; de Villiers, therefore, proposed a parley to discuss terms of capitulation.

Washington fearing treachery resolutely refused it, and as the rain was pouring down in torrents, operations were again suspended, although both parties lay suspiciously upon their arms. The French finally sent an officer, who succeeded in assuring Washington of the honesty of his commander's intentions, and the parley was accordingly had. Captain van Braam was sent to the French captain to ascertain what terms he proposed. The terms which de Villiers offered were most generous. The Americans were to march out of the fort with all the honours of war and everything they could carry. One of the swivels was allowed them; everything they could not carry was to fall to the French and Indians.

Washington having accepted them, the articles were reduced to writing by the French and brought back to camp by van Braam. The American officers, who knew no French, gathered around the Dutchman as he translated the French propositions to them. It was a difficult talk; the night had fallen and the rain was still pouring down; a solitary candle was hardly kept alight in the rain; van Braam stumbled through the blurred, blotted terms of the capitulation and Washington and his officers afterward appended their signatures to it.

To anticipate, after it was all over, they found they had formally acknowledged that they had assassinated young Jumonville. They knew no French. Van Braam reading hurriedly had mistranslated the word "*l'assassinat*," by "the death," or "killing." It is probable that he did it through carelessness and ignorance, for his knowledge of French was not comprehensive. At any rate the results of the blunder were sufficiently serious, for Washington found himself a self-proclaimed murderer, and it was a point over which the French made great capital in their subsequent discussions of the happenings in the Ohio valley. All this was in the womb of the future, however, at that time.

The next morning, the 4th of July, too, the fort was evacuated and Washington with a very dejected feeling set forth upon his retreat. His poor, tired, worn-out, half-starved men, staggered along the road, carrying on their backs or in hastily improvised litters, the wounded members of the regiment, the dead having been buried where they had fallen. Indians ran alonng by the side of the Virginians with menacing gestures and shouts for a long time, but they affected no one by their conduct. For seventy weary miles the Americans plodded on until they reached the storehouses at Wills Creek, where opportunity for rest and refreshment was afforded them. Washington left them there to recuperate and rode on to Williamsburg to make his melancholy report to the governor.

This, his first campaign, had ended disastrously. It had opened most auspiciously, but it had terminated in defeat. There was nothing dishonourable, however, in it. He had conducted himself well, defended his post bravely, and retreated with the honours of war before an over-whelming force. Yet he felt discouraged and dispirited. His feelings, however, were not shared by his countrymen, who received him with open arms and undiminished confidence.

Two phases of his career had passed. They had seen him first as a hardy and adventurous frontiersman, then as a bold if somewhat reck-less border fighter; and a year only was to elapse when they were to discover in him the most promising young soldier of his place and time.

2

The Second Failure

1. The Character and Career of General Braddock

In England, near the close of the seventeenth century, probably in 1695, there was born to Major General Edward Braddock, Lieutenant Colonel of the Coldstream Guards, a son who was named for his father. The origin of the family is unknown. The last one left no descendants and the family has vanished into the obscurity from which it sprang.

Though the name between father and son appears for over seventy years on the roster of the same famous regiment of the Guards—b, regiment so distinguished in English history that it was found necessary to caution its men lest they should bear themselves too arrogantly toward the soldiers of less favoured corps—but little is known of their history. It is vaguely surmised that they were of Irish extraction, though the name Braddock—query, broad oak?— does not bear out the speculation. How they obtained an *entree* into this exclusive body of soldiery and the means by which they were enabled to attain and retain their coveted station are equally unknown. Possibly in their capacity and merit, although these were but rarely rewarded at court, may be found the only explanation.

The son referred to became one of the most famous characters in English history; and, I do believe, one most unkindly dealt with by those who have tried to chronicle his actions. He was unlucky and hence unforgiven. To paraphrase an old proverb, "*Nothing defeats like defeat*," and poor Braddock has been overwhelmed with unmerited censure, his character and career made the subject of heartless jest, his misfortunes emphasized by undeserved obloquy, his reputation destroyed by insinuation and innuendo, and his good qualities—which

148

were many—have been almost totally lost sight of.

I hold no brief for England or the English. My own ancestors did fight under Forbes when he finally captured Fort Du Quesne, but that is their solitary instance of English service, of which I have record; their original nationality was Irish and they were invariably found in opposition to England. Some of them may have been in the Irish Brigade which opposed Braddock's own regiment of Guards at Fontenoy, yet in this story of a defeat as disastrous—not as disgraceful, I maintain, in opposition to popular opinion—as ever befell an English army, I shall incidentally strive to do justice to this unfortunate commander.

He entered the English service in 1710 as an ensign in his father's regiment, the Coldstream Guards aforementioned, being then about fifteen years of age, and he remained with it continuously until 1753, participating in all of the brilliant services in which it took part, including the famous battles of Dettingen and Fontenoy. Afterward, when "Butcher" Cumberland carried out his bloody campaign in Scotland Braddock was with him. His conduct at Culloden and afterward attracted the favourable notice of the duke, who thereafter became his firm friend and patron. To him Braddock owed his subsequent advancement.

In 1746, while still retaining his connection with the regiment, he was appointed brigadier general in the line and commanded a detachment in Admiral Lestock's expedition to Quiberon. He afterward returned to the Netherlands and remained there until 1748, distinguishing himself at the siege of Bergen-op-Zoom.

In 1753 he was detached from the Guards and sent to Gibraltar to take command of the Fourteenth Foot, an organization which had shown itself to be one of the most unruly and undisciplined in the service, and which needed some hard treatment to bring it into shape. He completely changed the character of the regiment, reducing it to order, drilling and disciplining it until it became noted for its efficiency; and it is stated, greatly to his credit, that the men of the regiment in spite of the breaking in he had given them, fairly adored him.

On the 29th of March, 1754, by the influence of Cumberland, he was appointed major general and commander of all His Majesty's troops then in, or to be sent to North America. So much for his record, which was one of constant, even brilliant, service, hard fighting, and steady promotion.

Now, as to his character. Walpole speaks of him as "desperate in his fortunes, brutal in his behaviour, obstinate in his sentiments." Let us examine these charges. When Braddock's father died the family consisted of two sisters and this one son. To each of the sisters was left about six thousand pounds and to the son probably the same amount. One sister died early leaving her estate to the other. Goldsmith records that the surviving sister expended her fortune and ruined herself to pay the debts of the man she loved, a creature unworthy of such a sacrifice, for finding her property was gone he promptly deserted her.

In despair poor Fanny Braddock resorted to the gaming table and eventually committed suicide, although nothing whatever could be brought against her moral character. Walpole writes that Braddock when he heard of the untimely end of his sister, remarked, "Poor Fanny! I always thought she would play until she would be forced to tuck herself up." Certainly it was a brutal thing to say—if he said it Walpole again relates a story of Braddock's robbing his mistress of her last guinea and then abandoning her. The incident was embodied in a play and Walpole ascribed it to this soldier. These two anecdotes are the main things by which he is discredited.

Walpole's statements are not above suspicion. In many instances he is palpably wrong and the accuracy of his judgment must often be questioned (as for instance when he calls Washington a "brave braggart" or a "*fanfaron*"—two things he certainly was not). In truth, Walpole had the habit of the gossip, and the gossip of the satirical kind at that; nothing escaped his heartless, caustic pen. He would sacrifice truth to a jest, accuracy to a witticism, reputation to an anecdote, honour to a trifle, without a compunction. As for instance, when the British army was toiling through the Alleghenies under incredible difficulties, Walpole coolly writes that "Braddock seems in no hurry to get himself scalped!"

While investigating various historical subjects I have found a number of misstatements in Walpole's Letters, consequently I am not disposed to rely entirely upon his statements or conclusions. To offset his deductions the following points are worthy of consideration. Braddock's income was something like three hundred pounds a year, and since Walpole stamped him as a man of broken fortunes the fact that he increased it slightly during his lifetime and left the sum of seven thousand pounds to Mrs. Anne Bellamy, gives the story the lie at once. Also, it is known that he freely drew upon his private funds for the furtherance of the king's business in America, which is significant.

Everybody admits that he was a man of the most determined courage. He could not have been enrolled for forty-five years in the finest regiment of the British army, whose officers were all men of birth and station, had he been a low, vulgar, brutal, tyrannical man. Mrs. Bellamy preserves one little anecdote about him which seems to refute the charge of cruelty and brutality. She says:

> As we were walking in the park one day, we heard a poor fellow was to be chastised; when I requested the general to beg off the offender. Upon his application to the general officer, whose name was Dury, he asked Braddock, how long since he had divested himself of brutality and the insolence of his manners? To which the other replied, 'You never knew me insolent to my inferiors. It is only to such rude men as yourself that I behave with the spirit which I think they deserve.'

He had served in many campaigns and always with credit. According to his standard he was a most accomplished soldier. Nobody ever claimed that he was a heaven-born leader, or that he was a great military genius, and when he was placed in conditions which no British soldier had ever faced and matched with foes whose tactics no British officer had ever fathomed, under circumstances hitherto unparalleled, he failed; but there was probably no soldier in the British army at the time who would not have failed, and those who succeeded subsequently, did so from experience gained by observing his failure.

In a day, moreover, in which peculation was universal and the public service was honeycombed with fraud and reeked with corruption, he was rigidly and sturdily honest—even Walpole admits this last and it does not accord with the character of a debt-ridden spendthrift.

And we must not forget that the men of the worst regiment in the service, whom he had trained, loved him. Wolfe sums up his character when he styles him "a man of courage and good sense, although not a master of the art of war,"—that last must have been said of nearly all English soldiers except Wolfe himself!

The evening before Braddock left England he called upon Mrs. Bellamy and as he bade her goodbye he told her she would never see him more, for he was going with a handful of men to conquer whole nations; and, producing a map of the country, he said that to do this they must cut their way through unknown woods and that they were to be sent like sacrifices to the altar.

It was Braddock's misfortune to be the first British soldier to conduct a campaign against Indians and savages in the wilderness, and unless he were possessed of the genius which would enable him to adapt himself to unknown and unfamiliar conditions, the first soldier was fairly enough doomed to defeat. I have a great sympathy for him and some admiration, which has arisen without design on my part from a study of the various authorities used in preparing this account. Arrogant, imperious, stubborn, self-willed, hard, he had his faults—and they were grave—but they were more than counter-balanced by his virtues.

2. THE MARCH TO THE VALLEY

But to return to the story. The king and his ministers were determined that the French should be driven out of the Ohio valley and when the campaign of Washington with its disastrous termination was reported in England, it was decided to send over to America such a force as would suffice—as they fondly thought—to settle the question.

France and England were still at peace with each other and were loudly proclaiming their mutual affection, while both parties were engaged in most formidable and warlike preparations. It was decided that the force for the reduction of Fort Du Quesne, with which we are immediately concerned, should consist of the Forty-fourth and Forty-eighth regiments of the line, then quartered in Ireland. Braddock was to have chief command in the colonies, with Shirley, governor of Massachusetts, as his second. Two more regiments of infantry, Shirley's own and Pepperrell's were to be raised in the colonies. The number of men in the Forty-fourth and Forty-eighth regiments, then containing about five hundred each, was to be increased to seven hundred each by enlistments in America.

The main force under Braddock was to take Fort Du Quesne, while auxiliary expeditions were proposed to seize Ticonderoga, Niagara, and various other points. All but that under the immediate direction of the commander-in-chief may be dismissed from our consideration for the present.

On the 25th of February, 1755, the famous ship-of-the-line *Centurion*, on which Anson had made his wonderful cruise around the world, arrived at Hampton Roads, in Virginia, with two other ships, the naval force being under the command of Commodore Keppel, afterwards so justly celebrated an admiral. Braddock and his staff were on this squadron. The remainder of the troops came straggling in at different dates on thirteen transports and three storeships, and it was not until the middle of March that the entire army waft landed upon the shores of Virginia.

A council of all the royal governors was held and preparations made to carry out the plans of the English Ministry. After incredible delays and infuriating experiences caused by dilatory and unruly colonial assemblies, by incompetent executives, and by jealousy, maladministration, and insubordination everywhere, which exasperated the general beyond endurance and caused him to voice his anger and disappointment in no measured terms, the necessary recruiting was completed, and the expedition in May reached Fort Cumberland.

It is noteworthy that Washington himself, on many occasions, was quite as severe in his strictures upon the incapable colonial governments and the inefficient militia as Braddock had been. The English general's most serious blunder was his contempt, freely and forcibly expressed, for the provincial troops; yet it was easy to understand. How could a man who had been trained a strict disciplinarian—a bit of a martinet indeed—think otherwise of such soldiers as the provinces produced? Knowing nothing of the conditions of the warfare in which he was about to engage, Braddock was not able to see possibilities of usefulness in anything but the rigidly drilled automata of the British line.

Fort Cumberland was a rude structure which had been built about the storehouses at Wills Creek on the Potomac to provide a base of supplies from which the army could begin the campaign proper. The two regular regiments had been recruited to seven hundred men each. In addition there were two companies of colonial troops, a company of guides or pioneers, a troop of light horse and a detachment of sailors from the squadron.

Sir John St. Clair, quarter-master-general, had been sent to America ahead of the others to make arrangements for the transportation of the army. He proved himself glaringly and woefully inefficient and accomplished practically nothing. Wagons and horses for the baggage and artillery train had been provided at last through the efforts of Benjamin Franklin, who had come upon the scene like a good angel and relieved the situation, after Braddock had almost despaired of securing transportation. Franklin had cunningly told the Pennsylvania farmers that their wagons and teams would be well paid for, adding that if they did not offer them voluntarily they would probably be taken for nothing—the king's business must not be delayed.

Poor Braddock in the midst of all his difficulties, described Franklin as the only man of parts and sense he had met in the country—although the shrewd philosopher did not reciprocate the opinion. There was one other man, however, whom Braddock had probably forgotten when he wrote, to whom he had wisely given his confidence, and that was Colonel Washington.

When the order had come the previous year making colonial officers of whatsoever rank junior even to ensigns who bore the king's commission, Washington had instantly resigned the service, although it was a serious blow to him to see all his hopes of military preferment vanish. He was a frequent visitor to the camp, which was established near Alexandria, however, and in company with the other gentry of the province extended much hospitality to the British general and his officers. He closely observed the drills and made himself master of the minutiae of army life as presented there. The lessons he learned were exceedingly valuable, indeed, it was there he laid the foundation of his knowledge of drill and discipline. It was the only school of the soldier he ever attended. It is greatly to Braddock's credit—let it be set down—that he readily discerned the soldierly stuff that was in Washington and in order to avail himself of his valuable service, offered him a position upon his own staff with the rank of colonel. There the high-spirited Virginian would be subject to no orders but the general's own. Orme and other members of the staff welcomed him gladly and Washington engaged in his new duties with becoming zeal and success, winning golden opinions everywhere. It was in many ways a most fortunate appointment for Braddock and his men.

By May 20th, the whole force was assembled at Fort Cumberland. On the 30th of May, having lost, it will be seen, some three months of precious time, which was in no sense the fault of Braddock, the advance began. Six hundred men were sent forward to open the road, which was a narrow Indian trail wretchedly cleared, winding through the woods. On the 7th of June, the first party followed under the command of Sir Peter Halket, colonel of the Forty-fourth; on the 8th the second party under Lieutenant Colonel Gage moved out, and on the 10th, the rear guard under Colonel Thomas Dunbar, of the Forty-eighth, broke camp. In ten days the army arrived at Little Meadows, having made less than two miles and a half per day!

They waited here for a week to recuperate and to receive belated provisions and forage which had been promised them but which were very slow in coming in. On the 18th of June, by Washington's advice, Braddock determined to press forward with what he called a flying column; although crawling column would be a better term.

Taking two hundred provincials and one thousand regulars, with four howitzers, four twelve pounders, twelve coehorns,[1] and thirty ammunition and artillery wagons, with the provisions on pack horses, and leaving the rest of the artillery train and the baggage with eight hundred of the poorest men under Dunbar—who took great umbrage at being relegated to the rear—to follow as best they could, Braddock set forth. On the 21st of June they entered Pennsylvania and by the 24th they had progressed, in five days, seventeen miles! Their way took them through a rough, wild, unbroken country, absolutely in its native state. Now they climbed lofty mountains, now they followed the winding course of rushing streams, now they defiled through narrow valleys. On the hills great woods of gloomy pine trees overshadowed them, and the rough road which the toiling pioneers managed to cut through the trees was hardly practicable even for pack horses.

Sometimes their slow progress lay through open forests, where the giant stems of oak and poplar, chestnut and maple, rose from a clean carpet of fallen leaves, or spread their leafy roof over wide stretching and luxuriant masses of rhododendrons and azaleas, just now in the very zenith of their bloom; at other times they were brushing between sombre walls of cypress and hemlock which hid the sunlight and the heat from dank, dark soils where the moss-grown carcasses of fallen trees lay heaped together in all stages of decay. Now the long column was clinging precariously to a precipitous hillside, beneath which some pent-up torrent churned and roared.

Now it was struggling—cattle, horses, wagons, and men—in some rocky channel, where a shrunken stream trickled amid the debris of its winter floods. Signs of the French and Indians were plentiful, but as yet they kept their distance, filling the measure of their hostility with taunts and ribald verses smeared upon the trees. Admirable discipline was maintained, and every precaution that prudence required was observed by Braddock. Men were thrown out upon both flanks marching abreast through the trees, while beyond these again scouting parties ranged the woods. A careless straggler was occasionally killed and scalped, but no party of the enemy ventured an attack upon the column, attenuated though it of necessity was.[2]

1. A small mortar for throwing grenades, usually carried by hand by four men.
2. *The Fight with France for North America* by Arthur G. Bradley, an excellent book. (Republished by Leonaur as *A History of the French and Indian War*.)

Map Showing the Route and Encampment of the
Expeditions of Braddock and Forbes in 1755 and 1758

They practically met no enemy, no friend. The silence about them to men accustomed to the crowded countries of Europe was menacing and unbearable. To the soldiers with their leather leggins, tight woollen coats, heavy knapsacks, tall mitred hats, the heat and fatigue of the journey were almost unsupportable.

The march dragged fearfully, as the long line plodded and struggled on. Instead of discarding every bit of parade and pressing rapidly toward Fort Du Quesne, Washington complains that they stopped to level every mole hill and build a bridge over every creek. Not a single practice of a European march was omitted, no point of military procedure was slighted. It might take them years to reach the valley of the Ohio, but they would do it as trained soldiers should. They set a fine example to the forest trees, since there was nothing else to see them. This was one of Braddock's greatest mistakes.

Yet in all the hardships of the journey the general, now a stout old man of sixty years, cheerfully shared. When the pack horses began to give out he set the example of surrendering his own for the service of the army; an example which was followed by the officers generally, as they toiled on slowly but surely through the wilderness.

Braddock has been accused of neglecting to employ any Indians and as despising these valuable allies. Whatever his opinions, and naturally he would not be greatly prepossessed in their favour, as a matter of fact he never had an opportunity to employ more than fifty and these, with the exception of eight, presently abandoned him. On the 3rd of July he encamped at Jacob's Creek and personally urged the remaining Indians to go forward on a scouting expedition. They at first refused to do this, but he finally persuaded them and they set forth on the following day. Christopher Gist, who had joined him, also departed upon the same errand. Dunbar with the rear guard meanwhile had started on the 2nd of July to follow the army.

On the 6th the scouting expeditions came back and reported that all was quiet in front of them and that the fort did not appear to have been heavily re-enforced. On the same day a convoy of provisions for which Braddock had been waiting reached him and he set forth again.

On the 7th he reached Little Turtle Creek on the bank of the Monongahela. He intended to cross this and proceed directly to the fort. If he had done so probably he would have succeeded in capturing it, but he was prevented by two circumstances; a report that was brought to him of the necessity for leading his army through a narrow pass between the river and the mountain, which could easily be held by the French, and by his inability to get his wagons across the creek on the ordinary road owing to the steepness of the banks. He was informed, too, that by turning to the left he would find a practicable crossing of the Monongahela and then after advancing a few miles another ford of the same winding river, which offered no difficulties to his passage. When he had crossed the second ford he would be within six miles, an easy striking distance, of the fort with no intervening obstacles worthy of mention. He determined, therefore, to try this road. Turning back from Turtle Creek, on the evening of the 8th he encamped near the first crossing of the Monongahela.

There Washington joined him. He had been ill of a fever and Braddock had compelled him to remain behind with Dunbar's force. Washington had only agreed to do this upon the assurance of the general that he should be brought up before the anticipated action, which he says he would not have missed for five hundred pounds. It gives a touch of homeliness to the narrative when we learn that Braddock solemnly enjoined Washington to take "Dr. James' powders," which he assured him were the finest powders in the world for fever! Washington was still ill and had been brought up most of the way in a wagon following the provision convoy. However, when he reached the others he was sufficiently recovered, although very weak, to mount his horse.

At three o'clock on the morning of the 9th of July, 1755, Braddock detached a strong party under Lieutenant Colonel Gage to secure the crossings. At four o'clock Lieutenant Colonel St. Clair, the quartermaster-general, was sent forward with a large working party to clear the roads. At six o'clock the general himself, with the rest of the army, broke camp. Four hundred men were posted on the heights covering the first crossing which the advance guards had declared unoccupied, and the whole army, baggage wagons, artillery train, pack horses, cattle, camp followers—including some thirty women!—safely made the passage. At eleven o'clock they reached the second ford, which was held in force by Gage and St. Clair. They were much surprised that no attempt had been made to dispute their passage in either instance.

It was a bright sunny morning. Thinking it probable that French or Indian scouts might be lurking in the vicinity Braddock determined to effect the second passage of the river in the finest military style. Companies were deployed and with the sound of trumpet and fife and roll of drum, the little army plunged into the water and marched across. A brave and splendid show they made; the red-coated regulars, the Virginians in blue, the sailors, the pioneers, the irregulars in their hunting suits; the martial music, the loud blasts of the trumpet, the rolling of the drums, the splashing feet in the sparkling waters, the sunlight reflected from the gleaming gun barrels and flashing bayonets, filled the scene with a martial display the like of which had never before been witnessed in America. The observers, of which there were not a few, were duly impressed—but not in the least dismayed.

The river where they crossed although six hundred feet broad was very shallow. They made the passage without difficulty and halted for dinner on the other side. At last they were within striking distance of the enemy. The last river was crossed, the last obstacle surmounted, the rest was to be plain sailing. Braddock and his officers were much elated. They had been a long time on this journey, but the end was near. Gayly they made their preparations for the final stage of their march. It never seems to have occurred to any one, not even to Washington, that they were approaching a most disastrous defeat—a slaughter, a rout. Everyone was sublimely and supremely confident of certain and immediate success, and in that fatuous but natural confidence they took up the final march.

3. THE DEFEAT ON THE MONONGAHELA

The ground on the east bank, the Du Quesne side, of the Monongahela sloped gently up from the bank of the river for some distance and was well covered with old trees with little or no underbrush. Near the crossing stood Frazier's house where Washington and Gist had received their timely succour a year before. It was now, of course, abandoned. Having seen his whole army safely across, about one o'clock Braddock gave orders for the advance. So far they had seen no one. Although they were near the fort no body of troops had come to oppose them. Nevertheless the English neglected no precaution which their experience and tactics suggested.

Lieutenant Colonel Gage was again thrown forward with an advance party with the guides and engineers; in front of them some of the Virginia light horse were ordered to scout. Flankers were extended through the woods on either side. Some little distance in the rear of Gage, who was accompanied by two pieces of artillery, came St. Clair with his party of road makers; then followed the general with the main body of the army and the artillery train, while Sir Peter Halket with some regulars and the colonial troops, amounting in all to some four hundred men, brought up the rear with the baggage train.

It was Braddock's intention to march until late in the afternoon, then encamp for the night and the next morning formally invest the fort. Neither he, nor Washington, nor anyone—unless it were shrewd old Benjamin Franklin back in Philadelphia putting a damper upon a fund which was being subscribed to celebrate the victory, by remarking that it would be better to raise such a fund when the victory came—seems to have doubted the result. Indeed, as Benjamin Franklin had said, if Braddock once succeeded in investing the fort its downfall would be certain. The only question in Franklin's mind was as to the likelihood of his getting there.

Fort Du Quesne was a stoutly built affair of logs, but was commanded by adjacent hills, and though it was impregnable to musketry, yet with Braddock's artillery train it would have been untenable. In fact de Contrecoeur had about decided that a defence was not feasible and that the only thing left for him to do would be to withdraw. He had, in fact, made every preparation for retreating when Braddock appeared. He had no doubt but that he would be permitted to leave with all the honours of war and had arranged to do so.

Fortunately for the French, however, the second in command of the post, the young Chevalier de Beaujeu, was one of those daring and adventurous soldiers to whom the idea of retreat is the last that presents itself, and he persuaded de Contrecoeur to allow him to take some seventy French regulars and one hundred and fifty Canadians with thirty-two officers and cadets from the small garrison of the fort, and, with such Indians as he could induce to follow him attempt, at least, to delay the advance. The French had assembled a large party of Indians from all over the northwest in the clearing about the fort, and influenced by Beaujeu's impassioned oratory and by the persuasions of such men as Charles de Langlade, a famous half-breed woodranger, and no less a chief than the afterward famous Pontiac, some six hundred and forty-seven of them at last volunteered to follow him. The total attacking forces numbered, therefore, less than nine hundred men.

Barrels of powder and bullets were broached before the gates and the Indians helped themselves. It was de Beaujeu's intention to dispute the passage of the river, but the delay in getting the Indians off, and Braddock's celerity—the one time he was quick in his movements—had forced him to abandon the effort. Although informed by his scouts that he had lost this favourable opportunity de Beaujeu determined to attack the British when he could and accordingly pressed on—a brave fellow indeed. This fact effectually disposes of the statement that Braddock was the victim of an ambuscade.[3]

Gage and his party preceded by Gordon, an engineer officer, and some of Captain Stewart's fleet light-horsemen, steadily advanced up the valley. A quarter of a mile from the river bank the hills rose to a maximum height of perhaps two hundred feet. As they marched along in the general direction of the river, though constantly swerving inward, the woods became thicker and the ground covered with underbrush. The marching column followed a narrow path a few feet wide which wound in and out among the trees, not much more than a trail in fact.

The axemen under St. Clair by cutting down trees did their best to increase the width of the road which presently made a wide detour away from the bank of the river to escape a swamp which was the termination of a rather broad shallow ravine, over which it was necessary for them to cross. One hundred and fifty yards farther another ravine parallel to the first stretched across the path of the invaders. From this ravine two smaller and rather deep depressions in the ground ran almost at right angles to it in a direction roughly paralleling the English advance.

The forest here was filled with shrubs and bushes and the two small ravines were hidden by trees, vines and a thick undergrowth. Back of the ravine upon the right arose a steep and commanding hill also thickly wooded. No one, neither French nor British, seems to have had the slightest previous idea of the existence of these smaller and parallel ravines. Unfortunately the flanking parties, preserving European military distances, were not thrown out quite far enough to detect them, and they were not visible until one stumbled into them. Between this quartet of ravines the battle happened to be fought; if the place had been made to order it could not have been more favourably constructed for the purposes of the French and Indians, and the luck was altogether against the British.

At half after two Gordon, the engineer officer with the advance party, being then a short distance from the second transverse ravine, suddenly became aware of a party of soldiers in French uniform directly in front of him. They seemed to the astonished Englishman to have sprung from the ground. They were led by a man in a hunting

---

3. This is a charge often made and is last repeated in Woodrow Wilson's *Colonies and Nation*. It is without foundation. There was no ambush.

shirt upon whose breast shone the polished silver *gorget* of an officer. Waving his hat the soldier turned to his men and spoke a short word of command. Instantly the forest rang with the report of arms followed by the shouts of "*Vive le Roi! Vive la France!*" Several of the English fell.

The horse having discovered the enemy very properly gave back to clear the front for the infantry, and Colonel Gage instantly deployed his men into such a line as the crowding trees permitted. A heavy volley from the British crashed through the woods in response to the French attack. The artillery was wheeled to the front and one or two vigorous discharges seemed to blow the advancing French away. The officer who had given the first command to fire was seen to fall. The French gave ground.

The British cheering madly began to advance. But before they had gone a few steps shot began to drop in on them from either flank. Here and there a dusky painted, feathered figure could be seen flitting from tree to tree, but nothing else. The Indians at that moment moved forward and stumbling upon the ravines immediately occupied them. Flashes of fire darted under the branches, drifts of smoke blew down upon the men in the open; the soldiers began to fall, they paused uncertainly, the shots came in from every side; they faced about, fired wildly, hesitated, began to retreat.

The French in front of them rallied and came on once more with loud cries; and then a new sound mingled with the cheering of the French. Upon those unaccustomed English ears for the first time broke the savage war cry in all its appalling, menacing fury. The retreat became a rout and in a wild run the advance came pouring through the woods abandoning their cannon. In vain Gage, who was wounded, tried to rally them, in vain the Virginia horse strove to intercept them.

Back at the crossing Braddock heard the sound which told him that the expected attack had at last begun. Leaving Halket and the rear guard with the baggage he immediately ordered up the rest of the army and pressed on toward the front himself. From both flanks and the front a fierce fire was being poured upon the advance parties, quickly extending on each side and rapidly enveloping the whole British lines. In spite of the most determined efforts of their officers Gage's men rushed upon the wavering ranks of St. Clair's detachment, not yet heavily engaged, which they threw into great confusion. The British had seen no one, did not see anyone thereafter—still the resistless rain of death kept up, still the men fell.

Meanwhile, M. Dumas, who had succeeded to the command on the death of de Beaujeu, in spite of the fact that his Canadian auxiliaries had retreated after the first disastrous discharge of the English, and in spite of the fact that the Indians had at first shown signs of withdrawing, succeeded in rallying them and his own men. At that moment the solitary chance of success for Braddock's men had presented itself. A prompt advance upon the French by Gage's party, a scattering of the other troops through the woods, fighting by taking advantage of every cover, would have routed the French regulars and sent the, at first, lukewarm Indian contingent into speedy retreat However, neither Gage nor St. Clair with the advance were able enough or experienced enough to recognize this opportunity and in a moment it was lost. Washington would have seized the chance probably, but he was still with Braddock, who knew nothing about it, and had he been at the front he had not sufficient rank or influence to have been heeded if he had suggested it.

Gage and St. Clair were both experienced soldiers. They called in their flankers, all who were left alive that is, and endeavoured to get their men into line. It was what they had been taught to do and what almost any other mere well-trained soldier would have done. It needed the bitter lesson of defeat to teach them differently. They got it. They knew nothing of forest fighting, but in that day they—or the watching world rather—learned something. Not for a hundred and fifty years would a British army be caught in such a position—their lesson lasted until they attempted to crush the South African republics the other day.

With the French officers and cadets and the regular soldiers, Dumas, with his second in command, de Ligneris, clung to the ravines in front of the British lines and the dangerous moment passed. The Indians recovered from their alarm and, guided and inspired by de Langlade and Pontiac and several of the French officers, they completely filled the two parallel ravines and a large body took shelter behind the trees upon the hill to the right, where they were practically safe from danger, and whence they poured in a withering and destructive fire.

As the main body of the redcoats came up the narrow road on a double quick the advance parties, now mixed in the helpless confusion of a retreat, precipitated themselves into the oncoming mass of their comrades. The two regiments became disorganized at once and were thrown into great confusion. They halted, hesitated, struggled

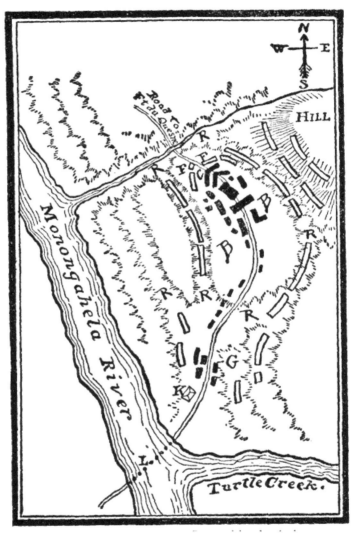

MAP OF BRADDOCK'S DEFEAT, PREPARED BY THE AUTHOR
B B, BRITISH; C, ADVANCE PARTY; C, REAR GUARD; K, FRASER'S
HOUSE; R R, RAVINES FILLED WITH INDIANS.

into broken disjointed lines and began firing wildly in every direction.

The Indians meanwhile continued to move along through the ravines on both flanks until they had the English practically surrounded. In fact, after a short time the savages were so far extended that they were enabled to engage Halket and the rear guard; although the colonials with him, taking cover and thoroughly understanding the savage way of playing the game, there put up a much stiffer fight. In vain did Braddock and his officers endeavour to restore a semblance of order to the disorganized men. The regimental standards were advanced and the men were besought to rally upon them. Officer after officer appealed to his men to follow him and charge upon the enemy whom they could not see yet whose presence was indicated by the encircling line of fire. But they could do nothing with their men. In their desperation in several instances the officers assembled in little parties hoping thereby to form a nucleus by which the men could be induced to advance.

In vain. The British soldiers remained huddled like sheep in the narrow lane in the tree-covered fields, thick with underbrush, blazing away in futile volleys at an enemy who shot at them from every direction. It was hardly necessary for the French and the Indians to take careful aim. All they had to do was to stand concealed in the ravines and point their guns over the edges at the huddled mass of red and blue showing through the smoke under the trees, and pull the trigger.

All that mortal man could do was done by Braddock and his officers. Such heroism as they showed on that field deserves the highest commendation. From the high hill to the right came the most galling fire. Colonel Burton, whose name was last upon the dying lips of Wolfe at Quebec, finally got together one hundred men to charge the hill and dislodge the enemy. Bravely he advanced, but after he had gone a few paces he found himself alone, the soldiers would not follow. One of the Virginia companies left the huddled mass of redcoats and advanced on the run until they gained the shelter of some fallen trees, when they began to pour a careful fire upon their foes. The excited British saw the smoke ahead of them, and thinking it came from an enemy, the artillery fired at it and over fifty of the Virginians were killed thereby. Indeed many of the English were killed by the fire of their comrades.[4]

4. It is sometimes alleged that Braddock was shot by one of his own men but the statement is undoubtedly false.

When the battle began the colonial troops, and the regulars who had enlisted in the colonies, having better knowledge of the demands of the situation, immediately sought the shelter of the trees and began to fire upon the Indians, endeavouring to fight them in their own way. Many of the British soldiers blunderingly essayed the same tactics. To hide behind a tree was in Braddock's mind the act of a coward, and the infuriated general actually beat the men out into the open with the flat of his sword, endeavouring to form and keep the line—and this in spite of the advice of Washington and the colonial officers!

Braddock's stubborn courage was magnificent. Freely exposing himself he held his men inflexibly in those unavailing lines of battle; hot, tired, hoarse, cheering them on and encouraging them to fight; horse after horse to the number of five shot under him, his clothes riddled with bullets—our hearts go out to the brave if stupid soldier. All his *aides* were disabled from wounds at last except the young Virginia colonel, and right gallantly did Washington second him that day. That young man heard bullets whistle then as he had never heard before. And he was the hero of the stricken field.

He was everywhere in the very thick of the fray, now striving to lead a charge, one moment springing from his horse and single-handed wheeling a cannon about and discharging it at the concealed foes; again heartening the frightened men, teaching them to take cover as he could, imploring them to make a brave stand; carrying the orders of the general here and there, begging him to allow the men to fight behind the trees; exposing himself freely, recklessly, to all the dangers of the battle, he raged about that field like a perfect incarnation of war. Two horses were shot beneath him and his clothing was riddled with bullets. Many of the Indians, it was told in after years, marked his tall figure and fired carefully at him again and again, but without avail. God was still protecting him for the great work of the future.

So the battle raged until nearly five o'clock in the afternoon. The long hours wore away and the woods were still filled with the continual crackle of the muskets and the roar of the heavier guns. The ground was covered with dead and wounded. Sixty-three of the eighty-nine officers had fallen. Washington in his excitement, writing while the story of the defeat was still fresh in his mind, called the British soldiers cowards, but men who can stand and fight an unseen enemy, for more than two hours while they are being shot down from every side, cannot properly be described as cowards. They stood helplessly in the forest glades dying in their tracks, the living blazing away ineffectually at the surrounding country while the Indians and the French made targets of them, until their ammunition was exhausted and Braddock himself at last commanded a retreat. Even to the brave, stubborn bulldog soul of the general the consciousness of defeat was at last borne. To stay long, was to invite destruction. With a breaking heart the proud old soldier gave the order.

He had not a single staff officer left unwounded except Washington. The British army had become completely disorganized. There was no semblance of order or organization left in it. The retreat at once became a rout. The men preserved no order and left the field on a wild run. Just as he gave the order to retire a bullet struck the general in the arm and passed through it into the lung, inflicting a mortal wound. Captain Stewart of the horse and Washington sprang to his assistance. Realizing that he had received his death wound the unfortunate leader begged piteously to be left to die upon the field where he had performed such prodigies of valour—in vain. Not heeding his request they lifted him upon a tumbrel or tool-cart, and dragged him after the rest. Everything was lost.

During the afternoon the Indians had extended their lines until they encompassed the rear guard, and though the Virginians who were with Halket had fought them off while their ammunition lasted, the rear had been at last overwhelmed like the rest. Sir Peter Halket, the best of the English officers, a man of the very highest character, had been shot and instantly killed. His son, a young lieutenant of the same regiment, stooping over him had met the same fate and had fallen dead upon his father's breast.

The guns and baggage were abandoned. The military chest with twenty-five thousand pounds of specie in it, was left behind. All of Braddock's papers fell into the hands of the pursuers. As the men fled they threw away their arms, equipments, and even divested themselves of their clothing as they could.

The tumbrel was also abandoned and the dying general was carried across the river in a silk sash, which officers going into action wore for that purpose. When the river was crossed he was mounted on a horse and carried a short distance farther when his pain became unbearable, and they were forced to dismount him. Washington, who was now the ranking officer unwounded, by the direction of Braddock strove to rally the men to form a rear guard. He succeeded in assembling about one hundred fugitives under Lieutenant Colonel Burton, but in a few moments they left him.

At the second crossing a like effort met with another failure. Yet how bravely the dying general strove to do his duty and check the rout and rally his men! Fortunately for the English the pursuit had stopped at the first crossing of the river. The Indians ranged over the field and with horrible ferocity killed all those who were so severely wounded as to be unable to get away. The French did what they could to restrain the savages from their brutalities, but they were too few in number to accomplish much. All but three of the unfortunate women were killed after such a fate as can painfully be imagined, and yet their experience was probably merciful contrasted with the fate in store for the three remaining.

Nearly nine hundred officers and men were killed and wounded, of whom the greater part were killed in battle or murdered after it.[5] There was scarcely an Indian engaged who did not dangle from his belt a reeking, gory scalp. The plunder and booty secured by the allies was immense, as the English succeeded in taking literally nothing across the river. Twelve unwounded Englishmen were captured by the Indians and reserved for a fearful end.

There was an American prisoner at Fort Du Quesne that day and he described the desperate anxiety with which de Contrecoeur waited during the afternoon for news from de Beaujeu whom the cowardly Canadians declared they had left in dire straits when they came running back after their desertion. It was late in the evening before the war party returned carrying with them the dead bodies of their heroic commander and three other Frenchmen who had been killed and bringing less than a score of wounded, which, with some sixty casualties among the Indians, represented the total loss sustained by the expedition. There was much joy in the garrison when the news of the crushing victory which they had obtained had been told.

The young American boy, the prisoner referred to, stood on the ramparts and saw the twelve British soldiers, who, utterly ignorant of the savage practices and customs, had surrendered themselves as prisoners of war, burned at the stake after having been subjected to the slowest and most agonizing of tortures. De Contrecoeur and his officers looked at the horrid orgy from the ramparts of Du Quesne while the white flag of France floated over the scene of shame to the eternal disgrace of its defenders.

---

5. The defeat of St. Clair in 1791 was a greater disaster, and was much more disgraceful; the casualties were larger, too, yet it is but little remembered—See my *American Fights and Fighters*, (also published by Leonaur).

But the French were not yet at ease. Within striking distance of the fort the English still had a force great enough to have effected its capture and de Contrecoeur waited in much anxiety for what might happen next. He would have been much relieved could he have divined the situation of his enemies.

Failing to get his men to make a stand Braddock was placed on a litter and borne slowly along the way which his army had so painfully followed in their advance in the morning. The soldiers had to be heavily bribed by Orme, one of the general's *aides*, and a friend of Washington—who has left us a vivid account of the campaign, by the way—to induce them to carry their commander. Braddock, who seems to have striven to do his duty even in the articles of death, that night despatched Washington to Dunbar's camp at Rock Fort, some sixty miles distant, to tell the story and give him orders to send men and wagons to receive the wounded.

Washington rode at reckless speed to discharge his errand. Fast as he went, however, the wagoners, colonists all, who at the first onset had cut the traces and galloped away, were ahead of him. They were the real cowards of the day. They brought the news of the annihilation of the army—the first one who came in actually declared he was the only survivor! Washington found Dunbar in a state of intense perturbation. Indeed, his fear amounted to cowardice. However, he sent a troop of soldiers out with the necessary wagons for the wounded. So panic-stricken had his men become that it was difficult to induce them to go forward. Washington led them back over the road.

On the 12th they met Braddock, who was slowly dying. They made him as comfortable as they could and finally brought him to Dunbar's camp at Little Meadows. There he died. He had lain all day in a stupor, saying nothing. Toward evening he revived a little and they heard him murmur again and again, "Who would have thought it, who would have thought it?" and just as the sands of life fled away he whispered softly, "We shall know better how to deal with them another time."

Alas, there was no other time for the defeated soldier. He had been given his opportunity and had lost it. He had done his best and he had failed, but he had yielded up his life in the failure. I think of him pityingly, kindly, tenderly.

They buried him in the gray of the morning in the road just a mile from Fort Necessity. There was neither pomp nor ceremony in his funeral. A few wounded officers and men followed him to his grave, where the tall young Colonial colonel read the solemn service of the Church of England, as they laid him away. I doubt if there was a volley fired even. They drew the wagons over his last resting place and marched the troops over it to conceal it lest it should be opened and violated by the Indians, and then marched on.

> *No useless coffin enclosed his breast*
> *Not in sheet or in shroud we wound him;*
> *But he lay like a warrior taking his rest.*
> *With his martial cloak around him.*
>
> *Few and short were the prayers we said,*
> *And we spoke not a word of sorrow;*
> *But we steadfastly gazed on the face that was dead,*
> *And we bitterly thought of the morrow.*
>
> *Lightly they'll talk of the spirit that's gone.*
> *And o'er his cold ashes upbraid him;*
> *But little he'll reck, if they let him sleep on*
> *In the grave where a Briton has laid him.*

Dunbar showed himself a coward—they called him "Dunbar the tardy" thereafter, and the adjective was, if anything, inadequate. Against the advice and entreaty of many he blew up and destroyed his stores and supplies and fled incontinently to Philadelphia. Shrewd Dr. Franklin was right. No subscription was called for to celebrate the victory. It had been a fearful campaign. Such a crushing defeat had probably never before been inflicted upon the English arms.

Poor Braddock—his memory rather—was made the scapegoat, yet the failure was not due so much to the man as it was to the inadequacy of the tactics in which he and his men had been trained and their utter uselessness in such an emergency; but he had opened the eyes of the world by his failure. Yes, he had opened the eyes of the colonies, too. The halo about the British regular was gone forever. Man to man in the country in which they lived, they knew themselves to be as good as, if not better, than he. Washington, Gates, Hugh Mercer, and stout old Daniel Morgan, a wagoner who had not run, and who had fought until severely wounded, had learned lessons that they never forgot.

For some insubordination Morgan had been punished—unjustly he claimed—by five hundred lashes. For every blow laid upon him the British one day paid a fearful price. The French and Indians builded better than they knew in their defeat of the English. They gave to America a demonstration of the possibility of success against the finest, best drilled, best equipped soldiers of Europe.

After the defeat and retreat of the British ensued a scene of horror in the west. Washington had not retired with the rest, and with a wretchedly ineffective provincial regiment of a thousand poorly provided men, he was left at Fort Cumberland to protect the thousand miles of helpless and otherwise undefended frontier from the incursions of savages who had quaffed blood upon the banks of the Monongahela and sought to drink deep of it with awful success before they were satiated. The homes of the lonely settlers were raided and destroyed, the men murdered, the women outraged and the children carried into captivity.

The consequences of the English disaster were thus visited upon the wretched inhabitants of the country. Washington did all that mortal man could do with the means provided to protect the people and check the savage onslaught. His countrymen thoroughly appreciated not only his brilliant conduct in the last campaign which might have been less disastrous had his advice been followed, but they also realized the importance of his service in protecting the frontier, although they did but little to help him. His situation was indeed deplorable.

Writes he to the governor:

> I am too little acquainted with pathetic language to attempt a description of these people's distresses. But what can I do? I see their situation, I know their danger, and participate in their sufferings, without having it in my power to give them further relief than uncertain promises. . . The supplicating tears of the women, and moving petitions of the men, melt me into such deadly sorrow, that I solemnly declare, if I know my own mind, I could offer myself a willing sacrifice to the butchering enemy, provided that would contribute to the people's ease.

Meanwhile, during all these happenings the flag of France still waved over the ramparts of Fort Du Quesne, and the Indians and French were yet masters of the valley of the Ohio.

3

The Final Success

1. Grant's Defeat

Five years have passed since young George Washington left Fort Le
Boeuf with the defiance of St. Pierre in his hand; years crowded with
thrilling experiences and hard campaigns; years filled with responsibilities which had developed the bold, reckless, adventurous young
man into a hardy, seasoned soldier. Once more at the head of a large
body of men we find him at Fort Cumberland.

It is late in the autumn of 1758. Since two years the false peace between England and France has been abrogated and they are engaged
in a life and death struggle for the domination of a continent. Amherst
and Wolfe have taken Louisburg, Abercrombie has been disgracefully
routed at Ticonderoga, Bradstreet, a hardy colonial soldier from Massachusetts, by a bold dash has captured Fort Frontenac on Lake Ontario, and Fort Du Quesne on the Ohio is at last cut off from its base of
supplies. The white flag still waves, however, over the ramparts of the
little fort, and the French as yet maintain their mastery of the valley.

Some thirty miles north of Fort Cumberland, near the little village
of Raystown, in a rude fortification called Fort Bedford, which gave
its name to the flourishing city which has supplanted it, lies an English
officer. He is desperately ill, unable to walk at all, and must fain travel
in a litter, prosecuting his campaigning under these disadvantageous
circumstances and drawing every breath in pain and anguish unspeak-
able. His name is John Forbes. Mark it well! He was a hero if ever
there was one, yet he is practically forgotten by everyone except a few
Philadelphians. There is no account of him for instance in the *Encyclo-
paedia Britan*nica, nor is he mentioned in that monumental work the
Dictionary of National Biography.

Perhaps the oblivion which has been attached to his memory is due to the fact that he did not participate either in a great victory or a great defeat, and his qualities were only exhibited in a hard, desperate and successful campaign. They were such qualities, however, as entitle him to a high and honourable place in the military records of his country. And he seems to have been as capable and admirable a man as he was a soldier.

The task which was set before him was one which had baffled the power of England and America for five years. In attempting to encompass it they had met a repulse and a most disastrous defeat. It was not less difficult when he essayed it than when Washington had tried it or when Braddock had attempted it. The campaign was to be carried on under exactly the same conditions and with much the same material, and the same difficulties were to be overcome; but this time the effort was crowned with success. The success was due to the commander.

John Forbes was a Scottish gentleman of parts and ability. He was born of a good family, at Petincrief, Fifeshire, Scotland, in 1710. When a young man he had studied medicine and had practised his profession until he had been able to indulge his inclinations by purchasing a commission in the British army. He had seen much hard service in the continental wars, notably at Fontenoy under Lord Ligonier, had been made colonel of the Scots-Grays in 1745, and afterward of the Seventeenth Foot. He had been adjutant general and was now promoted brigadier general and intrusted with the duty of reducing Fort Du Quesne. To facilitate him in accomplishing this task an ample force was allotted to him.

He had the Sixty-second Highlanders, twelve hundred and sixty strong, one battalion of the Royal Americans, mostly Pennsylvania Germans, numbering three hundred and sixty-three, and four thousand three hundred and fifty provincial troops. The regulars were thoroughly equipped and highly efficient, especially the Royal Americans, a regiment recently organized in this country, but the provincial troops were of varying quality indeed. Certainly the flower of these last were some seventeen hundred Virginians, commanded by Washing- ton. The others were mostly undisciplined, ill-equipped, indifferent soldiers in fact, and poorly officered, especially in the subordinate ranks.

Forbes was a man of liberal and enlightened views, courteous in his bearing and tactful in his methods, but determined—terribly resolute! By his generous and kindly manner he attached to himself those whom Braddock and his officers had alienated by their contempt. The army, with the exceptions noted, was well officered. The general was himself a host.

The command of all the colonial troops had been given to Washington, with such men as Armstrong, Byrd, and Lewis as his subordinates. Certainly Washington's experiences in the preceding five years made him an invaluable officer. Indeed it is not generally known that Washington had been a close student of military science and tactics; the lives and campaigns of the great masters of the art of war were—and they continued to be all his life—his favourite objects of research. This study and his practical experiences fairly entitled him to admission into the ranks of the professional soldier, in which category he takes no mean place. It is a mistake to consider him an untrained militia officer. He was a practised, drilled, trained, disciplined veteran; a most accomplished officer, indeed; one who could have commanded a regiment or an army even, with credit to himself and success to his cause anywhere.

Among Forbes' other officers was our whilom friend, Sir John St. Clair, just as obstinate, just as arrogant, just as stupid, just as incompetent as he had been in Braddock's expedition. He had his old place, too, and he made himself thoroughly and heartily detested. A man of a different stamp, however, was the second in command of the army, the lieutenant colonel commanding the first battalion of the Royal Americans. This last was a capital regiment. Its several battalions did splendid service on nearly every battlefield on the continent from Quebec to Du Quesne. The name of this officer was Henry Bouquet.

He was a Swiss soldier of fortune who had served the Dutch, the Sardinians, and the English, and was a veteran of the European wars. He was a man of much tact, address and resource; well able to adapt himself to the conditions of Indian warfare; after a little observation and experience he actually devised effectual means for beating the savages at their own game. There had been hot discussion as to the best method of approaching the object of their endeavour. Washington was inclined toward Braddock's road, which, by this time, for the major part of it at least, had become a thoroughly practicable way on account of the travel which made good use of it. Forbes, however, decided to cut his way through Pennsylvania, much to the disgust and disappointment of the Virginians.[1]

1. See map on page 156 for a portion of Forbes' route.

As a matter of fact, the making of a road would do much to open western Pennsylvania to settlement. As Virginia wished to monopolize the expected trade with the new country she was interested in preventing the building of this road, while Pennsylvania was correspondingly eager to bring it about.

It is an interesting question, for instance, whether the development of the Roman Empire was due to the prowess of the Legions or to the industry of the road builders. Certainly the conquests won by the sword could not have been held but for the toilsome labour of the axe, the pick, and the shovel. And that was to be the case in this instance.

When the decision had been arrived at, Colonel Bouquet[2] had been sent forward with two thousand men to make the road. He was now encamped at Loyalhannon, some forty miles west of Raystown, and about thirty miles from Fort Du Quesne. Forbes' idea was to dot his road with forts which would be capable of defending themselves against any force liable to be brought against them, which would act as storehouses and depots of equipment, supply resting places for his army in its various stages of progress westward, and would also afford rallying points by which to check retreat in case of defeat or disaster. He cautiously determined to leave nothing to chance.

The new way was to be no mere trail cut through the woods and over the mountains, but a fairly made road upon which great labour was expended. Washington, when the orders had reached him, with Colonel Byrd and Major Lewis, and the Virginians, had marched from Fort Cumberland to Raystown, and had thence proceeded to the advance post at Loyalhannon. The weather in Pennsylvania in the fall is usually mild and agreeable, but an exception to the ordinary conditions unfortunately prevailed, for the rain fell in torrents continuously, flooding the road, washing away the embankments and almost destroying the labours of the builders. Travel upon the new road, unless it was to be cut to pieces, was indefinitely suspended for some time.

While they were waiting, Bouquet, at the earnest solicitation of Major Grant, one of his subordinates, allowed him to take a detachment comprising six hundred of the Highlanders of the Sixty-second and make a reconnoissance in force of Fort Du Quesne. It was important that knowledge of the situation should be procured for the general, and Grant set forward with strict instructions to confine his

2. *Bouquet & the Ohio Indian War* by Cyrus Cort & William Smith, two accounts of the campaigns of 1763-1764, *Bouquet's Campaigns* by Cyrus Cort and *The History of Bouquet's Expeditions* by William Smith, also published by Leonaur..

efforts to observation and not to bring on an engagement. With him went two companies of Washington's regiment, commanded by Major Lewis and Captain Bullitt. Instead of the regulation outfit of the provincial soldiers, these men were dressed in hunting shirts and leggins, as were most of Washington's command, the prototypes in uniform of the famous rifle regiments which Daniel Morgan led "from the right bank of the Potomac" in the Revolution. Grant's total force was about seven hundred and fifty.

Lewis and Bullitt were experienced frontier fighters and the party guided by them and by some friendly Indians had no difficulty in reaching the ridge which overlooks Fort Du Quesne. The fort was now under the command of de Ligneris, who had so ably seconded Dumas at the battle on the Monongahela. It was night when they reached the heights and of necessity if they wanted to see anything they would have to wait until morning. Strictly speaking there was nothing for them to do but to reconnoitre if they kept within their orders. Grant being informed by his Indian scouts that the garrison was small—which was a mistake—and that there were but a few Indians about—which was another—conceived the rash design of enticing the French and their Indian allies into an ambuscade, which, if successful, would enable him to demand, and probably to receive, the surrender of the fort, which would be a thing greatly to his credit and certain to bring him high reward. He therefore detached Lewis to make a detour and get a position from which he could attack the hoped-for sallying party of the garrison in the rear, and then proceeded to make other arrangements for the expected onset.

Unfortunately in the thick darkness Lewis lost his way and when morning dawned had not yet secured the desired position, much to Grant's disappointment. In fact he was forced to bring his detachment back to the main body. He had not succeeded in getting anywhere. A little thing like that, however, did not amount to much in the mind of the British soldier who was laying his cunning plans, and when Lewis rejoined him after aimlessly inarching about all night, he stationed him with Bullitt and the Virginians on the ridge with the baggage of the detachment to allow his men to get a little rest.

He concluded that he could manage the affair with the Highlanders—the old story of the invincible British regular again—and he instructed Lewis to advance when the battle was joined and attack the enemy in the flank. Thus, at the beginning of the battle he deprived himself of his most experienced Indian fighters. Then having made such disposition of his canny Scots as he could, he determined to commence operations.

It was a damp, foggy morning, the 14th of September, 1758, and Grant had not yet been able to see much of the fort and the adjacent country. For the same reason the French appear to have been ignorant of his proximity. It was necessary to inform them of his presence in order to begin the game, so he actually directed his drummers and buglers to play the reveille! They played it and the French woke up. There were some fifteen hundred in the fort besides hundreds of Indians! They awoke with a promptness and completeness that was fairly dazzling. With their Indian allies they came swarming out of the fort in a hurry; so hasty were their movements that many of them were but partially dressed. They all had weapons, however, and they all seemed to know just what to do.

The ambuscade was a miserable failure of course. Neither Grant nor his Highlanders had the slightest practical knowledge of such a thing. Taking advantage of their thorough acquaintance with the topography and their long experience in this sort of warfare, the French and Indians soon surrounded the Highlanders and threw them into utter confusion. The opening scenes of Braddock's defeat were again enacted. This time, however, the Highlanders had sense enough not to stand up and be shot uselessly—or possibly they lacked a bulldog like Braddock to keep them up to their work. At any rate they broke and fled.

Lewis advanced promptly enough at the designated time, but the French had so manoeuvred as to throw Grant's men Entirely away from the path of Lewis' advance and the latter marched blindly into the open arms—firearms—of the French and Indians. His men, although surprised, put up a sharp fight but were overpowered and he himself was captured.

Meanwhile the Highlanders in frantic terror fled through the woods, the French and Indians in hot pursuit after them. Grant protesting unavailingly was swept along with them. As he was nearest the foe, having most reluctantly retreated, he was surrounded and his surrender demanded. "My heart is broke," he cried, "I will not survive the day." Stung with rage and mortification he refused to yield and proceeded to put up a most desperate fight until he was overwhelmed by numbers and captured.

Back on the ridge Bullitt and his Virginians had heard the firing and had seen the evidence of the rout and they made brave preparation to do their part to retrieve the day and cover the disaster. The Highlanders came streaming past them in panic terror and it was hard work for the little handful of colonial troops to resist the temptation to join in the rout, but Bullitt kept them well in hand and when the French and Indians appeared there began one of the hottest little engagements ever fought in Pennsylvania. The Virginians stood their ground manfully and showed the result of Washington's training. They were a great credit to him. The pursuit was checked and the flying Highlanders were enabled to get such a start that they were in no danger of being overtaken. After fifty of Bullitt's men had been killed and wounded the French gave over the attack and pursuit and returned to the fort, leaving Bullitt to march back to Loyalhannon with the honours of war.

The young man was highly complimented for his gallantry and skill and was at once promoted by Forbes. The loss of the foolish expedition was two hundred and seventy-three killed and wounded and a few captured. The remainder of the detachment straggled back to the camp after arduous experiences. It was a costly and needed lesson. The French, elated with their success, despatched a heavy force to attack Bouquet's position at Loyalhannon, but although they met with some success with the outlying detachments, they were presently beaten off after a smart engagement and forced to retire.

2 Forbes' Achievement and Death

A short time after this rout, the sick and suffering Forbes was brought up with the advance. The season was late, the weather still unpropitious and the sentiment of the army was in favour of postponing further attempt until the following year.

A council of war was had which unanimously reached this conclusion. That Forbes should determine to disregard the advice of such men as Washington and Bouquet and press on to complete the work is an evidence of his qualities. Not for nothing did they call this obstinate Scot "Iron Head." With unabated resolution he gave orders to continue the advance.

On November 18th, leaving the main body, which had at last reached Loyalhannon, at that place, they pressed on with some twenty-five hundred of the best men stripped to the lowest possible equipment and without tents, even. They marched rapidly, covering fifty miles in less than five days. They were much encouraged by news which they received from some deserters and friendly Indians that de Ligneris—taking it for granted on account of the lateness of the season and the disastrous losses the British had sustained in the defeat of Grant's detachment, that they would give over the attempt—had materially reduced his garrison by sending the greater part of it to Canada. There was another reason, however, for his action. He had not provisions enough to keep them in the valley during the winter. Bradstreet's destruction of the depot at Fort Frontenac had made it impossible for him to receive the usual supplies from Canada.

That was not the worst of it either. The cup of the French was filled by another circumstance. The Indians, who had been their stanch friends, supporters, and allies, had at last been alienated from them and they could neither get anything to eat from them nor could they count upon their support in the campaign. The credit for this important and vital move in detachment must be divided between two men. Forbes had realized the necessity, and at the same time fathomed the possibility of this undertaking.

The Indians were a purchasable commodity, in the market invariably at the command of the highest bidder. The cutting of the French line of communication and their failure to receive any supplies for bribery or barter, with which to subsidize and retain their savage allies, had already caused much discontent among the Indians. The savages were not without a shrewd idea, too, that the end of the French power had almost arrived in the valley. Forbes was setting about his work in a way which predicated success, and the Indian, like most people, was not averse to getting on the winning side. However, these dreams of Forbes would probably have come to naught had he not succeeded in finding an agent to undertake the labour of explanation and persuasion.

This was the Rev. Christian Frederick Post, a Moravian missionary endowed with a heroism, determination, and wisdom that might well have become a Jesuit This courageous and devoted man ventured into the Indian country. There he quaintly likened himself to Daniel in the Lion's Den, and the simile, if anything, is inadequate—it is an insult to the lions. I think the great-hearted follower of Zinzendorf and his Master was actuated and inspired by the knowledge that if he could detach the Indians from the French alliance there would be peace on the desolate blood-swept frontier.

Post had not only to persuade the Indians, but he actually had to do it in the very presence of the French emissaries and officers, who did everything possible to nullify his mission. Rewards were put upon his head by them and savage bands set on his track to capture and kill him, but God preserved him and he accomplished his end—a dauntless man indeed. The Indians generally were won over to the Americans, and for the first time since the beginning of the war western settlements were freed, in great measure, from apprehension of massacre and rapine.

There were councils galore, at which speeches were made, pipes smoked, hatchets buried, peace belts exchanged and agreements ratified. Amid them all the heroic Moravian stands supreme. Honour to Christian Frederick Post, Missionary and Man, as one of the defenders and protectors of the frontier. Yet, he, too, is another forgotten hero. One cause of Forbes' slow progress lay in the necessary delays to enable these various treaties and arrangements to be consummated.

But to return to the expedition. Urged on by the indomitable persistence of the dying soldier the march was resumed from Loyalhannon. On the 24th of November they reached a point about twelve miles from , the fort. As they encamped there, late in the evening, they were greeted by the dull reverberations of distant explosions. They wondered what could be the explanation, and many of them surmised the cause of it.

The next morning the march was taken up again. The army moved in three parallel columns; that on the right was commanded by Washington, that in the centre by Forbes still borne, like Marshal Saxe on his litter, and that on the left by Bouquet—a splendid trio for brilliant service.[3] Washington from his knowledge and experience had been constantly thrown in advance during the march and he now led the way. Presently toward evening they reached the ridge that overlooked the clearing where Grant had been defeated. As they gazed out from beneath the trees across the opening, they marked the courses of the Allegheny and the Monongahela, they could see where the two swept together to form the mighty Ohio, but where they had hoped to catch a glimpse of the bastions of the fort with the French flag waving over them, they saw nothing but blackened, smoking ruins. The French, surprised by the rapid approach and realizing that with their depleted garrison they could make no effective defence, had blown up the

---

3. The Indians had noticed and derided a commander who had to be carried on a litter, and to counteract their impression "it was given out by the English that the British chief had a temper so impetuous, irascible and combative, that it was not thought safe to trust him at large even among his own people, but that the practice was to *let him out on the eve of battle!*"

works and fled the night before.

Washington was among the first to enter the remains of the fort. Colonel Armstrong of the Pennsylvania Colonials hoisted the English flag over it and the French were forever dispossessed from the valley of the Ohio. It was a bloodless termination of much high endeavour and expensive effort, yet it was well worth the cost and it was most fit that the young man whose eye had marked it as the situation for a fort when the place was yet a virgin wilderness, should be in charge of those who floated the flag of England over the ruined walls at the last.

This was the end of their campaign. There yet remained to the victors two melancholy duties. As the Highlanders marched into the remains of the enclosure their hearts were filled with rage and fury, for upon rows of stakes were set the scalped heads of many of their comrades who had been killed in Grant's expedition. Below them on their mutilated bodies hung the plaids and kilts nailed up to express the derision of the French and Indians for what they were pleased to call "petticoat soldiers." They were unable to take any revenge, however, as the French were gone, and they could do nothing except to give the poor remains an honourable burial in the lone clearing by the banks of the Ohio.

One of the officers in Forbes' command was Brigade-Major Halket, the son of that commander of the Forty-fourth regiment who had fallen upon the banks of the Monongahela three years before. Led by some of the Indians who had participated in the conflict, but who were now their friends, a party of soldiery commanded by Washington visited the fatal field. They found it much as it had been left after the bloody defeat. The trees about the place where the British made their fruitless stand still showed the scars of bullets, many of which were found embedded in the trunks. Broken carts and weather-beaten, shattered equipments mingled with the bleaching bones which had been picked clean by wolves and vultures and had been whitened by the rains and snows and storms of the intervening years.

Near where the baggage had been, the remains of two skeletons were found, one apparently lying across the breast of the other. Major Halket identified that of his father by some peculiarities in his teeth, the other was that of his brother who had fallen and died in that position, and the chroniclers report that the bereaved soldier fainted at the ghastly sight.

The bodies of the two officers were reverently interred with military honours, and the men ranged over the field and gathered up all the other bones and put them in a common grave, paying them the last solemn rites of a soldier. Once again the roar of guns rang through the woods, but this time it was the requiem of those who had died so pitiably so many years before. It is said that Benjamin West, the great painter, was one of those who participated in this solemn ceremony. Would that he had made a picture of it!

Although it is not a matter of record that Washington did so, I have often surmised that, as he had read the prayers of his Church over the body of the general, so he may have done the same thing over the bones of his soldiery. What emotions must have arisen in the heart of that young man as he thought of all that had happened since he had first gazed upon that field, as he passed in review the incidents of that never-to-be-forgotten day of defeat?

If there was sadness in the retrospect, there was joy in the future. His soldiering was over. He had done his full share of campaigning, his service had been arduous and brilliant, and in the end successful. The French were driven from the valley, there was little fear of their return, the Indians had been pacified, the frontier was safe, no enemy menaced the Old Dominion, he could resign the army with honour. His approaching marriage rendered it desirable, as the successful campaign rendered it possible, for him to leave the service. The cause of the French was doomed, it was readily seen, and he was not needed elsewhere in bringing about the final downfall of their arms. So he retired from his command.

He had been elected a member of the Virginia Assembly and there is a pretty little story reported of a scene which took place the following year when he first took his seat. The thanks of the Assembly were unanimously voted to him for his courage and conduct. The young man, taken by surprise, rose to reply. He was only able to enunciate a few stammering sentences when he stopped in confusion, unable to proceed, staring at the speaker, blushing painfully the while.

"Sit down, Mr. Washington," said the latter smiling, "your modesty equals your valour, and that surpasses the power of any language I possess." This flattering remark probably added greatly to his perturbation! He had indeed deserved well of his country in his youth. And in his character and career men afterward read the prophecy of his future. What of the devoted Forbes?

After rebuilding the fort, or replacing it with a temporary structure which he called Fort Pitt, after the great war minister, and leaving Hugh Mercer with two companies of provincials to garrison it, he started back to Philadelphia—to die. Five hundred miles of the severest travelling intervened between him and his rest. He had been sustained and buoyed up in his illness on the advance,. by the prospect of the attainment of the object of his endeavour; but when his task was completed the inspiration to struggle was lost. In a pitiable condition from the deadly inflammation of the bowels from which he suffered, and from a complication of consequent ailments, he was carried back through the mountains toward Philadelphia. Every arrangement that was possible was made for his comfort by his solicitous soldiers, although that is not saying much.

A detachment was kept constantly ahead of the army with instructions to build a hut and kindle a warm fire in it ready for the general wherever a halt was made. On one occasion, through some misunderstanding, when evening terminated the day's march the unfortunate soldier found neither hut nor fire. He was forced to lie without shelter in the wintry cold for two hours. He nearly died then and there. Through the storm and cold of the winter he was borne slowly if steadily on, growing weaker with each passing day. It was a terrible journey, but it was ended at last when he reached Philadelphia on the 14th of January, 1759, amid the ringing of bells, the firing of cannon and the joyful enthusiasm of the people. He had completed his task and brought his army safely back to its base of supplies; then, having finished his course, he died on the 11th of March, having drawn his breath in pain and anguish for many days. Not many who died in that *Annus Mirabilis* have a better title to honour and remembrance than he.

> *When the souls of men are tried*
> *In old time or latest day.*
> *They who for our land have died—*
> *Count them not of common clay.*
> *God of battles in Thy keeping*
> *Guard the weary soldier sleeping.*

He is buried in the chancel of Christ Church, Philadelphia—the exact spot being undetermined—where a tablet to his memory has recently been erected by the Society of Colonial Wars. From it I quote:

> By a steady pursuit of well-conducted measures, in defiance of disease and numberless obstructions, he brought to a happy issue a most extraordinary campaign, resulting in the evacuation

of Fort Du Quesne, and made a willing sacrifice of his own life to what he loved more, the interest of King and Country.

An annual service within the walls of that ancient edifice recalls his services and awakens fresh local interest in his character and his name. Aside from that I do not think anybody particularly recalls him, yet the final expulsion of the French from that valley which is now teeming with industry, the home of a great, prosperous, and thrifty people, and the centre of worldwide activities, is due to his indomitable persistence, his unwearying determination, his lofty devotion, his utter self-sacrifice, which he carried out even to the giving up of his life.

No one who traverses that populous and prosperous section of our country can be indifferent to the story of the two men who are suitably conjoined by the possession of common characteristics as well as by personal associations. They wrested the valley of the Ohio from the French and the Indian and gave it to civilization and progress. These two are John Forbes and George Washington.

4

The Fighting Around Ticonderoga

1. THE GRAND EXPEDITION

While James Wolfe is winning his spurs amid the surf at Louisburg—Milesian mixture of metaphor, that—his great antagonist, to be, is demonstrating his capacity in the forests about Ticonderoga.

The genius of Pitt had conceived a plan for striking the French simultaneously at every vital point. John Forbes we have seen toiling through the mountains of Pennsylvania toward the valley of the Ohio. Boscawen and Amherst are battering away at the stone walls of Louisburg, Abercrombie is expected to pierce the centre by marching up the immemorial warpath of the nations formed by the valleys of the Hudson and the Richelieu. In other words, the centre and both flanks were to be attacked simultaneously in force. While the loss of Du Quesne and of Louisburg on either hand would be most serious, the shattering of the centre would be fatal, therefore, like a wise and prudent commander, Montcalm in person took charge of the preparations to repel Abercrombie.

That general was a respectable gentleman about fifty- two years of age, devoid of the faintest spark of military genius and as incapable a commander as ever "set a squadron in the field"—"a heavy man," "infirm in body and mind." Why Pitt ever allowed this mentally "imponderous rag of circumstance" to command this most important expedition, when, in every other instance, he had ruthlessly insisted upon appointing men upon whom he could depend, whose capacity, ability, and success, proved the accuracy of his judgment, is a mystery. It is stated, however, that out of deference to public opinion, which he was not yet strong enough to disregard, or rather which was not yet enlisted upon his side, and on account of certain influential connections of Abercrombie's, he was allowed to retain the command. Pitt sought to obviate the danger of such a situation by associating with him as his second, Brigadier General George Augustus, Viscount Howe, an officer of the highest merit and rare capacity, who was to have the real charge of the operations. Although young in years, thirty-four, his experience had been large and his successes brilliant. He possessed the family genius for war.

Of him Wolfe said he was "the noblest Englishman that has appeared in my time and the best soldier in the British army." High praise indeed and from such a source. In addition to his qualities as a soldier his personal characteristics were such as to endear him to every man, English or Colonial, in his following. He was, in fact, the very idol of the Provincial soldiery, and after his death Massachusetts erected a memorial to him in Westminster Abbey. Had he lived he might have made as great a name for himself on land as his brother and successor, Admiral Richard, Earl Howe, "Black Dick," did upon the sea. Had he not been killed in an obscure skirmish in the woods of America the American Revolution might never have been fought, or with him in command of the king's troops might have come a different conclusion to the struggle.

The bullets that struck down Henry Bouquet, James Wolfe, and George Howe did inestimable service, strange as it may seem to say it, to the cause of human freedom. They were great and heroic men, two of them at least did valiant service before they died, and the other bade fair to equal them. But they all died in early manhood. Their fate recalls to mind a phrase of Lew Wallace's. Speaking of Montezuma, after he had been spurned by his own people and struck down by their arms, the author of the "Fair God "describes his face as the face of a man breaking because he stood in God's way. Were these men laid low because standing they might have been in the way of God's plan for the achievement of civil liberty in a great continent? Who knows?

The force which Pitt had created for the advance up the valley was in every way ample. Abercrombie was in charge of six thousand British regulars and nine thousand Provincials. The Provincials were well organized and equipped and were in effect regular soldiers. There was a regiment of Rangers, too, under the command of the daring and successful partisan and pioneer, Robert Rogers, and a regiment of boatmen commanded by the dashing Colonial Colonel Bradstreet. In the British contingent Charles Lee, who had been one of Braddock's officers, and who was afterward the traitorous insubordinate second of Washington, held a commission.

Among the Colonial officers were two destined to national fame. Major Israel Putnam and Captain John Stark. Both of these men were honoured with the friendship of Howe, who was quick to detect their sterling worth. Among the British regulars the most noted body of men were the Forty-second Highlanders, familiarly known as the Black Watch,[1] from their sombre tartans of black, dark blue and dark green; they were under the command of Major Duncan Campbell of Inverawe.

The army was accompanied by a formidable artillery train and was well provided with every requisite necessary for successful marching or fighting. Great care had been exercised in every particular, and no better equipped body of men ever set forth upon a campaign. Under Howe's direction the unwieldy British uniforms had been discarded or altered to suit the men for such marching as they were expected to undertake. The long skirts of the coats had been cut off, the heavy cumbrous mitred hats had been thrown aside, leggins had been provided, the bright barrels of the muskets had been browned to give no sign of their presence in the woods, and so on.

It was expected that they would brush aside every obstacle and terminate their advance at Montreal. Nobody seemed to doubt that they would succeed in doing so. Between them and their goal, however, lay a little French army under the command of the military chief of Canada, the Marquis de Montcalm, a soldier of the first rank. Inconsiderable in numbers, it was high in quality, and was composed of some of the best troops of France.

Oh the peninsula of Ticonderoga, situated at the point where the waters of the river connecting Lake George and Lake Champlain flow into the latter, the French, in 1755, under the direction of the engineer Lotbinière, had erected a fort destined to be one of the most famous spots in American history.

Long before the *arquebuse* of Champlain rang the death knell of Indian supremacy there in 1609, the little peninsula had been the scene of many a bloody battle. Scarcely any place on the continent is so full of romantic reminiscence. The haughty Iroquois, the dashing French, the stubborn English, the stolid German, the hardy colonists, have all held the post in turn. Millions of money have been spent in fortifying it, and its soil is consecrated by the blood of hundreds of brave men. Here the dauntless Jesuit rested on those wild journeys where he bore the cross, told its story, and died upon it. Here Ethan

1. *The Black Watch at Ticonderoga*: by Frederick B. Richards also published by Leonaur.

Allen[2] had formulated his famous demand. Here men first heard of Benedict Arnold. Here Burgoyne enjoyed his one solitary moment of victory in that grand expedition of conquest which was to cut the United States in two.

The waters that laved these shores had borne the keels of the flotillas of Champlain, Frontenac, Montcalm, Abercrombie, and Amherst; upon the lake hard by, Arnold fought his hapless but heroic battle; and a generation later, MacDonough hammered the British fleet into defeat by the mighty broadsides of the *Saratoga*. A mass of crumbling ruins upon a low bluff marks the spot today, (as at time of first publication), and brings up before the thoughtful traveller the memory of much that is tragic and terrible in American history. Aye, 'tis hallowed ground!

The old fort stood between the lake and the river on a little plateau whose rocky sides dropped down toward narrow stretches of marshy ground bordering the water on either hand. The plateau extended in widening angle and with gradually increasing elevation for some distance inland until it reached a certain point, where it sloped gradually in all directions to the valley reaching on either aide to the water level. The spot was not particularly well chosen for defence against a skilled enemy provided with artillery, although English, French, and Americans, in succession, with singular fatuity, clung to the location as a suitable one for a fort. Across the river to the southward rose a difficult but not inaccessible mountain called in that day Rattle Snake Mountain, and now known as Mount Defiance. The distance from this mountain to the plateau was inconsiderable, for a battery of cannon placed upon the crest would have commanded it with ease. In fact, Burgoyne forced the evacuation of Ticonderoga in 1777 by that very expedient.[3]

The surrounding country save where it was threaded by a few Indian trails was an impenetrable wilderness, rocky and mountainous in the extreme as well. The river connecting the two lakes ran through a series of wild and romantic rapids impracticable for boats. A portage road, bearing a relation to the river like that of a string to a bow, had been cut by the French from the foot of Lake George to the river near to its entrance upon Lake Champlain, a short distance beyond the in-

---

2. *Ethan Allen at Ticonderoga During the American War of Independence* by Ethan Allen also published by Leonaur.

3. See my book, *American Fights and Fighters*. Saratoga Campaign, (also published by Leonaur.)

land termination of the plateau. This road was about two miles long. The French defensive works had been erected at the Lake George end of it, and at the other end a saw mill was placed.

On the 5th of July, 1758, the English army, which had been slowly assembling at the head of Lake George, embarked in boats and proceeded down the lake. There were nine hundred *bateaux* and one hundred and thirty-five whale-boats. The army advanced in three divisions, the regulars in the centre, in their brilliant uniforms of scarlet, Rogers and his Rangers[4], and Gage with the light infantry—we have seen him before also with Braddock in the lead; the Colonials in their new blue uniforms were in two divisions on either flank.

Lake George is one of the most romantic and beautiful sheets of water on this or any other continent. The shores now rise in graceful undulations to some distant tree-clad lofty mountain peak, or fade away in some blue range of far-off hills; or again they spring in awe-inspiring altitude in sheer and precipitous cliffs above the water's edge. The sparkling surface of the lake is dotted with lovely islands, the luxuriant trees of which overhang the banks, making cool, inviting retreats, restful and refreshing to boatman and voyager.

Now, it is surrounded by the homes of the care-free, the pleasure-loving, the wealthy. Then the tree-clad hills were untenanted save by the scouting parties of different armies, or bands of haughty and ferocious Iroquois ranging the forest glades. The vast flotilla, the largest armed force which had collected on the continent, moved rapidly and in orderly precision down the lake. The flags fluttered in the bows of the boats, bands sent the echoes of martial music ringing across the water and among the hills. And the picture was delightful, or would have been, had there been any spectator to mark their progress.

2 THE END OF LORD HOWE

Montcalm was in a fearful state of uncertainty. He had with him but three thousand men of whom four hundred were Colonial regulars and Canadian militia. No re-enforcement could by any possibility reach him at that date except a little party of some five hundred men under de Levis, a soldier scarcely less able than Montcalm himself.

The French general was too good a soldier not to realize the possibilities of the situation. He knew that successfully to maintain his po-

---

4. *Journals of Robert Rogers of the Rangers, Journals of the Siege of Detroit* by Robert Rogers and *Ranger: the Adventurous life of Robert Rogers of the Rangers* by Allan Nevins all published by Leonaur.

sition at Fort Ticonderoga—which, by the way, the French called Fort Carillon, from what sweet chime of bells, I wonder? Some priestly call, perhaps! or was it from the music of the river rushing over the rocky rapids hard by?—was a military impossibility.

In the first place its fatal weakness lay in the fact that it was commanded by Mount Defiance, so that if the English planted guns there they would have the garrison at their mercy. There were but eight days' provisions in the fort for his men, too. Should Abercrombie regularly besiege him, he would be starved out in a week. If he remained where he was the English force was large enough to allow one half of it to invest the fort while the other half could march up to Five Mile Point, where the lake narrowed to easy musket-shot range, and cut his communications and prevent his retreat. Yet to retreat without striking a blow, would be virtually giving up the whole of Canada south of the St. Lawrence. It would mean the abandonment of every French post south and west of Montreal, including the lonely forts in the valleys of the Ohio and the distant Mississippi.

He could not make up his mind to go. It was a terrible dilemma; either going or staying seemed to presage destruction. It is evident from his movements that he was in a state of great indecision. What he hoped to accomplish with three thousand men against twenty-five thousand, which was the number his scouts accredited to Abercrombie, is not clear. Yet he stayed, perhaps with the feeling that it were better to fight, even if defeated, than give up everything without a struggle.

Some of his officers were for retreat, others suggested that an intrenchment might be thrown up on the crest of the plateau which extended from the river to the lake, forming the base of the triangle of which Ticonderoga was the apex, and that the English might be met there with some chance of success. That would not materially alter the situation, however; the works would still be commanded from Mount Defiance, no intrenchments they could make would be of any permanence, as they could easily be destroyed by artillery. They could be blocked, intercepted, and starved out as before. Still, there could be no harm in trying it. In fact there was nothing else to do, and if they intended to fight they would need the breastwork. Montcalm certainly intended to fight, so he sent the regiment Berri to begin the intrenchment. Leaving a small garrison in the fort proper, with the main body of his troops he took post at the saw mill on the river, sending a strong party under de Bourlamaque to cover the beginning of the portage.

190

On the 6th of July, he despatched Captains Lagny and Trapézec with three hundred men to pass around on the western side of the connecting river and feel for the English. Abercrombie had stopped to rest his men at Sabbath Day Point, twenty-five miles down the lake, and twelve miles from the outlet, on the evening of the 5th, resuming his advance about eleven at night so that the next morning the army approached the foot of the lake. The French post covering the portage thereupon destroyed the bridges crossing the river, abandoned and set fire to their works, and retreated to Montcalm's camp. On the morning of the 6th, the English army passing down beyond the sheer face of Rogers rock on the left, debarked on the western side of the river in some open ground bordering the shore. Arrangements for the march were completed by noon. It was determined to march around the river until they came in touch with Ticonderoga, which they would formally invest, and then bring up the artillery and force a surrender.

Rogers with his Rangers led the advance. Following him came the army in four parallel columns, with Lord Howe and Israel Putnam at the head of the right centre column, which was slightly in advance of the other three. The *bateaux*, boats, guns, supplies, etc., were left at the landing place. There were no roads through the woods, the Indian trail would scarcely suffice for a single file of men; the bewildered guides soon lost their way, and the four columns disappeared and became hopelessly lost in the forest, which was thick, trackless, and choked with undergrowth. The density of the wood even obscured sounds, and half a mile away a watcher would have been ignorant of the fact that some fifteen thousand men were buried in the wilderness. Even Lagny, an experienced woodsman, became confused after a time, and lost all sense of his whereabouts, but wandered aimlessly in the waste of trees until late in the afternoon the French suddenly came in touch with the right centre column.

Howe and Putnam were still in the lead. Both parties were greatly surprised. The French, however, were quicker to recover themselves than the English, and they poured in a smart fire. Lord Howe fell dead at the first discharge, with a bullet in his heart. For a few moments the French drove back the startled and disorganized English, who outnumbered them ten to one, but Rogers heard the sound of firing and turned toward it. He happened to be within convenient distance. His men plunged through the wood and burst out upon the flank of the Frenchmen. Of the three hundred, one hundred and fifty were cap-

SKETCH OF COUNTRY AROUND TICONDEROGA AND
SIEGE OF LOUISBURG.

tured, one hundred were killed, and but fifty got away. The English loss was inconsiderable in number, but the killing of Lord Howe was an incomparable disaster. As Parkman says, "the death of one man was the ruin of fifteen thousand." In spite of their success in the encounter, the noise of the smart engagement, as he heard the firing through the trees, filled Abercrombie with apprehension that Montcalm was upon them with his whole army. The advance was halted and he kept the troops under arms all night. Early in the morning he withdrew from the forest and led the army back to the landing place. Under the circumstances it was the proper thing to do, and possibly the only wise thing the unfortunate commander ever conceived or attempted.

Tired, hot, and disgusted, worn out with a sleepless night, saddened by the death of Howe, the army waited the next move. His prisoners told Abercrombie that the force of Montcalm amounted to six thousand men and that a re-enforcement of three thousand more was expected immediately. He determined, therefore, to move up the portage road which Bradstreet with his Colonials had reconnoitred and found deserted, and to attack Montcalm the next morning, the 8th. Bradstreet had done more than reconnoitre. He had rebuilt the burned bridges and the road was entirely practicable not only for soldiers, but for artillery as well. In his hurry to get at the enemy, however, before that expected re-enforcement appeared, Abercrombie determined to carry the French position by a *coup de main*. He pushed his troops up the road therefore, on the afternoon of the 7th, and occupied the deserted French camp near the saw mill in the evening.

3 ON THE HILL OF DEATH

Montcalm had on the evening of the 6th at last come to a decision. His previous experience had not given him any great amount of respect for the English commanders, and he resolved to hazard himself and his army upon the chance that the English general would turn out to be a fool! It was a dangerous risk, but in the end was justified. Had it not been for the death of Lord Howe he would have failed. When he did make up his mind he acted with his usual energy. He decided to await the English attack on the crest of the plateau.

He broke camp at the saw mill that night and returned to the plateau where the regiment Berri had begun the intrenchment. The lines were traced in zigzag shape, much as the old-fashioned rail fence—snake fence—was laid out. They ran completely around the crest in three fourths of a circle, open in the rear toward the fort. On the low ground on either flank of the breastwork, strong parties were to be posted with such cover as they could make, to prevent the flanks from being turned—much like the men at the rail fence at Bunker Hill.

The lines having been marked out, the regimental flags were planted upon them early on the morning of the 7th, and everybody in the army without respect to rank, axe in hand, set to work. The French officers, stripped to their shirts, laboured with the rest. Such was the ardour with which they toiled, that in one day they had completed a breastwork of logs eight feet high, piled upon each other in this zigzag fashion, so that every part of it could be enfiladed.

For a musket-shot distance from the hill the trees on every side were cut down and left lying with their branches pointing toward the direction of the British advance. In front of the intrenchment where the ground was clearer, a rough and ready but exceedingly dangerous abattis of trees and branches with sharpened points toward the enemy had been laid. Loop-holes—in some instances three rows—had been cut in the logs, which were topped with bags of sand and sods, and behind which a small *banquette* had been erected. Mounted upon the work were a few small pieces of artillery, mainly swivels. The intrenchment was impregnable to musketry, but half a battery of field guns could have knocked it to pieces in an hour.

Our hearts go out even in this day to that gallant little band of Frenchmen, cheerfully facing fearful odds, outnumbered actually five to one, and in their imaginations, eight to one, lying behind a breastwork which, while it was dreadfully dangerous to infantry, could have stood the fire of artillery for no time. With but eight days' provisions in their haversacks, in imminent danger of having their retreat cut off, their courage was superb. Like every great soldier, Montcalm inspired the devotion and won the courage of his troops. They looked to him, trusted him, and confidently awaited the battle. In their confidence he could not share, and it is probable that he never passed a more anxious night in his life.

About noon on the 8th the French caught the first glimpse of their foes. Solid masses of red appeared just out of gunshot on the edge of the timber. Interspersed among the British regiments and extending to the right and left were the blue-uniformed Provincials, the hunting shirts of the Rangers, and there in splendid force, the one thousand tartans of the Black Watch. The French were ready. They were drawn up in three lines behind the breastworks. A generous breakfast had been served to them, and every preparation long since made. Montcalm in his shirt sleeves, for the day was warm, had visited every part of his intrenchment, cheering and inspiriting his men as he well knew how, and charging them not to fire until he gave the word.

On the slopes of Mount Defiance, toward which, doubtless, many anxious glances must have been cast by the French officers, expecting every moment to hear the roar of guns from the crest sounding the death knell of their hopes, a large body of Iroquois, some four hundred in number, under Sir William Johnson, opened a scattering rifle fire which at that distance proved entirely ineffective. During the rest of the day the savages contented themselves with watching the ghastly storm of battle going on beneath their feet.

Abercrombie's plan consisted in making a direct attack upon the works. His artillery lay at the landing place, inactive and useless. A young subaltern of engineers, named Clerk, a man of no experience whatsoever, who had been but six months in the service, had examined the French work from Mount Defiance and had reported to Abercrombie that it could easily be carried. There is no evidence that Abercrombie himself had ever seen it. Other men of less military prestige but more experience thought differently, and John Stark made strenuous representations which were unheeded. Stark and Howe had been great friends. Stark tells how he and Howe lying upon the same blanket a few nights before, had discussed the situation of Ticonderoga, with which Stark was familiar. So confident was Abercrombie of capturing the French work out of hand, that he gave strict orders to his soldiers that they should not fire, but that they should carry everything with the bayonet!

About one o'clock the attack began. The British, their drums beating, marched out from the shelter of the trees cheering loudly and made for the fort in three columns. Immediately they found themselves entangled in the fallen trees. Scrambling, climbing, and pushing their way through the interlacing boughs, they got over the awful obstacle at last, and with lines now utterly disorganized made a rush forward over the stump-encumbered ground toward the abattis and the intrenchment.

The white flags were fluttering gracefully in the gentle breeze over the fort, but otherwise there was not a sign of life until the British advance had almost reached the abattis. At that instant, the enclosure gave forth a sheet of flame followed by the crash of musketry and the roar of cannon. The heads of the columns were literally swept away by the sudden discharge repeated again and again by the French, with cheers and cries of "*Vive le Roi! Vive notre Général!*" The swearing, cursing, startled, helpless Englishmen were driven back until they struggled into the timber again, where, entangled in the branches, many of them were killed by the steady stream of bullets and grapeshot.

Disregarding the order about confining the attack to the bayonet they at once opened a furious fire upon the French, but it was only when some rash whitecoat exposed himself that they were able to do any damage. The New England sharpshooters in the trees, however, did some good service, and many of the French, incautiously leaving their shelter, were picked off. Again the English and Provincials, with splendid courage rallied, formed up, and with head down charged, bull-like at that death-dealing enclosure. Some of them actually forced their way to the foot of the wall in spite of the abattis, but there they stopped, they could do no more.

With dauntless courage they assaulted no less than six times during the course of the afternoon. They tried it on the right flank against de Levis, who with his five hundred had arrived that morning; they tried it on the left flank under de Bourlamaque, and in both cases were beaten back.

After the first attempt word was sent back to Abercrombie, who remained at the sawmill, asking what they should do, and his reply was a reiteration of his foolish orders. They should charge forward and take it. That was all. And "with the blind obedience of faithful soldiers the maddened regiments hurled themselves again and again upon the French line. It was magnificent, but it was not war." The general did send some *bateaux*, which had been transported from Lake George, down the river in an attempt to get in the rear of the French intrench-ments, but when they reached the desired position they were within range of the guns of the fort, which opened fire, and after three of them had been sunk the rest retired.

4. The Last Charge of the Black Watch

Meanwhile the services of the Black Watch were concentrated for one final attempt upon the extreme right of the fort. It was late in the afternoon when these magnificent soldiers in solid column burst from the trees and made for the white flag. With a deathless heroism which foreshadowed the conduct of that other Highland regiment, the Ninety-third, at a similar English defeat before New Orleans, in 1815, the men of the Forty-second advanced, led by their dauntless major.

They struggle through the trees, they cross the clearing, they reach the abattis. The way of their advance is lined with fallen men, but with the greatest courage, even the wounded, lying upon the ground forget themselves and shriek out that the regiment must go on and leave them lying where they fall. Desperate to the point of recklessness they surmount the abattis, tear aside, cut it down, get over it in some fashion. Major Campbell is shot down here, but they press on nevertheless. They reach the wall of trees, spring upon it. Their bonneted heads peer down upon the enemy, some of them leap over. They are in at last. The French at the point of impact give way.

Truly, it was superb, but useless, unavailing. Another Campbell with some twenty officers and men got into the fort. The situation was critical. There was fighting all along the line. At the same time another column of the English made a final demonstration against other parts of the intrenchments. Montcalm ran to the spot in person. The regiment Berri was held in reserve. De Levis put himself at their head and they moved down upon the Scotsmen. Those in the fort, disdaining to beg for quarter, fought desperately, back against the wall, until they were bayoneted where they stood. Those upon the outside were hurled back and the regiment at last doggedly and sullenly retreated, followed by the cheers of the Frenchmen, after having given such an exhibition of magnificent courage as has not often been seen in the history of war. Over half of them had fallen.

They carried with them the helpless body of their dauntless major, who had been shot beneath the walls and was severely wounded. It was the last effort of the English. They could do no more in that method of attack.

The fighting was over. More than two thousand Englishmen lay still and silent or writhing and groaning from terrible wounds, on the slopes of that ghastly hill. Men in red, men in blue, men in hunting shirt, men in the dark tartan—all were there mingled in common and dreadful death. Horrible to relate, some of them had been shot as they leaped at the abattis and their bodies were hanging impaled on the stakes—and some were yet alive in that situation. On the French side, so furious had been the British attacks, that in spite of the shelter of the fortification, no less than four hundred had been killed or wounded, including de Levis slightly, and de Bourlamaque, severely.

This is what Montcalm said about his victory in a letter to his wife. He exaggerated the force of, and the casualties sustained by, the English, but that is pardonable in his excitement over the result of the battle. The truth was enough:

"Without Indians, almost without Canadians or colony troops—I had only four hundred—alone with de Levis and Bourlamaque and the troops of the line, thirty-one hundred fighting men, I have beaten an army of twenty-five thousand. They repassed the lake precipitously with a loss of at least five thousand. This glorious day does infinite honour to the valour of our battalions. I have no time to write more. I am well, my dearest, and I embrace you."

And to a friend he wrote: "Ah, my dear Doriel, what soldiers are ours! I never saw the like. Why were they not at Louisburg?" He forgot that James Wolfe—and not Abercrombie—was there!

The day after the battle he erected an immense cross of timber upon the field which bore the following Latin legend composed by himself—he was a scholar as well as a soldier, it would seem:

Quid dox? quid miles? quid strata ingentia ligna?
En signum! en victor! Deus hic, Deus ipse triumphat.

Parkman translates the lines as follows:

Soldiers and chief and rampart's strength are nought.
Behold the conquering Crosa! 'Tis God the triumph wrought.

And he adds Montcalm's own paraphrase:

Chrétien! ce ne fut point Montcalm et la prudence,
Ces arbres renversés, ces héros, leurs exploits.
Qui des Anglais confus ont brisé l'espérance,
C'est le bras de ton Dieu, vainqueur sur cette croix.

So there you have the triumph celebrated in three languages.

The elation of the French at their tremendous victory can scarcely be imagined. They were, however, in a critical situation. Amherst had thirteen thousand men yet available and all his artillery. He might bring it up on the morrow and resume the battle, which would probably have a different termination. They expected he would do it. So did everyone else. Fortunately for the French, however, he did nothing of the kind. Imagining that the six thousand he supposed to have manned the intrenchments would be augmented by the three thousand which he had heard were coming, he broke camp the next morning and fled down the lake with all speed, abandoning valuable supplies and stores of all kinds in his possession!

The attempt to pierce the centre had failed lamentably, and in that failure the English had sustained prodigious loss. Cape Breton had fallen, and so, too, would Fort Du Quesne, but Montcalm and his veterans still held the heart of the continent, and it needed the grim wager of battle on the stern shore of St. Lawrence about Cape Diamond and Quebec before it should be determined who should master this half of the world. It was most fitting that the final arbitrament should be tried out by the two great captains in whose proud record of victories shone the names of Louisburg and Ticonderoga.

We scarcely know whether to marvel more at the audacity of Montcalm, the stubborn courage of his men, the stupidity of Abercrombie, or the magnificent hardihood of the soldiers he led. The battle was a shameful one, but the shame was with the general. The soldiers on that day had shown themselves to be worthy of the highest praise.

Nothing succeeds like success, of course, and the end seems tcl have justified Montcalm's acceptance of the desperate chance, but it is hard to conceive that any other man in the world would have so stupidly played into the hands of the French as the English commander had. Even after he was beaten the first time, there was no reason why he should not have resumed the campaign upon one of the practicable plans of which Lord Howe would have been prompt to avail himself.

5, The Legend of Inverawe

Almost every man who has told the story of this forgotten battle has mentioned a wild Scottish legend concerning the unfortunate commander of the Black Watch. Major Campbell was taken to Fort Edward with the rest of the army. His arm, which had been badly shattered, was in such a condition that it was necessary to amputate it at once and he died from the operation.

In the traditions of the Campbells there is a story that years before, when this same Duncan Campbell was alone in his castle at Inverawe one tempestuous night, a man in the direst extremity, panting with fatigue, almost exhausted, having been pursued nearly to death, appealed to him for hospitality and shelter, stating that he had killed a man and the avengers of blood were close on his track.

With romantic chivalry the Laird of Inverawe, as he was called after his castle, promised him protection and a safe hiding place, and at the earnest request of the stranger took oath upon the hilt of his dirk to hold him inviolate. He had scarcely concealed him when the pursuers burst upon the scene and informed Inverawe that they were seeking the murderer of his cousin—Donald Campbell! Bound by his oath and by his stern ideas of hospitality, Inverawe declared that he knew nothing of the man. That night, however, so the story goes, the ghastly figure of his murdered kinsman appeared at his bedside. From his blood-boltered lips fell in hollow tones these words:

"Inverawe, Inverawe, blood has been shed! Shield not the murderer!"

When day broke Campbell repaired to the place of concealment which he had allotted the stranger and, telling him of his dreadful night, ordered him to leave at once, as he could afford him protection no longer.

"You have sworn to do so upon your dirk," said the man, refusing to leave his shelter, and invoking the laws of hospitality of the wild age and people.

Finally Inverawe, who was naturally greatly perturbed by the deceit which had been practised upon him and the message of his ghostly visitor, induced the murderer to repair to a cave in a neighbouring mountain, where he left him, with a renewed promise that he would not betray him. His rest that night was broken again by the dread apparition and the same fearful words were rung in his ear. He could stand it no longer. In the morning he hastened to the cave, determined to warn him to go, or he would give him up, but the stranger was already gone. That night the spirit appeared once more, but with a different message, sufficiently fearful but less terrible than before:

"Farewell, Inverawe, farewell, until we meet at TICONDEROGA!"

After that night it returned no more. At that time it is probable that neither Campbell nor any other British officer had ever heard of Ticonderoga, but the mysterious aggregation of melodious syllables dwelt in his mind and he often recurred to it. Long afterward he joined the Black Watch, and in time became its major.

He had never forgotten the story, which he often told to the other officers. His horror, therefore, can be imagined, when he learned that his regiment was destined to attack Ticonderoga! A settled melancholy took possession of him. Before the day of the battle his officers entered into a little conspiracy and they met to assure him that the place they were about to attack was not Ticonderoga, but Fort Carillon, and that Ticonderoga lay further up the lake. They succeeded in reassuring him somewhat, but on the morning of the battle, he made them the startling statement that he had seen the apparition once again and it had uttered these fatal words:

"*This is TICONDEROGA!*"[5]

"I shall die today," he said to his officers, as he told the tale.

When he led the heroic advance of the Black Watch in the last effort to break the French line, therefore, he did it with the blind fatalism of a man who is conscious that he is marked for death and in that consciousness goes forward without fear and without hesitation. And to this splendid exhibition of reckless intrepidity on his part may have been due the partial success of the terrific attack.

He sleeps near Fort Edward near the scene of the fulfilment of the prophecy. His son. Lieutenant Alexander Campbell, of the same regiment, participated in the battle and was also severely wounded but survived. He, too, has left on record marvellous tales of the warnings of death which appeared to the ladies of the Campbells at Inverawe, on the day when the Laird of the castle fell before the gory abattis on that awful hill across the sea.

There are more things in heaven and earth, Horatio,
Than are dreamt of in your philosophy.

---

5. Indian name "*Cheonderoga*," which in the Iroquois tongue signifies "Sounding Water."

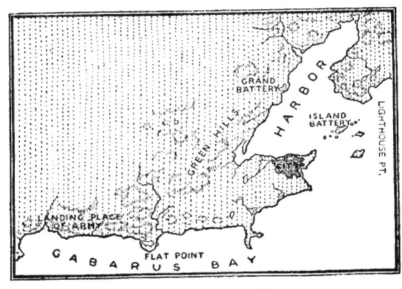

MAP OF LOUISBURG, 1758.
(See also map on page 192.)

5

Before Louisburg Again

When we left Louisburg thirteen years ago, in 1745, the flag of England flaunted in triumph over its half ruined walls while the hardy colonists under stout William Pepperrell, their drums beating gayly, marched through the battered gates. Yet on this 1st of June, 1758, the strong eastern wind sweeping in unimpeded course across one thousand leagues of Atlantic seas, whipped out from the end of the lofty staff the lilied banner of France! All the labours, sacrifices, hardships, gallantries and pleasant humours of the New Englanders had come to naught; for, when the peace of Aix-la-Chapelle terminated King George's War, by subtle and persistent diplomacy the French managed to have the fortress at Louisburg returned to them. And on the day mentioned it stood in the possession of its original owners, more formidable and menacing to England and her colonies than ever.

The old works had been repaired and strengthened at an expense of more than a million pounds sterling. It was amply garrisoned by four thousand men, the greater part of whom were French regular soldiery. Nearly two hundred and forty cannon and mortars were mounted upon the walls and outworks. The Island battery where the English had met such a disastrous repulse, had been strengthened and was now heavily armed. Within the spacious harbour five splendid ships-of-the-line, a fifty-gun ship, and six saucy frigates, mounting nearly six hundred guns, swung at their anchors. Admiral Desgouttes and is three thousand seamen constituted a formidable auxiliary to the defence. The whole was under the charge of the Chevalier de Drucour, a veteran and experienced soldier of much skill and proven courage. He was not to be caught napping as the unlucky Du Chambon had been years before, and every practicable landing place was lined with intrenchments and batteries.

At intervals during the stormy months of spring, out of the mist, and fog, and rain, and the tempests that beat almost incessantly upon the dangerous rock-bound shores a little squadron of English ships varying in size, but high in quality, could be seen beating to and fro across the entrance to the harbour where the huge rollers seethed and foamed over the reefs, endeavouring to maintain a blockade. They were not very successful in their efforts; conditions were against them, and the force was too small, so the French ran in and out at will, hence the presence of the men-of-war in the harbour. Indeed even after the arrival of the great English fleet, *Le Bizarre*, 64, and *La Comete*, 30, as we shall see later on, succeeded in getting away on the 8th of June, while the attempt at landing was being made. Practical freedom of access being thus assured the fortress was fully provided for a siege, and de Drucour awaited with confidence the expected attack.

It was not long in coming. When the French awoke on the second day of June, they were astonished at the sight which greeted their eyes in Gabarus Bay, south of the town. No less than one hundred and fifty-seven ships lay straining at their anchors. Twenty-three of these were ships-of-the-line, eighteen were frigates, and the rest were transports. From the masthead of the *Namur*, 90, flew the flag of stout old Admiral Edward Boscawen, the naval commander of the expedition; old "Dreadnought," or "Wrynecked Dick," as he was indifferently called by the sailors, had Royal Stuart blood in his veins, but in despite of that he was a gallant officer and a splendid sailor.

On the transports were some twelve thousand troops; there were Highlanders, Provincial Rangers, two battalions of Royal Americans, and a regiment of light infantry, batteries of skilled artillerists to man a train of one hundred and forty guns of various calibres, while grenadiers, engineers, and troops o{ the line made up the rest. This land force was under the command of Major General Jeffrey Amherst, who had for his brigadiers, Lawrence, Whitmore, and James Wolfe, his first entry upon the pages of American history.

Hazardous indeed was the undertaking, desperate the problem before the soldiers and sailors. The officers searched with their glasses the desolate, storm-beaten shore, or rowed along its granite face in boats, and could find but three practicable places at which a landing could be effected. Further reconnoissance discovered the fact that each of these points was covered by strong fortifications and apparently heav-

WASHINGTON AT BRADDOCK'S DEFEAT ON THE MONONGAHELA,
AND THE DEATH OF BRADDOCK.

CUTTING OUT OF LE PRUDENT AND LE BIENFAISANT

ily garrisoned. Discouraging indeed was the prospect. They had arrived off Cape Breton Island *via* Halifax, after a long and tedious passage across the ocean, and now within sight of their goal the obstacles before them appeared well-nigh insuperable.

What would the admiral decide upon? The determination of course, was left entirely to him. The troops could not disembark without the aid of the sailors who were entirely under his orders. It was an anxious time indeed for Amherst and his young brigadiers and for Boscawen as well. What should he do in this emergency? Should he hold a council of war and be governed by its conclusion? Then good-by to any hope of aggressive action. He was pressed to do this by numbers of his captains and the decision would inevitably have been to abandon the attempt and retire.

Councils of war had ruined the career of many officers and the fate of Admiral John Byng, who had been shot on the quarter-deck of his own flagship the previous year, for not fighting—it was alleged—as valiantly and successfully as he might, and should have done, was still fresh in the minds of everyone. An old Scottish sea officer named Ferguson, the captain of the *Prince of Orange*, 60, turned the scale. What little things, sometimes scarcely noticed, more often unknown, determine great events! The sturdy representations of the brave old seaman who advised Boscawen to hold no council, and to land the troops or to make a desperate endeavour to do so, at last prevailed, and the admiral announced his determination to do what he had come so far to do.

2. The Landing in the Surf

It was resolved after consultation between Amherst and his generals, that three brigades of the army should be embarked in three divisions under the command of the three brigadier generals, that the divisions of Lawrence and Whitmore should make a feint at landing at those two of the available points nearest the fortress, but that the real landing should be made by the left division under Wolfe, and the point where the attempt was to be made was a little bay called by the French *Le Coromandière*, by the English Fresh Water Cove. The beach here was crescent shaped for about a quarter of a mile with rocky cliffs at each end.

The place was as strongly fortified and as formidable as the rest; and, as they afterward learned, was garrisoned by nearly a thousand men, under the command of Lieutenant Colonel de St. Julien. But it was the most practicable of access, apparently. The defensive works were on a bluff about fifteen feet above the sea level and were composed of trees and earth, protected by a rough abattis of felled trees and mounting several small pieces of artillery planted to sweep the beach, and hidden by evergreens stuck in the ground in front of them.

A further distraction to the enemy was afforded by another feint of landing a regiment far to the northward of the town near a place called Lorembec, beyond Lighthouse Point. Preparations having been speedily concluded they awaited a favourable moment for the attack. Dense fogs and fierce gales prevailed, however, for a week, during which the frigate *Trent* was lost, and it was not until the 8th of June that the weather permitted them to essay their task. During the night the men embarked in the boats of the fleets the frigates were sent in shore, and anchored as close to the cliffs as they dared. When day broke with every gun that bore they opened a furious cannonade upon the French, while the larger ships moved up opposite Louisburg proper and with their heavy guns engaged the fortress as they could.

Such a roar of artillery woke the solitudes as had never been heard before in the western hemisphere. Under the cover of this furious fire, to which the French made spirited reply, the three divisions of boats dashed toward the shore. As Wolfe's brigade drew near Fresh Water Cove, they were for a time unmolested, but when they got within close range the French suddenly opened fire upon them. The sea was still rough and only the uncertain motion of the boats, tossing about in the huge waves, which disconcerted the aim of the gunners, prevented them from being sunk. The flagstaff of Wolfe's boat was cut down and several men were hit. As soon as the flotilla of boats got into calmer water nearer the shore, they would be cut to pieces. After scanning the position Wolfe reluctantly decided to give over the attempt at that time. The difficulty may be inferred from that decision. He signalled the other boats of his flotilla therefore, to retire. On account of the loss of his flagstaff Wolfe gave the signal with his hand.

Three boat loads of light infantry on the extreme right commanded by Lieutenants Hopkins and Brown and Ensign Grant, either did not understand him or deliberately disregarded his signal. These officers thought they had found a practicable landing place under the shelter of the cliffs which, so long as they remained on the beach, would protect them from the fire of the enemy. Taking not only their lives but their reputations in hand, they dashed at it. If their observations were erroneous, and their deductions false, they would be court-martialed and shot.

They were all right, however. It was a difficult and dangerous place to debark an army, but they succeeded in getting ashore. They were followed by Major Scott, who commanded the light infantry, and the Rangers. His boat was stove but he sprang ashore and with ten men at once clambered up the cliff. At the first volley five were shot down, but the rest took cover and each moment added to their number, as the men from the other three boats followed Scott's example. Wolfe marked their success, countermanded his orders and headed his own boat for the same spot. In his eagerness he leaped into the water as soon as the depth permitted and, with a small cane in his hand, led his soldiers forward. The men as fast as they landed scrambled up the cliffs and at once found themselves in hot action with the French.

Boat after boat was wrecked on the beach as they dashed at it and many of the soldiers were drowned and the powder of the rest was rendered useless. The French opened fire upon the English as fast as they appeared, but under the shelter of the trees Wolfe at last got them formed up for a solid attack. With fixed bayonets they made for the French. There was a fierce discharge at them which did not stop them, and then followed a brief *mêlée* in which something like one hundred and fifty of the French were killed and wounded, when the rest were driven from their intrenchments.

The divisions of Lawrence and Whitmore were now making a landing where Wolfe had succeeded in gaining a foothold. The boats of the fleet with the rest of the army were also putting for the shore. The French colonel reasoned that unless he made good his escape when he had opportunity, the English would interpose between him and Louisburg and cut him off, so he fled up the coast at full speed with his men, abandoning the several batteries which had been erected.

They were hotly pursued by Wolfe at the head of his light infantry, a corps of men whom he had specially trained after notions of his own, which were then thought fantastic, but which are now accepted by military authorities of all nations. They were lightly equipped but formidably armed, were taught to move in open order and to take advantage of every possible cover in advance or retreat. The heavy massed line of battle was not for them. All useless articles of baggage, uniform, and equipment were discarded.

Meantime during all that day the boats of the ships continued landing the soldiers. Although more than one hundred boats were smashed in the breakers and on the rocks, the total loss of the English in killed and wounded and drowned in this brilliant feat of arms was scarcely more than one hundred. The pursuit of the flying French continued until Wolfe came within range of the guns of Louisburg. Amherst now came on shore and assumed direction of the operations. A siege was regularly begun.

3. The Fortress Beleaguered

In front of the line of works extending across the peninsula from the ocean to the bay and forming the base of the triangle enclosing the town, lay a huge impassable morass. Louisburg was approachable, however, on firm ground from either flank, by the seashore or inland. The English steadily advanced their batteries nearer the town with each succeeding day. The Grand battery which lay opposite the mouth of the harbour had been burned and abandoned by de Drucour as soon as the English landed. The French ships were moved across the bay and anchored under the protection of the walls.

Admiral Desgouttes had pleaded that he might be allowed to leave the harbour and escape while he could, but de Drucour desired the services of the ships and men and had refused to permit him, which was a tactical blunder. The ships were too few to fight Boscawen's great fleet. They could not materially aid in the defence of the city and they had to be protected from the British attack, therefore their presence was a source of weakness, although their crews were most useful in the siege. If by any means the city were captured, the ships would be lost too. All this was pointed out to de Drucour, but to no avail. The ships therefore joined with the batteries of the town in returning the fire of the English.

One vessel especially, the frigate *Aréthuse*, placed in the land-locked basin, or inner harbour, called Le Barachois, from her position was enabled to enfilade the English batteries. She was in charge of Captain Vauquelin, a brave and successful officer. The English at last succeeded in planting a battery which commanded her and they riddled her with shot, but she pluckily stuck to her station until near the end of the siege. Two of the frigates which attempted to get away were captured, after hot engagements, by British frigates outside.

By Amherst's direction, on the 12th of June, Wolfe took his light infantry the circuit of the harbour and erected a powerful battery on Lighthouse Point, with which he succeeded in silencing the Island battery. There was nothing now that would prevent the British from sailing into the harbour. Therefore, Desgouttes and de Drucour determined to block it up. They sank the fifty-gun ship, and the two remaining frigates in the mouth of the harbour; and then, withdrawing the *Aréthuse* from her untenable position, they patched her up, waited for a dark night and towed her through the obstructions and sent her to France, which she safely reached bearing an appeal for help—too late.

Meanwhile the indefatigable English batteries were regularly approaching nearer the walls of the town, the men actually making solid ground with fascines and earth in the marsh, upon which to mount their guns. On the night of the 6th of July the French made a sally which was repulsed with severe loss to them and but little to the English. De Drucour made a second and more determined effort to dislodge the steadily approaching enemy. On the night of the 9th of July he sent out one thousand picked men who fell upon the light infantry like a storm. The English were driven back from the first line of intrenchments and the probability of a serious repulse was imminent when Wolfe himself appeared on the scene, reanimated his men, led a charge against the French, and after some severe hand to hand fighting, drove them back, disheartened and defeated.

Wolfe's men on the 16th of July succeeded in occupying a hill called Gallows Hill, the place of execution, within three hundred feet of the Dauphin's Bastion, erecting a battery thereon which did no little execution.

The fire of the English batteries, in which the ships participated whenever the weather permitted, was simply appalling. They rained shot and shell on the devoted town. Every building of wood, including the barracks, was consumed by fire, and the chief storehouses and other buildings of stone were battered into hopeless ruins. There were many fishermen and women and children within the walls who were left houseless, and forced to seek shelter of the casemates and bomb proofs.

Madame de Drucour, the wife of the governor, proved herself a heroine indeed; daily appearing with her husband on the ramparts and encouraging the soldiers by sometimes firing the guns with her own fair hand. More and more guns were landed from the ships, some of them manned by sailors. Nearer and nearer the English approached to the works and the pounding the walls got was terrific.

The walls presently began to succumb to the tremendous battering they were receiving. Unfortunately, as is often the case with national contracts, some of them had not been completed and much of the work had been badly done; in their need the French had eked out the wanting masonry with fascines. Great gaps appeared here and there, cannon after cannon was dismounted, the citadel was laid in ruins, but still the besieged held out heroically.

4. Destruction of the Fleet

On the night of the 21st of July, however, they met with a great catastrophe. A bomb shell fell upon the deck of *Le Célèbre*, 64, and set her on fire. In spite of the efforts of her depleted crew—most of her complement being ashore in the batteries—she burned furiously and breaking from her moorings at last drifted down upon *L'Entreprenante*, 74, and then fell foul of *Le Capricieux*, 64. They both caught fire from the first one; the English turned their guns upon them, and the three devoted ships, a mass of flame, their guns firing in every direction, finally drifted ashore and burned to the water's edge, or blew up with tremendous explosions.

This left but two ships of the line out of the twelve vessels which had originally found refuge in the harbour, and their fate was soon determined. Boscawen arranged to destroy them by a boat attack. Commanders Laforey and Balfour were placed in charge of six hundred British seamen in forty boats. There were no troops or marines concerned in the enterprise. Two boats from each ship, manned by their regular crews heavily armed with cutlasses, pistols, pole-axes, and muskets and bayonets, with a lieutenant aft and a midshipman forward, were detailed to make this attack. It was a picked force and nobly did it carry out the undertaking.

A little after midnight on the morning of the 26th of July, the boats got under way. It was a dark, foggy night well suited to their undertaking. With muffled oars and in perfect silence, they stole past the watchers on the Island battery and entered the harbour. As they had started from the ships a signal from the *Namur* had been given and the English had at once engaged the town.

Under the roar of the furious cannonade the boats succeeded in getting into the basin absolutely unnoticed. They rowed in as far as the Grand battery, so as to be able to approach the ships from the landward side, from which an attack would scarcely be expected. Separating in two divisions, Captain Laforey, with three hundred men dashed at *Le Prudent*, 74, which was nearest the shore. Commander Balfour, with a like force, made for *Le Bienfaisant*, 64.

The attack had been beautifully planned. The boats of the two flotillas deliberately circled about the devoted ships to reach their appointed stations. A sentry on each finally gave the alarm, but the small French crews on board had scarcely time to tumble out of their hammocks and seize their arms, before the English were upon them. They boarded over the bows, through the gangways, upon the quarters, in fact from every side, with loud cheers, and immediately fell to work. There was a brief, fierce *mêlée* upon each ship, and the English were in possession.

It was graying toward morning by this time and the noise and confusion of the attack apprised the garrison within the town, a short distance away, of what was taking place. They sprang to the guns of the water batteries and opened a heavy fire upon the captured ships, which cut them up severely. The English were too busy to make any reply. The tide was at low ebb. Laforey found that *Le Prudent* was aground. It was impossible to lighten her to bring her off, so he set her on fire. He and his men remained on the ship until she was burning hopelessly, then, after releasing and disarming the French prisoners, giving them their own boats and a schooner, lying alongside, with which to get ashore, the English abandoned her. They got into their boats and rowed over to *Le Bienfaisant*. By hard work Balfour's party had got their ship afloat, and the two boat divisions deliberately towed her out of range of the batteries under a tremendous fire, and anchored her safely under the lee of the Lighthouse battery that Wolfe had established to the north of the harbour.

It was a splendid feat of arms and at daybreak the hearts of the besieged weakened. Boscawen immediately prepared to enter the now defenceless harbour with six of his ships. The garrison was worn out. The sick and wounded were exposed to a continuous fire. No part of the works was safe from the guns of the enemy. Nearly two thousand men were incapacitated by wounds or illness, and upward of a thousand had been killed. The casemates were filled with terrified women and children. The English batteries had successfully breached the walls. The guns opposite the English army, with the exception of three or four, had been dismounted and put out of action. The citadel was a hopeless ruin. De Drucour had made a gallant defence. He could do no more. By the advice of his officers he sent out a flag asking for terms.

He thought at least that his splendid defence would entitle him to march his garrison out with the honours of war, and he made such a proposition. But Amherst was no sentimental soldier, neither was Boscawen. Their answer to the governor's proposition was a demand for an instant and unconditional surrender, under threat of an immediate assault in force. De Drucour and his officers indignantly rejected these terms and declared themselves willing to endure an assault rather than surrender the town under such circumstances.

A messenger was sent carrying their rejection to Amherst, but as soon as the rejection became known to the inhabitants of the town, numbering about four thousand, they crowded around the governor and his staff with such pleas and representations, such lamentations as to their certain fate, and the fate of the women and children, that they at last moved him to surrender unconditionally.

Another messenger was despatched post-haste to recall the rejection, which fortunately for the French, had not yet been delivered. Poor de Drucour signed the capitulation at midnight of the 27th, and on the morning General Whitmore marched in and took possession. The French soldiers threw down their arms before him with tears of mortification and gestures of rage; the white banner was again hauled down and for the second time the Gibraltar of America passed under the English flag. It stayed there as long as it had any existence. The French power was forever driven from the Atlantic seaboard.

The English loss in killed and wounded had been a little over five hundred. De Drucour surrendered about fifty-six hundred soldiers, sailors and marines.

This was one of the most successful feats of arms in the war. Its success was made possible by the hearty cooperation between Boscawen and Amherst, and the patient perseverance of the latter, but above all by the dashing audacity, sound judgement, and brilliant military genius of James Wolfe.

"He is mad," said one of the incapables about the person of the king, when he read of Wolfe's daring tactics, his wonderful innovations.

"Mad is he?" growled the old king, with a vivid memory of some of his cocked-hatted failures, "then I only hope he'll bite some of my generals!"

Among the officers in Wolfe's brigade who was fore- most in all the exploits and undertakings of the siege, was a young ensign, who was promoted to a lieutenancy by that general himself for conspicuous courage and gallantry. His name was Richard Montgomery, a man whose career in the American Revolution was as brief as his fame was great. He was destined to die years after under the walls of Quebec, fighting against the very flag to which, in this campaign, he had given such ungrudging and brilliant devotion.

6

The Fall of Quebec

Come, each death-doing dog who dares venture his neck,
Come, follow the hero that goes to Quebec;
Jump aboard of the transports, and loose every sail.
Pay your debts at the tavern by giving leg-bail;
And ye that love lighting shall soon have enough:
Wolfe commands us, my boys; we shall give them Hot Stuff. [1]

1. THE STAKE, THE GAME, AND THE PLAYERS

On the 29th of February, 171 2, when Louis XIV, old, broken, and defeated, was closing his long reign, a little boy was born in the south of France. Fifteen years later, on the 2nd of January, 1727, another lad saw the light in the England of George the First. Born under different governmental systems and springing from different "racial stocks, standing for different ideas, the lives of these two children were destined to be strangely intermingled. They were to be the chief factors in a great contest in which the stakes were a future empire the like of which the world had not seen. They were to play their great game upon a theatre of unparalleled magnificence and before an audience which comprised the world.

There were circumstances of great dramatic interest in the career of both, and in the end each laid down his life in defence of his principles on the same bloodstained field. The Frenchman was the son of a great nobleman; the Englishman, a child of the sturdy middle class. Both were soldiers. There were brave days for soldiers then, and both of them saw much hard fighting and arduous campaigning. Both had risen rapidly, and both had been chosen for positions of importance

---

1. These words are from a contemporary song; they prove, for one thing, the antiquity of the supposedly modern phrase "Hot Stuff."

which they had neither sought nor desired, but which both had accepted from the very highest sense of duty and love of country.

As we have just seen, Montcalm had signally demonstrated his capacity by inflicting upon the English an overwhelming defeat in the pine woods of Ticonderoga, and Wolfe had shown his ability at the siege of Louisburg. They were now to be matched in a struggle for a point more vital than the fortress in the pine-clad hills or that on the iron-bound coast of Cape Breton. The rifle shots of the Virginians under George Washington in the forest glades of western Pennsylvania, which struck down young Jumonville, had kindled a conflagration of war which had swept like a besom of destruction from the St. Lawrence to the Ganges, and which had involved every power in the world in a gigantic struggle—England, Prussia, and the American Colonies *contra mundum!* On the icy plains of Russia, 'neath the shadows cast by the Himalayas, and in the forests primeval of the New World the conflict raged.

On this continent two great ideas had stood at sword's point with each other from the landing of the Pilgrims and the voyage of Cartier. In a thin strip upon the Atlantic seaboard from the Penobscot to St. Augustine, the beginning of a government "*of the people, by the people, and for the people*" had been established; and a nation, frugal and industrious, hardy and bold, was in the travail pains of existence. The several English colonies embraced a population of over a million souls. On the back of the continent, with one hand on the great river of the north, the other clutching the great river of the south, lay the power of France, a country still the most formidable in the great family of nations. A thin chain of military posts dotted along the two rivers and the great lakes represented the barrier by which the advocates of the feudal system—decaying in France, but which it was hoped might be revived in America—strove to hold back the inundation of men already beginning to break upon the mountain chains of what was then the West.

Though the province had been most assiduously fostered by the crown, the number of inhabitants in New France did not exceed, at the very highest estimate, seventy thousand; but every male in the population was liable for military service, and the *seignors* of the villages and rude chateaux and the officers of the posts were men of high stamp, bearing some of the noblest names of France. In war they could bring to their assistance hordes of ruthless savages, who, under the teaching of the Jesuits, had added to their natural vindictiveness and ferocity the machinery of the warfare of the time. There were, in addition to the population, some five thousand regular soldiers in the country, battalions of picked men from some of the finest regiments of the incomparable French infantry. Therefore, while the odds against the French were heavy, their case was not desperate.

Various disjointed attempts had been made at different points during the Seven Years' War, but after the reduction of Louisburg in 1758, Pitt determined to attack New France at every available point at once, making use of his great numerical superiority and command of the sea for that purpose. Amherst was to move up Lake Champlain, Prideaux and Sir William Johnson were to attack Fort Niagara, Stanwix was to sweep the posts on Lake Erie, and Forbes, with Washington, was to effect the reduction of Fort Du Quesne. The main expedition was directed against Quebec itself, and comprised twenty-two ships of the line, with accompanying frigates and transports, under the command of Vice Admiral Saunders, convoying nine thousand men under James Wolfe.

The genius of Pitt had led him to select this young man from hundreds of others his seniors in rank—an unprecedented proceeding, by the way—and he had given him the temporary rank of major general for the American campaign. His force, consisting of English and Provincial troops, all regulars, was one of the best that had ever been assembled under the British flag. Wolfe's brigadiers, Monckton, Townshend, and Murray, were also young and capable soldiers. The army was officered by young men. Pitt's idea was that an army was to win battles and campaigns, and not to become a plaything for incompetent officers who possessed nothing but rank.

On the 21st of June, the expedition anchored off the Isle of Orleans, a few miles below Quebec, in the noble river St. Lawrence. Leaving the different garrisons along the frontier to defend themselves as best they might, Montcalm had concentrated his army at Quebec. He had under his command a force probably of fourteen thousand men, of which not more than four thousand were regulars. Of the balance, some were Canadian militia, and the larger number partisans, Indians and undisciplined peasants.

The city he had elected to defend commanded the St. Lawrence, the great way of communication through the country. Its site was one of the most magnificent on the continent, if not in the world. "Que Bec!" had exclaimed the rough sailor of Dieppe in 1535, when he first caught sight of the rock of Cape Diamond, towering for over three

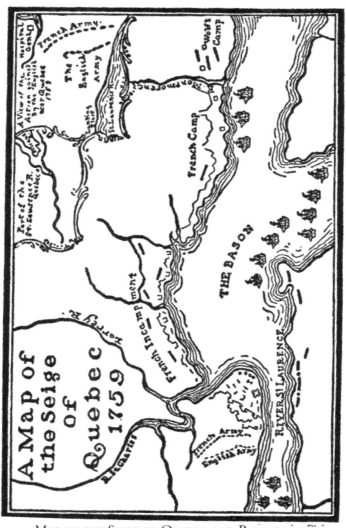

Map of the Siege of Quebec and Plan of the
Battle on the Plains of Abraham

hundred feet in the air, overlooking the deep land-locked basin which made the magnificent harbour. Upon the crest of this tremendous mass of granite which stands almost perpendicular to the river had been erected a fortress. Toward the north the rock sloped gently down until it was broken by a rugged plateau half way to the water's edge, and upon it stood a walled town containing the Cathedral, the Laval University, the Ursuline Convent, and the Chateau St. Louis, the residence of the governor. Still farther down on the strand was the lower town, bounded on the north by the river St. Charles.

Along the banks of the St. Lawrence for seven miles to the northward straggled the villages of Charlesbourg and Beauport. The St. Charles emptied into the St. Lawrence through a broad expanse of mud flats almost impassable at low tide and guarded by heavy fortifications at high water, together with a barrier and two floating batteries. These fortifications were continued for seven miles along the edge of the bluffs of Beauport, and terminated on the deep gorge of the rapid and practically unfordable Montmorency River, which, just before it reaches the St. Lawrence, leaps down the cliffs in a sheer fall of two hundred and fifty feet, in a glorious and beautiful cataract. Beyond the citadel on the southern side of the city for eight miles there was a continuation of the plateau. The tableland terminated on the river coast in sheer and precipitous rocks overgrown here and there by stunted patches of trees and shrubbery. On the south, at Cap-Rouge, it was protected by another gorge and river, and on the other side by rocky and impracticable slopes to the valley of the Charles. One or two places where the cliffs could be scaled were guarded, though their existence was unknown to the English.

Montcalm, after properly garrisoning the town, wisely chose to await attack in the intrenchments at Beauport. But the situation on the French side was not pleasant. The governor of New France, Philippe de Rigaud, Marquis de Vaudreuil, a captain in the French navy, was a jealous incompetent. No sort of harmony existed between him and Lieutenant General Montcalm. The general administration of affairs was under de Vaudreuil, while Montcalm was supreme as to military matters, with the limitations of power not well defined between them. To further complicate matters, finance and trade were controlled by François Bigot, one of the most consummate thieves and scoundrels who ever lived. The administration of internal affairs was thoroughly corrupt. The king was robbed on the one hand, the people on the other. While the people starved, and the army lived on half rations, de

Vaudreuil and Bigot and their satellites rioted in luxury on the plunder of their country.

Montcalm, a stern and simple soldier, struggled vainly against this state of affairs, but he was without power except so far as military matters were concerned. Before the expedition of Wolfe had arrived, realizing the importance of the possession of Quebec, he had sent his lieutenant, Bougainville, afterward the celebrated circumnavigator, to France to beg aid. The king, busy with his Pompadour and his *Parc aux Cerfs* and other similar matters of state, had sent him a promotion, a star, some four hundred men, and some scanty supplies, with instructions to hold on to the province at all hazards! "A little is precious to those who have nothing," sadly remarked Montcalm, when Bougainville exhibited the results of his labours. He said that he would save the colony or die in it. The words meant much from him.

The gallant little marquis was a domestic man, and was ever sighing for the advent of that day when he might return to France to his beloved country-seat at Candiac and pass his days in peace in the society of his wife and children. Bougainville had brought him word of the death of one of his children, which had been reported just before the ship sailed, and the poor man never found out which child had been taken from him until he met her in heaven. His letters to his wife and mother, read today, after a century and a half of silence, still touch the heart with their tenderness and love.

2. The Repulse on the Montmorency

The problem that met Wolfe was one of the most gigantic with which the human mind had ever grappled, and how to compass it he knew not. As a preliminary to the enterprise, however, he captured the Isle of Orleans and the heights of Levis, a bold promontory opposite the city. On the latter, he erected batteries, which, by vigorous bombardments soon reduced the lower town to ruins, though neither from the batteries nor the ships was he able to secure sufficient elevation to throw shells into the upper town, much less the citadel. For offensive purposes his ships were more or less useless, for the water was shallow on the Beauport shore and the batteries were so placed that they could fire upon the ships with impunity. But they lent mobility to his force, which doubled its effectiveness and signally illustrated the advantage of sea command in warfare.

Wolfe's first attempt was to land his men on the north bank of the Montmorency River and then try to find some way through the dense virgin forests to cross the river and turn Montcalm's left. The condition of the country made this impossible. There was but one doubtful ford, which was guarded. One of Wolfe's advance parties was badly handled by the French and Indians. The open season in the latitude of Quebec lasts but a few months and the whole army, working during the whole time, could not have opened a road for the advance. The plan was necessarily abandoned.

The cliff over which the Montmorency River rushes to meet the St. Lawrence is several hundred feet back from the low water mark, and when the tide, which ebbs and flows in the river as in the ocean, was out, it was possible to ford the smaller stream; so Wolfe next decided to make an attack upon some detached fortifications which apparently constituted the extreme flank of Montcalm's line, commanded by de Levis. He trusted that, if he could gain them, he might turn the flank of the line, make the intrenchments untenable, and force Montcalm to fight. Therefore, with the cooperation of the navy, which was always cheerfully given, he determined upon this desperate plan.

On the morning of July 31st, the line-of-battle ship *Centurion*, 64, with two armed transports, moved down opposite to the destined spot. The transports went so far in shore that they grounded on the flats, but all opened a furious bombardment on the redoubts. When the tide was completely out, Wolfe, leading in person the grenadiers, the Royal Americans, and the Highlanders, which had been embarked in boats, made for the land. At the same time, Monckton's brigade started down from the intrenched camp upon the heights of Montmorency to support the attack from the river.

The Royal Americans and the Grenadiers first reached the shore. Without waiting to be formed and with no attempt at order, disregarding entirely the commands of their officers and without the support of Monckton's column, they rushed impetuously pell-mell toward the redoubts, the French retreating before them as they came on. Swarming over the redoubts they attempted to ascend the hill, which, they discovered too late, bristled with fortifications commanding every slope. They were met by a deadly fire and in a few moments were driven tumultuously down the hill where they took shelter behind the useless redoubts. Over four hundred had been killed and wounded in a few moments.

A violent rainstorm now came up, and after it was over, Wolfe, who had kept the Highlanders well in hand, seeing the futility of further attack, ordered his men to their boats. Acts of great gallantry were performed by many of the men in bringing in the wounded, whom the Indians were already creeping down the hills to scalp. Monckton's brigade did not get in action at all.

Wolfe severely censured the reckless and disorderly conduct of the Grenadiers and Americans; but while the censure was deserved, it is difficult to see how any different result could have been expected. The transports were burned. The French exulted greatly over the repulse.

3. On the Plains of Abraham

About this time the English general, whose physique was of the frailest, was seized by a low fever and prostrated by a wasting disease, and his life was despaired of. To the great joy of the army, however, he recovered, in part at least, and resumed command. As the season was drawing on and they had made no progress, in his desperation, he suggested to his brigadiers several plans of attack upon Beauport, Charlesbourg, and the lower town, which they wisely rejected as impossible. There remained but one other thing to be tried. If by any means he could get a foothold upon the plateau above Quebec, he could force Montcalm to come out in the open and fight, and in that event, he had no doubt of the issue. A Scotsman, Captain Stobo, who had been taken as a hostage from Washington's command at Fort Necessity and had been detained for many years at Quebec, had effected his escape that spring, and joined Wolfe's army. He informed the commander that there was one practicable path up the cliffs, in a little cove called Anse de Foulon, and he offered to conduct a party to that point. It was their last chance, and Wolfe determined to embrace it.

The army and fleet had not been idle; at different intervals during the summer many ships had succeeded in running the batteries of Quebec, and had anchored in the river above the town. Various expeditions had been undertaken, some to ravage the country on every side, and others to menace Cap-Rouge and vicinity, to stop the provisions from coming down the river from Montreal. Several attempts to destroy the fleet by French fire-ships had been thwarted by the vigilance of the officers and the daring of the men. Montcalm had detached some two thousand men under the command of Bougainville, who was stationed at Cap-Rouge. Saunders had warned Wolfe that whatever he did he was to do quickly, for the near approach of the Canadian winter rendered it imperative for him to take his ships out of the harbour if they were not to be frozen up until the next spring.

The French had about concluded that all danger for the year had passed, but Montcalm had not relaxed his vigilance in the slightest degree. The Canadian peasants, watching the burning of their farmhouses and the devastation of their country from the shores of Quebec, were deserting in great numbers. Provisions were short, and supplies were shorter. Still Montcalm held on, hoping that the cold weather would relieve him from the presence of his persistent enemy; he counted without his host.

On the 3rd of September, the camp at Montmorency was abandoned, and troops to the number of thirty-six hundred were embarked on the ships of Holmes' squadron above the town. Wolfe, in a small boat, carefully examined the shore, and verified the existence of Stobo's path. By the white tents at the top of the hill he saw that it was guarded, but he thought there was a possibility that the guard might be negligent and that he could surprise it. On the 4th, he fell desperately ill again. Only his indomitable energy kept him alive. He said to the surgeon that he knew his end was near, but he begged him to patch him up for a few days to enable him to complete the undertaking.

On the 7th, he was so far recovered as to order a feint at Cap-Rouge. The ships ran into the cove of the river, and smartly engaged the batteries and Bougainville's troops. The next two days it rained, to the great discomfort of every one, and for three days thereafter the ships moved up and down the river with the tide, making feints at landing at different points and completely wearing out the Frenchmen on shore.

On the evening of the 12th, they anchored off Cap-Rouge again. It was the night selected for the undertaking. Wolfe had depleted the garrisons at Orleans and Point Levis to the danger limit, and twelve hundred men marched up the opposite shore, and lay on their arms until the morning. The total force of the expedition, therefore, was about forty-eight hundred men. Wolfe had lost over one thousand in killed and wounded in the different attacks and in raids, and there were many sick and disabled in the hospitals. A fortunate circumstance prepared the way for the attack. It had been learned from a deserter that arrangements had been made to float several boatloads of provisions from Cap-Rouge down to Quebec under cover of the darkness. The plan was abandoned, but the sentries on the river were not notified of the change. In the cabin of the *Sutherland* the young commander sat waiting for the ebb.

With him was a young naval officer named John Jervis, who had been a schoolfellow and boy friend in England. He lived to become one of the greatest of English admirals, and he related afterward that Wolfe, after charging him with messages to his mother, took from his neck a miniature of a beautiful young woman, Miss Lowther, to whom he was betrothed, and whose picture he had habitually worn; that he gave it to his friend with instructions as to its disposition after the action, which he felt assured he would not survive. I like to dwell upon him as he sits there, a dying man, in the flickering lamplight in the rude cabin of the ship, on the eve of his desperate hazard, thinking of home and mother and sweetheart and friends.

About two in the morning, the night being very dark and rainy, the boats were cast off, and silently drifted down the river with the young ebb, the ships following a little later. In the first boat was Wolfe himself with his staff. An officer of the Highlanders, who spoke French like a native, was stationed forward. In this boat and the next were twenty-four men from the light infantry who had been chosen from numberless volunteers as a forlorn hope to lead the assault. They were under the command of Lieutenant Colonel William Howe, who later crossed swords with Washington from Long Island to the Brandywine. Not a light was shown in any boat, and in perfect silence they swiftly floated down the river.

The stillness of the night, the desperate nature of their attack, the mysterious loneliness of the towering shores, must have filled their hearts with awe. In Wolfe's boat, he himself broke the silence by reciting some of the verses of Gray's famous *Elegy*. Those who were with him love to recall that he said afterward that he would rather have written that poem than capture Quebec. As they passed one of the jutting curves of the Palisades, a sharp voice from the shore broke the silence with the challenge "*Qui vive!*"

"*France,*" was the instant reply made by the Highlander.

"*A quel regiment?*"

"*De la Rein,*" said the officer with great presence of mind, naming a regiment which was known to be at Cap-Rouge. That was all. The hearts of the officers and men in the boats must have stood still. If they were discovered they were lost; but the sentry, apparently satisfied, said nothing more, and they drifted on. They were hailed again, and the same Highlander answered that they were provision boats and that silence must be kept or they would be betrayed to the English, The current bore them swiftly around a great headland and into a little cove to the landing place; so swiftly in fact, that the boats brought to the shore somewhat below the destined spot. It was after four in the morning now.

Led by the Scotsman, they soon reached the foot of the path. On the top of the hill the lights of the small encampment could be seen. Montcalm had ordered the place carefully guarded. A picket of a hundred men was stationed there under the command of Captain de Vergor. This captain had been tried for cowardice and gross neglect of duty, of both of which he was undoubtedly guilty, while in command of the fortress of Beausejour. Bigot and de Vaudreuil had, however, interfered to procure his acquittal. In disobedience of his orders, he had now allowed the larger portion of his party, who were Canadian militia, to leave their posts and go home to harvest their crops. He himself was fast asleep, and a negligent watch was kept. A part of the battalion Guyenne, which had been ordered to camp near the spot, by some mistake had never left the Charles River. There were batteries scattered here and there along the shore at Samos and Sillery. Apparently all were asleep and unsuspecting.

As the men disembarked, Wolfe and his officers advanced to the narrow path trailing up the face of the cliff. They found it had been barricaded. Howe and his men, however, thought they could get up the side of the cliff, which is here somewhat less precipitous and is thickly wooded, by clinging to the projecting trees. "You may try it," said Wolfe, "though I do not think you will succeed." In silence he and his companions watched the forlorn hope scale the palisades, while boat after boat its load and went back to the ships for more. There was a crashing here and there among the trees and bushes as they disappeared, then silence. Presently the eager listeners heard the sound of a rifle shot, and then more and more, a perfect fusillade, then a British cheer! Concealment was at an end. The men at a nod from Wolfe sprang at the barricades on the path and soon tore them to pieces, and then, in a long sinuous, red line, they toiled up the cliff toward the top, Wolfe among the first.

De Vergor, the coward, had attempted to fly, and had been wounded and captured. The fall of New France rests absolutely upon his shoulders. With his picket he could have kept down Wolfe's whole army. As fast as the regiments climbed the hill they were deployed. The day was just breaking. Meanwhile, the boats had been sent back for the party on the other shore, and it was being rapidly ferried over. The sailors of the squadron dragged up two small pieces of artillery. The batteries at Samos and Sillery were attacked at once, and carried by surprise.

At the other end of the long line, Montcalm, supremely confident, was held in his intrenchments by Admiral Saunders. Boats filled with soldiers and marines moved to and fro in front of the Beauport shore, and the ships of the fleet dropped down and opened a furious cannonade upon the line, as if to cover an attack. Montcalm was up all night, watchful and ready. He was astonished, therefore, when a courier galloped breathlessly up to him, threw himself from his horse, and shouted that the English had established themselves on the Plains of Abraham. "They have got to the weak side of us at last, and we must crush them with our numbers," was the reply. There was galloping in hot haste in every direction. With quick intelligence he realized now that he had to fight a battle, whether he would or no, and that the fate of Quebec hung trembling in the balance. He took horse at once, and stopping a moment to speak with de Vaudreuil, he rode in haste toward the town, with fixed look, saying nothing.

In the gray of the morning the soldiers of Beauport and Charlesbourg took up the line of march, trampling over the bridge, passing through the streets of the startled town. Some of the famous battalions of France—Bearn, La Sarre, Guyenne, Languedoc, and Royal Rousillon—were under Montcalm's command, backed by large numbers of militia, *coureurs de bois* in leather hunting-suits, and painted, plumed Indians. He hoped to drive Wolfe into the sea. Sending expresses to de Vaudreuil to bring up the militia and de Ramesay to send him artillery from the battery of twenty-four field pieces in Quebec, he rode in person to the scene of the conflict.

About six in the morning, the English, who had breakfasted, were drawn up in the battle formation of that day in three ranks. As the line was not long enough to stretch from one side of the plateau to the other, the left flank under Townshend was refused. One regiment had been thrown backward to hold in check Bougainville. Another was held in reserve, leaving about thirty-five hundred men on the fighting line. The field was an open one, partly cultivated, with clumps of trees and thickets on either side. Already the underbrush was filling with savages and partisans, and the bullets were beginning to fall in the English line, the men lying down and skirmishing heavily. The sky was overcast, and the rain fell in fitful showers.

Wolfe commanded in person. He walked up and down exhorting and encouraging his men while he waited for Montcalm. Not an heroic-looking man, with his long, pointed nose, receding forehead and chin, red hair, with a head set upon sloping shoulders; a slender,

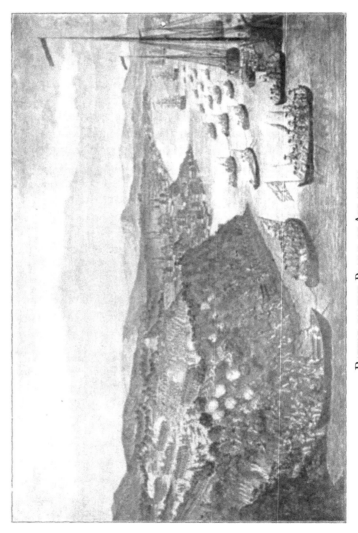

BATTLE ON THE PLAINS OF ABRAHAM

DEATH OF WOLFE.

emaciated figure over six feet in height; but there was a flash in his eye and a look in his bearing which proclaimed a soldier, and all the men of his army loved him. His illness was gone, and he seemed full of vigour and energy. As he passed down the lines they greeted him with cheers.

Presently, over the crest of a little hill which shut off the view of Quebec, appeared the white coats of the enemy. Very pretty they looked against the green grass that rainy morning. There was much manoeuvring to and fro, readjusting of lines, deploying of battalions. There were men on horseback there too. The great Frenchman had his moment of parade. He too had ridden up and down his line, sword in hand, calling upon the chivalry of France for a last effort to sweep the hated English into the sea, and with equal spirit they had responded. The three field pieces which de Ramesay had grudgingly sent forward began to play on the two naval guns of the English. Throwing a mass of militia, Canadian woodsmen and Indians on the left flank, to turn it if possible, and opening a heavy fire from the trees and bushes on both sides, at ten o'clock, the French army, numbering about four thousand five hundred, began to move with Montcalm leading in person.

The generalship of Montcalm in making this attack has been questioned. There was no question as to the necessity of fighting. His position was untenable, his communications broken, his supplies stopped, unless he could drive the English from the position; but the necessity for fighting at that moment was not apparent. There were at Cap-Rouge two thousand good troops under Bougainville, an officer of great merit; back of him, at Beauport, were perhaps five thousand more, rather indifferent, but still counting for something, if de Vaudreuil could be induced to bring them up. A delay and a more imperative order probably would have brought him more guns than those de Ramesay had sent him. By waiting he might have strengthened his army, and with Bougainville's assistance taken the English between two fires.

We can only suppose that he underrated the strength of the thin red line across the green sward under the great red flag, and that he imagined from his previous experiences with the English, which had been fortunate, that he could easily beat them. He did not realize that they were led by a hero of heroes, that they were among the finest soldiery in the world, that they had their back against a precipice, and that they must conquer or be exterminated. So in a fatal hour, he ordered the advance.

The regiments came on in some little confusion, but still presented a brave show. They were pouring their fire into the stolid, silent English ranks; the skirmishers had withdrawn on the main body, the men were ready. Wolfe had given strict orders that the fire of his army should be held. The bullets of the French opened gaps here and there; men fell and lay groaning, or still, on the sod. In obedience to his quick orders, the ranks were continually closed, and the grim front presented itself unbroken. The leader was everywhere cheering and animating his veterans. The French were nearer now, the bullets were coming harder. They were but sixty yards away—fifty—forty—twenty—the English soldiers could see the whites of the eyes of the French. A sharp word of command rang out, the gun-barrels came down; with a crash like the discharge of a battery of cannon, the front rank fired a volley. A moment after, the second rank delivered its fire, and as soon as the smoke cleared away, the third rank poured in a deadly discharge.

The head of the French army literally had been blown to pieces. The advance was halted. The ground was covered with writhing figures, the white coats, bloodstained, showing plainly upon the green grass. The line was reeling to and fro like a drunken man. There were not so many horsemen now. Montcalm, Senezergues, and the other officers made frantic efforts to reform the lines. The French regulars responded gallantly, rallying and returning the fire, but nothing could stand before the deadly regularity of the English discharges. Volley after volley rang out over the plain. The partisans in the bushes still kept up a fire. Townshend led his men forward and cleared the left flank, and then turned on the centre, where the French still fought on. Monckton was badly wounded.

The battle was not yet over. "Forward! Forward!" cried Wolfe, his soul aflame, and he leaped to the front of the Louisburg Grenadiers on the right. With wild cheers the army advanced, first on the double-quick and then in a wild run. Frazier's Highlanders, throwing aside their muskets and waving their terrible claymores, led them all. Menaced on three sides, there was fight in the French yet. The shattered battalions met the advance with all the heroism and gallantry of their noblest traditions.

A bullet struck Wolfe in the left wrist. He caught his handkerchief about it, and pressed on; another hit him in the body, still he kept his place at the head of the grenadiers. Presently a third struck him, in the abdomen, inflicting a dreadful wound. "Don't let me fall!" he cried to those nearest him, "lest I discourage the men." One or two sprang to his side, caught him in their arms, and laid him down on the grass. The grenadiers who had seen it all gritted their teeth, and pressed on with red revenge in their hearts. There was a hand to hand *mêlée*. The French regulars died gallantly, the Canadian volunteers fled, the Indians had gone long since; but nothing could stop the British bayonet, the Highland steel. The French broke and ran; the real fighting had lasted but a quarter of an hour!

4. THE DEATH OF THE GREAT CAPTAINS

Back on the grass the life blood of Wolfe was ebbing away. "It is all over with me," he said to one of the bystanders; and a moment after as he heard one of them cry "They run! They run!"

"Who run?" he asked, opening his eyes.

"The enemy, sir. They give way everywhere."

"Go, one of you to Colonel Burton," he returned, still intent upon his duty in the very articles of death, with the clear instinct of a soldier still undimmed; "tell him to march Webb's regiment down to Charles River to cut off their retreat from the bridge! "

It was his last order. He turned on his side exclaiming, "Now, God be praised, I will die in peace," and when they looked at him again he was dead.

Montcalm, still on horseback, commanding, imploring, entreating, was swept back by the flying crowd toward the town. Just before he reached the St. Louis gate a bullet passed through his body. He would have fallen had not two soldiers supported him on either side. Inside the gate the townspeople were listening with bated breath to the roar of the battle outside the walls. As he entered, they saw his white shirt covered with blood.

"*O, mon Dieu! mon Dieu! le Marquis est tué!*" (Alas, alas, the marquis is killed), cried a woman.

"*Ce n'est rien, ce n'est rien; ne vous affligez pas pour moi, mes bonnes amies*" (It is nothing, it is nothing! Have no anxiety for me, my good friends), he replied.

Those of the army who could do so found shelter in the city. The greater number poured down the Cote St. Genevieve toward Charlesbourg bridge to regain their intrenchments. A little body of Canadians threw themselves into a thicket, and opened a hot fire upon the advancing English to protect the retreat, and by their courage redeemed their reputation. They were dislodged by the Highlanders after a furious fight The delay enabled the fugitives to cross the bridge in safety. In the French camp all was confusion. The English army was recalled from pursuit, and at once threw up intrenchments. When Bougainville appeared it was too late for his small detachment to do anything.

The casualties on both sides had been frightful. The English had lost some seven hundred killed and wounded, including Wolfe killed and Monckton wounded. The French had lost upward of fifteen hundred, among them Montcalm and Senezergues, both mortally wounded. There was much that the French could have done; but the spirit went out of the army when Montcalm was stricken down, and they fled precipitately to Jacques-Cartier, thirty miles away, abandoning Quebec to its fate.

The great Frenchman lay dying within its walls. When the surgeon told him that his wound was mortal. "I am glad of it," he replied; and when he was told, in answer to his question, that he had scarcely twelve hours to live, he remarked, "So much the better; I am happy that I shall not live to see the surrender of Quebec." He spoke in complimentary terms of Wolfe and of his own successor, de Levis.

When de Ramesay, the commandant of the garrison, came to get orders from him, he refused to give any, remarking, "I have much business that must be attended to of greater moment than your ruined garrison and this wretched country."

A different ending from that of the great English soldier! Yet he still thought of his men. One of his last acts was to send the following note to Townshend, who had succeeded to the command:

> *Monsieur*, the humanity of the English sets my mind at peace concerning the fate of the French prisoners and the Canadians. Feel toward them as they have caused me to. feel. Do not let them perceive that they have changed masters. Be their protector as I have been their father."

The Bishop of Quebec, himself in a dying condition, administered the last sacraments, and at four o'clock in the morning, on the 14th of September, Montcalm quietly entered into his rest. The wife and the children would wait long for him; he would never return to his beloved Candiac. No one could be found to make a coffin, and an old servant of the Ursuline Convent, procuring a few boards, nailed them together to form a rough box. In it they laid the body of the dead captain, and in the evening of the same day they buried him. There was no escort, no funeral pageantry; the officers of the garrison and some of the people, mostly women and children, joined the silent procession along the deserted streets. A shell bursting under the floor of the Ursuline Convent had made a deep cavity, which had been shaped into a rude grave. There they laid him away, and as the clods fell upon his coffin, they sounded the death knell of New France. On the 18th of the month, de Ramesay surrendered the town to the English.

A month later, a great fleet approached the chalk cliffs of England. On the quarter-deck of the line-of-battle ship *Prince William* lay a coffin. It contained all that was left of Wolfe. A few days before the battle on the Plains of Abraham, Wolfe had sent a frank and despondent letter to Pitt, in which he told of his failures and the slender prospect of success. It had been made public, and the English people were not prepared for the news of the splendid achievement which arrived at the same time as the dead body of the commander.

Oh, what a homecoming was there! Such manifestations of joy have not often been seen in England, as when the story of his great victory, the tale of his great success, had been spread abroad. Bonfires blazed on every hill, and the people fairly went mad with enthusiasm; but no sound reached the dull ear of the dead soldier on the great ship, in peace after so much suffering, so much struggling, so much heroism, such high endeavour.

There was quiet in one little hamlet where a bereaved mother thought that not all the Empire of the West, which had been won at the point of his sword, could compensate for the loss of her son; and in another home, another woman bowed her head over a miniature placed in her hand by a gallant sailor who told her the story of that last interview in the cabin of the ship on the eve of the decisive battle,

O Captain! my Captain! our fearful trip is done,
The ship has weathered every rack, the prise we sought is won.
The port is near, the bells I hear, the people all exulting,
While follow eyes the steady keel, the vessel grim and daring;
But O heart! heart! heart!
O the bleeding drops of red.
Where on the deck my Captain lies,
Fallen cold and dead.